COMING TO TERMS WITH LANGUAGE

COMING TO TERMS
WITH LANGUAGE:
AN ANTHOLOGY

Edited by
RAYMOND D. LIEDLICH

JOHN WILEY & SONS, INC.
NEW YORK   LONDON   SYDNEY   TORONTO

Library of Congress Cataloging in Publication Data:

Liedlich, Raymond D.   comp.
Coming to terms with language.

1. Communication.   2. Content analysis
(Communication) I. Title.

P93.L5   808.5   72-10382
ISBN 0-471-53435-8

Printed in the United States of America

10-9 8 7 6 5 4 3 2 1

This book was set in Palatino by Cherry Hill Composition, and printed
and bound by Semline Inc. The designer was Paddy Bareham. The editor
was Vivian Kahane. Phyllis D. Lemkowitz supervised production.

Cover credit : Reprinted by permission of Oliver A. Kingsbury, Vice
President of Schneider, Smith, Wilbur, Inc., Advertising, New York City,
from *Time* magazine, January 5, 1970. Designed by Art Director Bob
Cohen, original art by Jeri-Gale, copy by Norton Amerman.

To Martha, who uses language better than anyone else I know

CONTENTS

3. UP AGAINST THE WALL:
RHETORIC AND REVOLUTION

4. COLOR SCHEMES: LANGUAGE AND RACE

5. THE SILENT LANGUAGES:
VERBAL AND NONVERBAL COMMUNICATION

6. THE LAST WORD: LANGUAGE AND CULTURE

PREFACE

This volume brings together 30 essays on language and communication in their contemporary social contexts. Written in nontechnical language and, with few exceptions, for a general audience, they deal with such subjects as advertising, politics, war, obscenity, youth, violent protest, revolution, race, nonverbal communication, and cultural differences. Upon completing the book, students should be in a better position to appreciate the importance of language and communication in their lives, to recognize how the abuse and misuse of these resources contributes to many of our current problems, and to develop a greater sense of responsibility in their own handling of language situations and the communication process.

Coming to Terms with Language differs significantly from other language readers in that (1) it treats only those aspects of the subject that have demonstrated their appeal to a wide range of students; (2) it emphasizes their social and cultural implications and thus deals extensively with contemporary issues; (3) it focuses on practical applications rather than theory; and (4) it consists entirely of contemporary selections, most of them written for a general audience.

Following an introductory essay to establish perspective, the book is divided into six parts: Language and Reality, The Use

and Abuse of Language, Rhetoric and Revolution, Language and
Race, Verbal and Nonverbal Communication, and Language and
Culture. Each selection is accompanied by introductory notes that
indicate its central concerns and point out some of its relationships to the other readings. In addition, the essays are followed
by Suggestions for Discussion and Writing. Many of these encourage students to relate the reading to their own experience;
others help them to make the connections between one essay and
another; still others lead them to investigate the subject further.
Most of the suggestions are as adaptable to speech situations
as they are to writing.

Coming to Terms with Language leads students to explore the
ways we perceive experience, the role of language in shaping our
thoughts, the current trend of distorting and exploiting language
and the consequent dehumanization it entails, the breakdowns
and gaps in communication, and the means available to overcome those breakdowns and reach across those gaps to understand other people and cultures. Such matters are of interest and
importance in several different types of courses. My own classroom experience with this material has been in freshman English
courses in both composition and communication, but it might
also be used in Speech, Semantics, or English language studies.
Although the book is substantial enough to be used as a basic
text, I have tried to keep it brief enough to serve as a supplement
as well. In either case, I have found that most of the selections
are quite accessible to first-year college students, and the subject
matter of even the more difficult essays will sustain the interest
of those students.

The sixty-first annual convention of the National Council of
Teachers of English passed two resolutions on language. One
called for members to "find means to study dishonest and inhumane uses of language by advertisers, to bring offenses to
public attention, and to propose classroom techniques for preparing [students] to cope with commercial propaganda." The
other urged them to "find means to study the relation of language to public policy, to keep track of, publicize, and combat
semantic distortion by public officials, candidates for office,
political commentators, and all those who transmit through the

mass media." Although I had begun this book long before those resolutions were passed, they nevertheless clearly reflect the kinds of concerns that led me to undertake it. I hope that in this volume teachers may find one means toward achieving those ends.

For their perceptive and encouraging reviews of the manuscript, I am grateful to Walker Gibson, Director of the Rhetoric Program, University of Massachusetts at Amherst; and Frederick Warner, Chairman of the Language Arts Department, Portland Community College. And once again, I am indebted to my wife Martha, to whom this book is dedicated, and to Terri and Bobbi for their patience and understanding.

                                        Raymond D. Liedlich

COMING TO TERMS WITH LANGUAGE

We make ourselves real by telling the truth.
Thomas Merton

BY WAY OF INTRODUCTION

NOT BORN FREE:
ESTABLISHING PERSPECTIVE

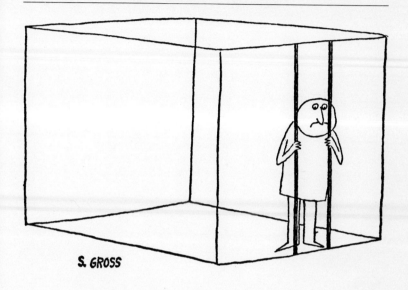

S. GROSS

1

Peter Farb

MAN AT THE MERCY OF HIS LANGUAGE

Studies in the relationship between language and culture indicate that, in a linguistic sense, man is—as Peter Farb says here— not born free. That is, he inherits a language, and his language is more than a tool for reporting ideas; it actually shapes those ideas. In this selection, Mr. Farb explains the significance of the pioneering studies by linguists Edward Sapir and Benjamin Lee Whorf, who were among the first scholars to develop the hypothesis that language reflects basic differences in the world view of various cultures and the manner in which they understand their environment. The author is a free-lance writer and researcher in the science and natural history of North America.

Linguistically speaking, man is not born free. He inherits a language full of quaint sayings, archaisms, and a ponderous grammar; even more important, he inherits certain fixed ways of expression that may shackle his thoughts. Language becomes man's shaper of ideas rather than simply his tool for reporting ideas. An American's conventional words for directions often limit his ability to read maps: It is an apt youngster indeed who can immediately grasp that the *Upper* Nile is in the *south* of Egypt and the *Lower* Nile is in the *north* of Egypt. Another example: English has only two demonstrative pronouns ("this" and "that," together with their plurals) to refer either to something near or to something far away. The Tlingit Indians of the Northwest Coast can be much more specific. If they want to refer to an object very near and always present, they say *he; ya* means an object also near and present, but a little farther away; *yu* refers to something still farther away, while *we* is used only for an object so far away that it is out of sight. So the question arises whether even the most outspoken member of American society can "speak his mind." Actually, he has very little control over the possible channels into which his thoughts can flow. His grammatical mind was made up for him by his culture before he was born.

The way in which culture affects language becomes clear by comparing how the English and Hopi languages refer to H_2O in its liquid state. English, like most other European languages, has only one word—"water"—and it pays no attention to what the substance is used for or its quantity. The Hopi of Arizona, on the other hand, use *pahe* to mean the large amounts of water present in natural lakes or rivers, and *keyi* for the small amounts in domestic jugs and canteens. English, though, makes other distinctions that Hopi does not. The speaker of English is careful to distinguish between a lake and a stream, between a waterfall and a geyser; but *pahe* makes no distinction among lakes, ponds, rivers, streams, waterfalls, and springs.

A Hopi speaker, of course, knows that there is a difference between a geyser, which spurts upward, and a waterfall, which plunges downward, even though his vocabulary makes no such distinction. Similarly, a speaker of English knows that a canteen of water differs from a river of water. But the real point of this comparison is that neither the Hopi nor the American uses anywhere near the possible number of words that could be applied to water in all of its states, quantities, forms, and functions. The number of such words is in the hundreds and they would hopelessly encumber the language. So, to prevent the language from becoming unwieldy, different kinds of water are grouped into a small number of categories. Each culture defines the categories in terms of the similarities it detects; it channels a multitude of ideas into the few categories that it considers important. The culture of every speaker of English tells him that it is important to distinguish between oceans, lakes, rivers, fountains, and waterfalls—but relatively unimportant to make the distinction between the water in a canteen in his canoe and the water underneath the same canoe. Each culture has categorized experience through language in a quite unconscious way—at the same time offering anthropologists commentaries on the differences and similarities that exist in societies.

The possibility of such a relationship between language and culture has been formulated into a hypothesis by two American linguists, Sapir and Whorf. According to Sapir, man does not live in the midst of the whole world, but only in a part of it, the part that his language lets him know. He is, says Sapir, "very much at the mercy of the particular language which has become the medium of expression" for his group. The real world is therefore "to a large extent unconsciously built up on the language habits of the group . . . The worlds in which different societies live are distinct worlds, not merely the same world with different labels attached." To Sapir and Whorf, language provides a different network of tracks for each society, which, as a result, concentrates on only certain aspects of reality.

According to the hypothesis, the differences between languages are much more than mere obstacles to communication; they represent basic differences in the "world view" of the various peoples and in what they understand about their environment. The Eskimo can draw upon an inventory of about twenty very precise words for the subtle differences in a snowfall. The best a speaker of English can manage are distinctions between sticky snow, sleet, hail, and ice. Similarly, to most speakers of English, a seal is simply a seal, and they have only that one word to describe it; if they want to say anything else about the seal, such as its sex or its color, then they have to put an adjective before the word "seal." But the Eskimo has a number of words with which to express various kinds of sealdom: "a young swimming seal," "a male harbor seal," "an old harbor seal," and so forth. A somewhat similar situation exists in English with the word "horse." This animal may be referred to as "chestnut," "bay mare," "stallion," and other names that one would not expect to find in the vocabulary of the horseless Eskimo.

The Eskimo, of course, is preoccupied with seals, a primary food source for him, whereas some speakers of English seem to be taken up with the exact particulars of the domesticated horse. The real question is: Do these different vocabularies restrict the Eskimo and the speaker of English, and do they force the speakers of different languages to conceptualize and classify information in different ways? Can an Eskimo look at a horse and in his own mind classify it as a "a bay mare"? Or, because he lacks the words, is he forever blind to the fact that this kind of animal exists? The answer is that with a little practice an Eskimo can learn to tell apart the different kinds of horses, just as an American can learn about the various seals, even though the respective languages lack the necessary vocabularies. So vocabulary alone does not reveal the cultural thinking of a people.

But does the *totality* of the language tell anything about the people who speak it? To answer that, look at the English verb "grab." An English speaker says, "I grab it," "I grabbed it," "I will grab it," and so on. Only the context of the situation tells the listener what it is that is being grabbed and how it is being done. "I grab it" is a vague sentence—except in one way. English is remarkably concerned about the tense of the verb. It insists on knowing whether I grab it now, or grabbed it some time in the past, or will grab it at a future time. The English language is preoccupied with time, and so is the culture of its speakers, who take considerable interest in calendars, record-keeping, diaries, history, almanacs, stock-market forecasts, astrological predictions, and always, every minute of the waking day, the precise time.

No such statement as "I grab it" would be possible in Navaho. To the Navaho, tense is of little importance, but the language is considerably more discriminating in other ways. The Navaho language would describe much more about the pronoun "I" of this sentence; it would tell whether the "I" initiated the action by reaching out to grab the thing or whether the "I" merely grabbed at a horse that raced by. Nor would the Navaho be content merely with "grab"; the verb would have to tell him whether the thing being grabbed is big or little, animate or inanimate. Finally, a Navaho could not say simply "it"; the thing being grabbed would have to be described much more precisely and put in a category. (If you get the feeling the Navaho is an exceedingly difficult language, you are correct. During World War II in the Pacific, Navaho Indians were used as senders and receivers of secret radio messages because a language, unlike a code, cannot be broken; it must be learned.)

Judging by this example and by other linguistic studies of Navaho, a picture of its speakers emerges: They are very exacting in their perception of the elements that make up their universe. But is this a true picture of the Navaho? Does he perceive his world any differently from a White American? Anthropological and psychological studies of the Navaho show that he does. He visualizes himself as living in an eternal and unchanging universe made up of physical, social, and supernatural forces, among which he tries to maintain a balance. Any accidental failure to observe rules or rituals can disturb this balance and result in some misfortune. Navaho curing ceremonies, which include the well-known sandpainting, are designed to put the individual back into harmony with the universe. To the Navaho, the good life consists of maintaining intact all the complex relationships of the universe. It is obvious that to do so demands a language that makes the most exacting discriminations.

Several words of caution, though, about possible misinterpretations of the Sapir–Whorf Hypothesis. It does not say that the Navaho holds such a world view because of the structure of his language. It merely states that there is an interaction between his language and his culture. Nor does the hypothesis maintain that two cultures with different languages and different world views cannot be in communication with each other (the Navaho and the White American are very much in communication today in Arizona and New Mexico). Instead, the hypothesis suggests that language is more than a way of communicating. It is a living system that is a part of the cultural equipment of a group, and it reveals a culture at least as much as do spear points, kinship groups, or political institutions. Look at just one of the clues to culture that the Sapir–Whorf Hypothesis has already provided: Shortly after the hypothesis was proposed, it was attacked on the basis that the Navaho speak an Athabaskan language and the Hopi a Uto-Aztecan one, yet they live side by side in the Southwest and share a culture. So, after all, asked the critics, what difference can language make in culture? Instead of demolishing the hypothesis, this comparison actually served to reveal its value. It forced anthropologists to take another look at the Navaho and the Hopi. As the hypothesis had predicted, their world views are quite far apart—and so are their cultures.

The Sapir–Whorf Hypothesis has alerted anthropologists to the fact that language is keyed to the total culture, and that it reveals a people's view of its total environment. Language directs the perceptions of its speakers to certain things; it gives them ways to analyze and to categorize experience. Such perceptions are unconscious and outside the control of the speaker. The ultimate value of the Sapir–Whorf Hypothesis is that it offers hints to cultural differences and similarities among peoples. . . .

SUGGESTIONS FOR DISCUSSION AND WRITING

1. What is the relationship between this article and the preceding cartoon of the man behind bars? What common idea do both convey about the way in which human beings view the world and perceive their environment?

2. We have all had the experience of realizing that we held a narrow or limited view of something or someone. Write an essay about such a realization, discussing what might have caused you to hold that view and how the realization came about. Be sure to consider whether language played any significant part in the experience.

3. Persons learning a foreign language often experience difficulty in trying to "think" in the new language. Why? Would this problem lend any credibility to the Sapir–Whorf Hypothesis? Write an essay about the difficulty you may have had in learning a second language because of the difference between your way of thinking in your native tongue and in the foreign language.

4. Discuss the differences in perception or world view of two

cultures with which you are familiar, noting the extent to which language influences these differences. (If this assignment appears at first to be beyond your range of experience, you might consider the cultures of youth and age as the basis for your discussion.)

5. Investigate Sapir's or Whorf's ideas about the relationship between language and culture (see Bibliography) and prepare a report of your findings.

A WORLD OF WORDS:

LANGUAGE AND REALITY

"THERE'S A TOUGH BUNCH. UNDER THE V.C. THEY SURVIVED LIBERATION, ORIENTATION, AND TAXATION. FROM US THEY TOOK DEFOLIATION, INTERROGATION, AND PACIFICATION."

2

John Cogley

WORDS

*This first group of readings shares the common theme that many
contemporary Americans are failing to exercise responsibility in
their use of language and employing it in thoughtless and dishonest ways. The resultant corruption of language not only
undermines the communication process but distorts the very
basis for our perception of reality. As editor of* The Center Magazine, *John Cogley expressed his deep concern over this problem
in the following editorial.*

Words have a way of creating their own reality. As George
Orwell and others have pointed out, corruption of language can
lead to the corruption of political life. During recent years, this
truth has been spectacularly obvious. Words are being fired liked
ammunition in the wars that polarize us.

The calculated use of obscenities on the part of campus dissidents stirs up outrage and self-righteousness in the users and
blind rage in those on the receiving end. Words, mere words,
then, create the atmosphere in which violence becomes not only
possible but almost inevitable. At the other end of the political
spectrum, apologists for the carnage in Indo-China use soft,
patriotic words to camouflage what America is doing there, putting minds at ease and stirring up love of country to overwhelm
the claims of conscience.

Abroad, the people of Vietnam are reduced to "gooks," the
easier to kill them. At home the police are reduced to "pigs," the
easier to defy them. In both cases men are reduced to less than
men for political purposes. Who, then, can take either side

Reprinted, with permission, from the July/August issue of *The Center
Magazine,* a publication of the Center for the Study of Democratic Institutions in Santa Barbara, California.

seriously when they talk solemnly about the dignity of man?

If man is inviolable, it is blasphemy to talk of Vietnamese, North or South, as gooks; it is sacrilegious to speak of policemen as pigs. It is an outrage to refer to black men as niggers. The outrage is approved when white men in turn are spoken of as honkies.

Either one believes in the dignity of man or one doesn't. The disdain found in the words of contempt that are used so freely deny the central idea behind that proposition. Those who indulge in the general downgrading reduce not only their enemies but themselves.

But, alas, dehumanizing by language is now found on all sides. The President himself has played the game, referring to dissident students as "bums." The Vice-President has learned to make headlines by choosing his words with malice aforethought. Mr. Agnew has made a practice of arousing audiences by encouraging, even inciting, them to express disdain for their fellow men. For all his piety, he denies human dignity in every other sentence—as do so many youthful rebels when they spit out their contempt for fellow human beings, as well as racists of whatever hue, and political partisans, left or right, who confront opponents not with arguments but personal epithets.

Seen one way, words of course are merely syllables uttered to convey meaning. But that is only part of the story. The skillful selection of words, we all know, can turn evil into good or good into evil in the minds of those who hear them.

When words are used to serve emotions rather than reason, they can change a normally attractive coed into a screaming harridan, a normally reasonable man into an inciter of violence, a normally peaceful community into a ranting mob crying for blood. This is happening.

We can deceive even ourselves by accepting words that make evil look good, the ugly appear beautiful, or the sick look healthy. This marks the greatest victory of propagandists, and it has frequently left wreckage in its path.

Modern history has made it clear that whole nations can lie to themselves this way. They have been known to turn in fury against the lonely individuals who hold out for the integrity of language.

The corruption of language, especially when it is rationalized by more corrupt language, can lead to incalculable harm. It is often responsible not only for the destruction of reason and responsibility but for the actual killing of innocent men and women. The abuse of language is at the root of almost every case of mob violence. And still it goes on, with even the most ardent advocates of peace playing thoughtlessly with the loaded weapon of words.

It is not enough to respond that even exaggerated language can serve the truth and when it does that is enough justification for its use. There is also such a thing as a mode of truth. The one who uses words to sentimentalize the truth or turn it into a partisan weapon, who employs it to do violence to fellow human beings, vulgarizes it, sectarianizes it, or treats it as an instrument of hate, does as much violence to the truth as the worst liar on earth. For, misused, even the truth can create monstrous realities.

SUGGESTIONS FOR DISCUSSION AND WRITING

1. Since editorial opinions are subject to space limitations, they usually contain unsupported generalizations. Point out some in this essay. Do they weaken the argument? Why or why not? See if you can provide specific support for some of these generalizations.

2. The author says that "Either one believes in the dignity of man or one doesn't." Is this statement valid? Why or why not?

3. In the same paragraph the author goes on to say, "Those who indulge in the general downgrading (by speaking contemptuously of others) reduce not only their enemies but themselves." How might it reduce a white man to call a black man "nigger" or a black man to call a white man "honky"?

4. *Point out the ways in which this essay agrees with Peter Farb's "Man at the Mercy of His Language."*

5. *The author provides several examples of the ways in which words may create their own reality. See if you can recall from your own experience some way in which words created a reality for you.*

3

Melvin Maddocks

THE LIMITATIONS OF LANGUAGE

As many of the selections in this book point out, man lives in a world made of words. Melvin Maddocks, writing for Time *magazine, warns in the following essay that our perception of that world is being distorted by an overload on our verbal circuits. Maddocks defines the problem as "semantic aphasia," that is, a "numbness of ear, mind and heart—[a] tone deafness to the very meaning of language—which results from the habitual and prolonged abuse of words." He shows how both the Counterculture and the Establishment have contributed to the problem through oversimplification on the one hand and "overcomplification" on the other. And Maddocks sees beyond the surface of this language pollution to its deeper implications.*

In J. M. G. Le Clézio's novel *The Flood,* the anti-hero is a young man suffering from a unique malady. Words—the deluge of daily words—have overloaded his circuits. Even when he is strolling down the street, minding his own business, his poor brain jerks under the impact of instructions (WALK—DON'T WALK), threats (TRESPASSERS WILL BE PROSECUTED), and newsstand alarms (PLANE CRASH AT TEL AVIV). Finally, Le Clézio's Everyman goes numb—nature's last defense. Spoken words become mere sounds, a meaningless buzz in the ears. The most urgent printed words—a poem by Baudelaire, a proclamation of war—have no more profound effect than the advice he reads (without really reading) on a book of matches: PLEASE CLOSE COVER BEFORE STRIKING.

If one must give a name to Le Clézio's disease, perhaps semantic aphasia will do. Semantic aphasia is that numbness of ear, mind and heart—that tone deafness to the very meaning of

Reprinted by permission from *Time,* The Weekly News-magazine; © TIME Inc. 1971.

language—which results from the habitual and prolonged abuse of words. As an isolated phenomenon, it can be amusing if not downright irritating. But when it becomes epidemic, it signals a disastrous decline in the skills of communication, to that mumbling low point where language does almost the opposite of what it was created for. With frightening perversity—the evidence mounts daily—words now seem to cut off and isolate, to cause more misunderstanding than they prevent.

Semantic aphasia is the monstrous insensitivity that allows generals to call war "pacification," union leaders to describe strikes or slowdowns as "job actions," and politicians to applaud even moderately progressive programs as "revolutions." Semantic aphasia is also the near-pathological blitheness that permits three different advertisers in the same women's magazine to call a wig and two dress lines "liberated."

So far, so familiar. Whenever the ravishing of the English language comes up for perfunctory headshaking, politicians, journalists, and ad writers almost invariably get cast as Three Horsemen of the Apocalypse. The perennially identified culprits are guilty as charged, God knows. At their worst—and how often they are!—they seem to address the world through a bad PA system. Does it matter what they actually say? They capture your attention, right? They are word manipulators—the carnival barkers of life who misuse language to pitch and con and make the quick kill.

So let's hear all the old boos, all the dirty sneers. Paste a sticker proclaiming Stamp Out Agnewspeak on every bumper. Take the ribbons out of the typewriters of all reporters and rewritemen. Force six packs a day on the guy who wrote "Winston tastes good *like* . . ." Would that the cure for semantic aphasia were that simple.

What about, for example, the aphasics of the counterculture? The ad writer may dingdong catch phrases like Pavlov's bells in order to produce saliva. The Movement propagandist rings his chimes ("Fascist!" "Pig!" "Honky!" "Male chauvinist!") to produce spit. More stammer than grammar, as Dwight Macdonald put it, the counterculture makes inarticulateness an ideal, debasing words into clenched fists ("Right on!") and exclamation points

("Oh, wow!"). Semantic aphasia on the right, semantic aphasia on the left. Between the excesses of square and hip rhetoric the language is in the way of being torn apart.

The semantic aphasia examined so far might be diagnosed as a hysterical compulsion to simplify. Whether pushing fluoride toothpaste or Women's Lib, the rhetoric tends to begin, rather then end, at an extreme. But there is a second, quite different variety of the disease: overcomplication. It damages the language less spectacularly but no less fatally than oversimplification. Its practitioners are commonly known as specialists. Instead of unjustified clarity they offer unjustified obscurity. Whether his discipline is biophysics or medieval Latin, the specialist jealously guards trade secrets by writing and speaking a private jargon that bears only marginal resemblances to English. Cult words encrust his sentences like barnacles, slowing progress, affecting the steering. And the awful truth is that everybody is a specialist at something.

If the oversimplifier fakes being a poet, the overcomplicator fakes being a scientist. Perhaps it is unfair to pick on economists rather than anybody else—except that they are, after all, talking about money. And as often as not it turns out to be our money. Here is a master clarifier-by-smokescreen discussing the recruiting possibilities of a volunteer army if wages, military (W_m) are nudged seductively in the direction of wages, civilian (W_c): "However, when one considers that a military aversion factor must be added to W_c or subtracted from W_m, assuming average aversion is positive, and that only a portion of military wages are perceived, the wage ratio is certainly less than unity and our observations could easily lie on the increasing elasticity segment of the supply curve." All clear, everyone?

The ultimate criticism of the overcomplicator is not that he fuzzes but that he fudges. If the cardinal sin of the oversimplifier is to inflate the trivial, the cardinal sin of the overcomplicator is to flatten the magnificent—or just pretend that it is not there. In the vocabulary of the '70s, there is an adequate language for fanaticism, but none for ordinary quiet conviction. And there are almost no words left to express the concerns of honor, duty or piety.

For the noble idea leveled with a thud, see your nearest modern Bible. "Vanity of vanities, saith the Preacher . . ." In one new version his words become, "A vapor of vapors! Thinnest of vapors! All is vapor!"—turning the most passionate cry in the literature of nihilism into a spiritual weather report. The new rendition may be a more literal expression of the Hebrew original, but at what a cost in grace and power.

Who will protect the language from all those oversimplifiers and overcomplicators who kill meaning with shouts or smother it with cautious mumbles? In theory, certain professions should serve as a sort of palace guard sworn to defend the mother tongue with their lives. Alas, the enemy is within the gates. Educators talk gobbledygook about "non-abrasive systems intervention" and "low structure–low consideration teaching style." Another profession guilty of non-defense is lexicography. With proud humility today's dictionary editor abdicates even as arbiter, refusing to recognize any standards but usage. If enough people misuse disinterested as a synonym for uninterested, Webster's will honor it as a synonym. If enough people say infer when they mean imply, then that becomes its meaning in the eyes of a dictionary editor.

Con Edison can be fined for contaminating the Hudson. Legislation can force Detroit to clean up automobile exhausts. What can one do to punish the semantic aphasics for polluting their native language? None of man's specialties of self-destruction—despoliation of the environment, overpopulation, even war—appear more ingrained than his gift for fouling his mother tongue. Yet nobody dies of semantic aphasia, and by and large it gets complained about with a low-priority tut-tut.

The reason we rate semantic aphasia so low—somewhere between athlete's foot and the common cold on the scale of national perils—is that we don't understand the deeper implications of the disease. In his classic essay, *Politics and the English Language*, George Orwell pointed out what should be obvious—that sloppy language makes for sloppy thought. Emerson went so far as to suggest that bad rhetoric meant bad men. Semantic aphasia, both men recognized, kills after all. "And the Lord said: 'Go to, let us go down, and there confound their language, that they may not understand one another's speech.' " Is there a more ominous curse in the Bible? It breathes hard upon us at this time of frantic change, when old purposes slip out from under the words that used to cover them, leaving the words like tombstones over empty graves.

How, then, does one rescue language? How are words repaired, put back in shape, restored to accuracy and eloquence, made faithful again to the commands of the mind and the heart? There is, sadly enough, no easy answer. Sincerity is of little help to clichés, even in a suicide note, as Aldous Huxley once remarked. Read, if you can, the Latinized techno-pieties of most ecologists. Good intentions are not likely to produce another Shakespeare or a Bible translation equivalent to that produced by King James' bench of learned men. They wrote when English was young, vital and untutored. English in 1971 is an old, overworked language, freshened sporadically only by foreign borrowings or the flickering, vulgar piquancy of slang. All of us—from the admen with their jingles to the tin-eared scholars with their jargon—are victims as well as victimizers of the language we have inherited.

Concerning aphasia, the sole source of optimism is the logic of necessity. No matter how carelessly or how viciously man abuses the language he has inherited, he simply cannot live without it. Even Woodstock Nation cannot survive on an oral diet of grunts and expletives. Mankind craves definition as he craves lost innocence. He simply does not know what his life means until he says it. Until the day he dies he will grapple with mystery by trying to find the word for it. "The limits of my language," Ludwig Wittgenstein observed, "are the limits of my world." Man's purifying motive is that he cannot let go of the Adam urge to name things—and finally, out of his unbearable solitude, to pronounce to others His own identity.

SUGGESTIONS FOR DISCUSSION AND WRITING

1. Politicians, journalists, and advertising writers are groups frequently criticized for abusing language. Do you consider such criticism justified? Why or why not? The author also charges the Counterculture with debasing the language. Is this criticism justified? Again, support your answer.

2. Explain what the author means by both oversimplification and "overcomplification"; then see if you can find some examples of each.

3. The author says that educators and lexicographers ought to "serve as a sort of palace guard to defend the mother tongue." What does he want to defend it against and how would they go about it? What should educators and lexicographers do for the language? According to the author, what have they done to it? Do his charges strike you as well founded?

4. The author quotes philosopher Ludwig Wittgenstein's statement "The limits of my language are the limits of my world." What does that statement mean to you? Is it negative, positive, or something of both? Discuss the statement in relation to some of the previous selections and illustrations.

5. Explain the basis for the author's optimism in the final paragraph. What does he mean by the "logic of necessity"? How does it provide a basis for optimism? Do you agree with that outlook? Why or why not?

4

Henryk Skolimowski

THE SEMANTIC ENVIRONMENT IN THE AGE OF ADVERTISING

Any treatment of the effect of language on contemporary culture must, for obvious reasons, eventually deal at some length with the subject of advertising. In this essay, Henryk Skolimowski, who teaches philosophy at the University of Southern California, shows that the semantic environment has a greater influence on our behavior and attitudes than most of us realize. In light of this, he charges advertising with a distortion of language, which has led to a corresponding distortion of values.

David Ogilvy is a very successful advertising man. In addition, Mr. Ogilvy has turned out to be a successful writer. His book, *Confessions of an Advertising Man*, was a best-seller in 1965. His confessions are in fact intimate whisperings of one adman to another. These whisperings, however, turned out to be interesting enough to make his book one of the most readable and lucid stories of advertising ever written. What is so fascinating about this book is not the amount of linguistic contortions which he advocates, but the amount of truth which is expressed there incidentally. There is nothing more comforting than to find truth accidentally expressed by one's adversary. *Confessions of an Advertising Man* provides a wealth of such truths.

Mr. Ogilvy tells us that "the most powerful words you can use in a headline are FREE and NEW. You can seldom use FREE," he continues, "but you can always use NEW—if you try hard enough." It is an empirical fact that these two words have a most powerful influence upon us. This fact has been established by scientific

Reprinted from *Etc.*, Vol. 25, No. 1, by permission of the International Society for General Semantics.

research. Whenever these words appear, they are used deliberately—in order to lull and seduce us.

The word FREE is especially seductive. Whether we are aware of this or not, it has an almost hypnotic effect on us. Although we all know "nothing is for nothing," whenever the word FREE appears, it acts on us as the light of a candle acts on a moth. This is one of the mysteries of our language. And these mysteries are very skillfully exploited by advertising men.

Apart from the words FREE and NEW, other words and phrases "which make wonders," as Mr. Ogilvy's research has established, are: "HOW TO, SUDDENLY, NOW, ANNOUNCING, INTRODUCING, IMPORTANT, DEVELOPMENT, AMAZING, SENSATIONAL, REVOLUTIONARY, STARTLING, MIRACLE, OFFER, QUICK, EASY, WANTED, CHALLENGE, ADVICE TO, THE TRUTH ABOUT, COMPARE, BARGAIN, HURRY, LAST CHANCE." Should we not be grateful to Mr. Ogilvy for such a splendid collection? Should we not learn these "miraculous" phrases by heart in order to know which particular ones drive us to the marketplace? To this collection I should like to add some of the phrases which I found: SIMPLE, SAVE, CONVENIENT, COMFORT, LUXURY, SPECIAL OFFER, DISTINCTIVE, DIFFERENT, RARE.

Having provided his collection, Ogilvy comments upon these words that make wonders (and this comment is most revealing): "Don't turn up your nose at these clichés. They may be shopworn, but they work." Alas! They work on us. What can we do about their merciless grip? Nothing. Language and its workings cannot be controlled or altered through an act of our will. The cumulative process of the development of language used as the instrument of tyranny or as the bridge to God through prayers; as a recorder of everyday trivia or as a clarion trumpet announcing new epochs in human history; as an expression of private feelings of single individuals or as a transmitter of slogans to the masses—this process has endowed some words with incredible subtleties and others with irresistible power. The only thing we can do about the influence of language on us is to become aware of it. This awareness may diminish the grip language has on us.

It is very gratifying to know that nowadays advertising is so punctilious, so systematic, and so scientific in its approach to the customer. Mr. Ogilvy in *Confessions* relentlessly repeats that "research has shown" so and so, "research shows" this and that, "research suggests" that, "research has established" that, etc. This constant reference to research is not an advertising humbug. It is through systematic research that we are "hooked" more and more thoroughly. With perfect innocence Ogilvy informs us that "Another profitable gambit is to give the reader helpful advice or service. It hooks about [was this a slip of the tongue, or intentional, plain description?] 75 per cent more readers than copy which deals entirely with the product."

Madison Avenue has, above all, established that through words we may be compelled to perform certain acts—acts of buying. This conclusion is not to be found in Ogilvy. Whether it is an historical accident or not, it is a rather striking fact that, independent of semanticists and logicians and linguistic philosophers, advertising men have made some important discoveries about language. And they have utilized these discoveries with amazing success. They are probably not aware of the theoretical significance of their discoveries and are no doubt little interested in such matters.

J. L. Austin, one of the most prominent linguistic philosophers at Oxford during the 1950's, developed a theory of what he called *performative utterances.* He observed that language is systematically employed not only for stating and describing but also for performing actions. Such utterances as "I warn you to . . ." or "I promise you x" are performances rather than descriptions. They function not only on a verbal level, but also as deeds, as concrete performances through words. The discovery and classification of performative utterances is an important extention of ordinary logic—that is, logic concerned with declarative utterances. On the other hand, it is an important finding of the hidden force of language in shaping our social and individual relationships.

Quite independently, advertising men have developed and successfully applied their own theory of performative utterances. They may be oblivious to the logical subtleties involved; however, they are not oblivious to the power of their medium—that is, the verbal utterances through which they induce our acts of buying. Again, there is very little we can do about it. This is the way language works. We can only recognize this fact. But once we recognize it, we acquire some immunity.

Now, we all know that advertising messages are conveyed in words. Usually, there are not only words, but pictures and images which suggest appropriate associations to the person reading the words. The images are projected to be psychologically appealing. Psychologically appealing images are those which appeal to our seven deadly sins: sexual urges, vanity, snobbery, gluttony, greed, etc.

Many analyses of advertising have shown the mechanism of psychological associations built into the ad message. In particular they showed that the level of most of these appeals is that of sheer brutes, of ultimate half-wits whose only desire is to satisfy their most rudimentary biological urges. However, not many analyses of advertising, if any at all, show how frail the link is between the picture set to evoke emotional reactions and the linguistic utterance which, in the final analysis, is the message of the ad. We must remember that it is the verbal message which ultimately draws us to the marketplace. The analysis of this verbal or linguistic level of the ad is our main concern here.

Language is, of course, basically a medium of communication. To be an adequate medium, language must be flexible. But to be flexible is one thing; to be entirely elastic and malleable is another. These other two characteristics, extreme elasticity and malleability, are required from the language which is set to infiltrate people's minds and contaminate their mental habits. It is in this latter capacity that admen want to employ language. And consequently, they do everything conceivable, and sometimes inconceivable, to make language infinitely flexible and as malleable as plasticene.

The point is very simple. If language is made a plasticene, the meaning of concepts is so stretched that words are deprived of their original sense and end up with whatever sense the wild imagination of the admen equips them. Since the language of ads often departs radically from ordinary language, advertisements could in one sense be regarded as pieces of poetry.[1]

[1] The idea that advertising is a kind of bad poetry was first forcibly and tellingly expressed by E. E. Cummings in his "Poem, or Beauty Hurts Mr. Vinal" (1926). See also "Poetry and Advertising," Chapter XV of Hayakawa's *Language in Thought and Action* (rev. ed., 1964).

A piece of poetry should have a nice ring to its words, pleasant or extraordinary association of ideas, unusual combinations of meanings. The factual content is not important. For communication, as I shall use the term here, the factual content is most important. It is the content that we wish to communicate, and this is conveyed in messages. Consequently, messages must contain factual information. If there is no factual information in the message, the message does not communicate anything. Usually the actual content of the message may be expressed in many different ways. What is important is the content, not the manner of expression. If the manner of expressing a message is more important than its content, then the message does not serve the purpose of communication. It may serve many other purposes, but it does not serve the purpose of conveying factual information.

And this is exactly the case with advertising. The advertising messages are pseudo-messages, not genuine messages. They do not contain factual information. At any rate, this is not their main purpose. Their main purpose is not to inform but to force us to buy. It is clear that if the content of advertising were of any importance, then the same message worded differently would serve the same function; namely, of informing us. This is obviously not the case with advertising: the overwhelming majority of ads would have little effect, if any, if they were phrased differently.

In art, our emotional involvement is the source of our delight. It is the uniqueness of the form that inspires our thoughts and arouses our emotions. The meaning and significance of the work of art hinge upon the uniqueness of its form. Once the form is destroyed or altered, the work of art does not exist any more. If the validity of advertisements depends on preserving their form intact, then they pretend to be pieces of art, but not the carriers of factual information. The trouble is that they *do* pretend to give factual and objective information—but in a rather peculiar way: in such a way that the "information" would force us to acquire the product which is the substance of the message.

Communication is for humans. It is the mark of a rational man to grasp the content of a message irrespective of the form of its presentation—that is, irrespective of its linguistic expression. The nature of any communication in which the actual information conveyed is less significant than the manner of its presentation is, to say the least, illogical. The illogical man is what advertising is after. This is why advertising is so anti-rational; this is why it aims at uprooting not only the rationality of man but his common sense; this is why it indulges in exuberant but deplorable linguistic orgies.

Distortion of language, violation of logic, and corruption of values are about the most common devices through which advertising operates. This is particularly striking in endless perversions of the word FREE. Since this word has such a powerful impact on us, there is no limit to its abuse. In his novel *1984*, George Orwell showed that what is required for establishing a "perfect" dictatorship is perhaps no more than a systematic reform of language. The condition is, however, that the reform must be thorough and complete. "Doubletalk" as a possible reality has, since Orwell's novel, been viewed with horror, but not with incredulity. The question is whether doubletalk has not already become part of our reality, has not already been diffused in our blood stream through means different from those Orwell conceived of. Isn't it true that advertising has become a perfect Orwellian institution?

Nowadays there is in operation a doubletalk concept of freedom according to which protecting the public from fraud and deceit and warning people about dangers to their health is but "an erosion of freedom." This concept of freedom is, needless to say, advocated and defended by advertising agencies. In the opinion of admen, "freedom" for people means protecting people from their common sense and ability to think. For many admen "freedom" means freedom to advertise in whatsoever manner is profitable, freedom to force you to buy, freedom to penetrate your subconscious, freedom to dupe you, to hook you, to make a sucker of you, freedom to take away your freedom. Anything else is for them but an "erosion of freedom." Hail Mr. Orwell! Hail doubletalk!

Now to turn to some concrete illustrations:

MUSTANG! A CAR TO MAKE WEAK MEN STRONG, STRONG MEN INVINCIBLE.

Do not say that we do not believe such obvious blusterings. We do. It seems that the art of magicians—according to which some incantations evoke events, bring rain, heal wounds; some amulets bring good luck, prevent bad luck or illness—has been re-established by contemporary advertising. Motor cars in particular are the amulets of the atomic age. They possess all the miraculous qualities you wish them to possess—from being a substitute for a sweetheart (or mistress, if you prefer) to being a soothing balm to a crushed ego. Dictionaries usually define an automobile as a self-propelled vehicle for the transportation of people or goods. The car industry and car dealers are of a quite different opinion. Perhaps lexicographers are outdated in their conception of "automobile."

Roughly speaking, motor cars are advertised to be amulets of two kinds. The first casts spells on us and makes us happy, or builds up our personality, or adds to our strength, or makes us invincible if we are already strong; the second casts spells on others and, while we drive this magic vehicle, makes other people see us as more important, more influential, more irresistible. As yet, there are no cars which, being driven by us, would bring punishment upon our enemies. Perhaps one day this will come to pass. The question is how many of us can really resist the incantations of car dealers and remain impervious to the "magical" qualities allegedly embodied in the modern automobile. How many of us can remain uninfluenced by the continuous flow of messages, in spite of our ability to see the nonsense of each one individually?

Our civilization has often been called the motor-car civilization. But in no less degree, it is the drug civilization; it is also the detergent civilization. Each of these elements is apparently essential to the well-being of our society. But it is by no means only detergents, cars, or drugs that offer us full happiness "as a reasonable price." Nowadays, practically any product can give you happiness.

Happiness Is To Get (or Give) a Bulova

The only problem is to believe it. Whether Bulova is a yellow canary, a black watch, or a green giraffe, it unfortunately takes a bit more to achieve happiness then getting or giving a Bulova. But of course the counter-argument can go, "happiness" in this ad was not meant literally but only figuratively. Admen today are like poets; we must allow them poetic license. But must we? And how figuratively would they really like to be taken? It seems that they (and the producers of the products they advertise) would be very unhappy if we took all their messages figuratively. On the contrary, they want their messages to be taken as literally as possible. It is precisely their business to convince us about the "loveliness" of soaps, "happiness" in Bulovas, and "delights" of a cigarette puff. The poetic language they use is meant to break our resistance, to produce desirable associations which we usually associate with poetry.

The sad part of the story is that in the process of serving advertising, poetry has gone down the drain. Poetic expressions are poetic so long as they are in the context of poetry; so long as they evoke unusual emotional reactions, serve as a substance of an esthetic experience—the experience of delight. In its exuberant development, advertising has debased almost the entire poetic vocabulary. And advertising seems to be responsible for a decline of the poetic taste and for a considerable indifference, if not hostility, of American youth toward poetry.

The nausea which one experiences on being bombarded by the pseudo-poetry of advertising may recur when one approaches genuine poetry, unless one has developed love for poetry *before* becoming aware of advertising—which is impossible for young people nowadays. It is quite natural that such a reaction would develop. We are not likely to seek nausea deliberately, and so we would rather avoid whatever reminds us of it. It seems that if the process of debasing and abusing language by advertising is carried further, we may discover a new value in absolute simplicity of language. Perhaps one day, when the traditional poetry is completely ruined, we shall count as poetry some simple and concrete descriptions like this: "There is a table in the room. The table is brown. There are three chairs at the table. A man is sitting on one of the chairs."[2]

The main point is more significant. By applying highly charged emotional terms like "lovely" to soaps, and "bold" and "proud" to automobiles, advertising pushes us to consider objects as if they were human beings. Through the language of advertising, we participate in the process of constant personification of objects which we should "love," be "enchanted by," be "delighted with," and "be happy with." Unconsciously we have developed emotional attachments to objects surrounding us. We have become worshippers of objects. Advertising has been a powerful force in this process.

My thesis is that the semantic environment has a more profound influence on our behavior and our attitudes than we are aware. If this thesis is correct, it may throw some light on the phenomenon which we usually attribute to the population explosion and the mechanization of our lives; namely, the depersonalization of human relations. I should like to suggest that perhaps a transfer of attitudes through the change of the semantic environment has taken place. Previously, highly emotional expressions were applied to human beings. Nowadays, they are constantly and massively applied by the admen to objects. We have thus developed loving fondness for objects which we worship. Dehumanizing of human relations seems to be the other part of this process. It is quite natural that when we become more and more emotionally involved with objects, we tend to be less and less involved with people. As a consequence, attitudes traditionally reserved for objects are now displayed toward people. In love, in friendship, and in the multitude of other human relations, detachment, lack of interest, and coldness seem to prevail. Human beings are treated like objects.

To summarize, the success of advertising and our failure to defend ourselves against it result mainly from our obliviousness to some of the functions of language. We think that language is

---

[2] Perhaps some poets have discovered this principle already. Here is the complete text of "The Red Wheelbarrow" by William Carlos Williams: "so much depends/ upon/ a red wheel/ barrow/ glazed with rain/ water / beside the white / chickens." (*Collected Poems 1921-1931*, Objectivist Press, 1934.)

a tool, an indifferent piece of gadgetry which simply serves the process of communication and that the only relation we have to language is that *we use language*. We do indeed use it. But this is only part of the story. The other part, which is usually overlooked, is that *language uses us*—by forming our personal and emotional habits, by forming our attitudes. Language is thus not only our servant; it is also our master. No one knows this better than the adman!

The relation between language and us is more complicated than we usually are prepared to admit. To escape the tyranny of language, we have to recognize the double role of language in human relations, (1) as a carrier of messages we send, and (2) as a shaper of the content of human relations. We cannot reduce or nullify the influence of language on us by simply denying the existence of this influence. The only reasonable thing we can do is to recognize the force of language: its strength, the way it works, its theater of operations. By identifying the traps of language, by identifying the linguistic strategies of the admen and other propagandists, we shall be able to cope with the semantic environment much more effectively than we have done hitherto.

SUGGESTIONS FOR DISCUSSION AND WRITING

1. *Survey some recent advertisements to see how frequently the "wonder-making" words such as those mentioned in the essay appear.*

2. *Locate and study several advertisements that reveal how the language has been made so flexible the words have been deprived of their usual sense.*

3. *"The main purpose of advertising," according to the author, "is not to inform but to force us to buy." Examine a number of advertisements to see what proportion actually informs us about the product and what proportion merely influences us to buy.*

4. One of the major faults with which the author charges advertising is the way it treats objects like humans and humans like objects. Can you provide examples of advertisements that support that charge?

5. The author says that "The only thing we can do about the influence of language on us is to be aware of it. This awareness may diminish the grip language has on us." How do we go about becoming aware, and how might such awareness diminish that grip?

5

Paul Dickson

THE WAR OF THE WORDS

Alice in Wonderland may at first seem far removed from the subject of this essay: the role of the United States in the Vietnam War. But free-lance writer Paul Dickson argues that at least one aspect of that fiction—"Humpty Dumptian semantics"—has a factual equivalent in our government's creation of a language that aims less at clarifying than obscuring the nature of that war and our role in it.

"When I use a word," Humpty Dumpty told Alice, "it means just what I choose it to mean—neither more nor less." This scornful statement was delivered to Alice in *Thorugh The Looking Glass* after she objected to his interpretation of the word "glory" as meaning "a nice knockdown argument." Such an unflinching attitude towards language is significant in light of the war in Vietnam because it is obvious that "Humpty Dumptian semantics" have been and are today a major tenet of unwritten official policy.

Wars have always presented a semantic challenge to those managing them because armed conflict is ever so much harder—if not impossible—to start and maintain in an atmosphere of official candor. Each war generates its own terminology—the Korean war, for instance, brought forth the phraseology of the "police action." If there is a strong sales challenge involved in putting over a war, the number of new coinages and official redefinitions increases. Consequently, the Vietnam war has required more than just a new set of terms but rather a veritable language (which some call Vietlish) of sometimes subtle and sometimes not-so-subtle deception. Unlike the more ambitiously constructed falsehoods of the war disclosed in the Pentagon Papers, the words

Reprinted with permission from *The Progressive*, April 1972.

and phrases used and created by the Government have been compact little lies, ruses, dodges, distortions, and euphemisms. Linguistically, the Pentagon Papers are interesting because the same officials who had no delusions about the larger fictions of the war had brought their own deluding language and used it in their top-secret memos—apparently without embarrassment.

Thus far the war has manifested itself in three linguistic periods, each presenting a distinct dialect of the mother tongue. The first period, characterized by the dialect of "UnWar I," began with the earliest U.S. involvement and lasted to 1965. This was followed by the dialect of the "dirty little war" period from 1965 to 1968 which, in turn, was followed by the period from 1968 to the present in which the dialect of "UnWar II" is spoken. As a careful student of "Humpty Dumptian semantics," I have set down the linguistic record of these three periods.

I. UNWAR I

Early in the war Vietlish was geared to understatement, and the efforts to prove that our actions in Vietnam were not "war" but UnWar were far more exhaustive than the campaign to make 7-Up the "UnCola." Or as Peter Lisagor, Washington correspondent of the *Chicago Daily News* recently recalled, "A whole language was created to minimize that we were in war, and didn't know how to fight it."

It was during this first period that some of the classic obfuscations were coined. Most famous were those "advisers" who were not "troops" even when more than 20,000 of them were roaming the Vietnamese countryside. Included in the advisory group were large numbers of pilots who, as several writers of the period pointed out, dropped bombs and seldom if ever advised against dropping them. "Adviser" stands as one of the euphemisms of the war that was so important to Washington it had its own elaborate support force. Prior to April, 1965, when the adviser ruse was officially dropped, all American adviser-pilots had to be accompanied by a South Vietnamese ("Even a mail clerk would do," according to the *Los Angeles Times* back then) so that if the craft crashed or was shot down, the Vietnamese could be named as the pilot.

The words most often used to describe our increasingly combative role during this period were "indirect," "economic," "political," or "tutorial." It was made to sound like a faraway graduate school rather than a war. "Counterinsurgency" was a technique which the United States taught rather than practiced, and when an American flyer-"adviser" did not return to his "training base" his death was noted as a "training mission" loss. The job of declaring that the United States was actually at war in Vietnam fell to the press and individual legislators.

II. "DIRTY LITTLE WAR"

After the Tonkin Gulf Resolution was put into effect in 1965, the UnWar ruse was officially dropped in favor of the "dirty little war"—so called because no matter how big or nasty it got, it was still officially framed in diminutive terms inferring something of the size and scope of an Excedrin headache. The word "dirty" was a reference to the enemy and served as a built-in rationale for the counter-dirty tactics employed by the home team. Although the actual term "dirty little war" was most common it had its variant forms such as "mean, dirty struggle" (Secretary of State Dean Rusk) and "dirty, brutal and difficult" (President Lyndon Johnson).

One of the most apparent changes from the first period to second period dialect was the shift in the predominant tense of official pronouncements. During the UnWar phase, statements were presented in the noncommittal present, giving no hint that the war had a future. From the beginning of the second period, the predominant tense moved to the future, indicating that the war had had a beginning, was in the middle, and would soon have an end.

Semantically, the most difficult aspect of this period was that of building up the war without making it too obvious. One of the few detailed studies of the verbal accomplishments of this period was conducted by psychiatrist Isidore Ziferstein. In his paper,

"Psychological Habituation to War," he follows the U.S. build-up in terms of conditioning the homefront:

"Each step appears to evolve as a logical consequence of a previous small and seemingly insignificant step toward greater involvement. And the new step equally logically prepares the ground for the next small and seemingly insignificant step." The result is to leave the citizen "bewildered, helpless, and apathetic."

One of the habituation techniques Ziferstein cited is that of "psychological backing and filling," which is ideally suited to periods of escalation. Ziferstein reduced the process of escalation to a simple formula which works like this: "First step: highly alarming rumors about escalation are leaked.' Second step: the President officially and dramatically sets the anxieties to rest by announcing a much more moderate rate of escalation, and accompanies this announcement with assurances of the Government's peaceful intentions. Third step: after the general sigh of relief, the originally rumored escalation is gradually put into effect, after all."

The handmaiden of habituation is euphemism, and the second period—the "dirty little war"—was euphemistically the richest of this war and perhaps of any war. Many of the terms were replays of terms long ago spotted as outrageous misrepresentations but which were nonetheless effective. In his 1946 essay, "Politics and the English Language," George Orwell pointed out that because many political actions are too brutal to face without flinching, the language describing such actions has to consist largely of "euphemism, question-begging, and sheer cloudy vagueness." Among Orwell's 1946 illustrations were these: "Defenseless villages are bombarded from the air, the inhabitants driven out into the countryside, the cattle machine-gunned, the huts set on fire with incendiary bullets: this is called *pacification*. Millions of peasants are robbed of their farms and sent trudging along the roads with no more than they can carry: this is called *transfer of population* . . ."

Mario Pei, in his book *Words in Sheep's Clothing*, says that in such fields as advertising, economics, and education, euphemisms —or, as he terms them, "weasel words"—are generally gross overstatements. However, in the field of war and destruction the trend is to minimize the implications. This, of course, was the operating principle in effect during the second period of the war.

Once the "advisers" had become "troops," the words "defend" and "defenders" received much official play. The first Marines in Danang were sent to "defend" American installations, and then more Marines were sent to "defend" the "defending" Marines. Words like "offensive" and "attack" (as in "sneak attack") were reserved for the other side. The United States never attacked but rather initiated "an Allied drive," began an operation (like "Operation Cedar Falls") or, to use President Johnson's oft-used term, "took positive action." And while the other side could only "ambush" American and South Vietnamese troops, the Allies could only "encounter" their adversaries.

The innocuous-sounding "area denial" was a "concept" invoked to describe a variety of acts ranging from the incessant use of "anti-personnel devices" (which Mario Pei calls the total euphemization of the term "killer weapon") to the wiping of villages off the map. The forced transfer of civilians was invariably given a nice "operation" or "program" title like "Operation Independence" or "Operation Sunrise." Such transfers were officially termed "compulsory relocation" and the civilians involved were either moved to "strategic hamlets" or "resettlement centers"—locales that were often no more than what were called "refugee camps" in other wars. As a *New York Times* reporter observed a few years back, "A few people were driven together, a roll of barbed wire was thrown over their heads, and the strategic hamlet was finished."

"Operation Ranch Hand" was the folksy name created in 1965 for a series of concentrated airborne chemical defoliation missions during which, according to officials at that time, the chemicals being dropped were likened to "weed killers"—even though they could kill a plant fifteen miles from the point at which they were dropped. Terms like "Ranch Hand," "weed killer" ("the same as you buy in the hardware store at home," said an American official in 1966), "routine improvement of visibility in jungle areas," "non-toxic," and "resources control" conspired to make defoliation and crop destruction sound like a major 4-H Club project. Other terms were created to give the adventurer the

aura of a Boy Scout hike. The thirty-four dollars given to families of South Vietnamese civilians killed by mistake were officially called "condolence awards," and gross bombing errors were
seldom termed anything more incriminating than "navigation
errors," "misdirections," or "technical errors." The titles given to
U.S. attacks and operations were given obfuscating American
names like Harrison, Lincoln, Garfield, Jim Bowie, Yankee Team,
Dewey Canyon, Phoenix, White Wing and Pierce Arrow.

Just as terms for U.S. operations, concepts, and hardware
tended to sugar-coat their lethal reality, terms for their enemy
counterparts were given more imposing names. Not content with
announcing "harass and destroy" missions against rather innocuous-sounding junks, sampans, and barges, the Navy officially
began calling them "waterborne logistic craft." Not content with
Vietcong, many U.S. pronouncements opted for "hard-core Vietcong." For a long time such titles as "National Liberation Front"
and "People's Army of North Vietnam" did not exist, officially,
unless accompanied by the disdainful modifier, "so-called." The
conspiratorial-sounding term "infrastructure" was liberally applied in lieu of the civil government when officials explained that
villages had to be cleared to "deny the use of the civilian infrastructure" to the Vietcong, or Pathet Lao, depending on what
nation's villages the Americans were "saving" at the time.

One of the outstanding linguistic innovations of the war crop-
ped up as a facet of the "dirty little war" dialect. Known as
"before and after" terms, they were created to meet the demand
for "results" from Washington where the war was being fought
on charts at Pentagon press briefings. Such terms mostly revealed
themselves after an object was destroyed and not only gave
dignity to that which was gone but—as with other facets of
Vietlish—made it all seem less horrific. A good primer in "before
and after" terms appeared in 1966 in a letter from a bomber pilot
in Vietnam to the editors of *Aviation Week and Space Technology* which pointed out that once destroyed a "straw-thatched
hut" officially became "a structure," a dead pig or goat a "pack
animal," a splintered set of logs felled across a stream "a bridge,"
and a sunken one-man dugout a "boat."

Called "target verification," these curious postmortems were spotted by others. For instance, more than one news dispatch from the war told how a "hootch" or hut, once destroyed, became an "enemy building," and bomb shelters blasted were seldom called that after their demise but rather "VC bunkers" or "a network of tunnels." A non-destructive example of "before and after" Vietlish has been the instant renaming of a "civilian refugee" to a "defector" or "returnee" as soon as he walked into a Chieu-Hoi (Open Arms) camp. The late Bernard Fall reported that in 1966 the United States claimed a total of 20,242 "defectors" who carried 1,963 weapons among them. Fall concluded that most were unarmed civilians "surrendering" at the peaceful camps to escape the horrors of war rather than defectors from the other side.

During this period officially-adopted modifiers helped mitigate a multitude of sins. "V.C. rice" was inevitably the only rice ever confiscated or pinpointed by airborne herbicides. Moreover, such enemy rice was invariably found in "caches" or "hoards" while AID rice came packaged in bags. Righteous-sounding "counter-terrorists" was the U.S. term for our allied South Vietnamese specialists practicing the same black arts of destruction and assassination attributed to "Vietcong terrorists." "Counter," by the way, has long been in vogue as a soothing military modifier employed in such constructions as "counter-force deterrence" —a resonant, almost musical term that has what poets call liquidity which is produced by the absence of frictional consonants and the liberal use of r's.

Perhaps the most abused and abusive adjective of the war has been the provocative "hostile," especially when used to modify "civilians." Writing in *The New Yorker* in 1967, Jonathan Schell pointed out that during the land-clearing "Operation Cedar Falls" the Army faced a major semantic problem in deciding what to call the people it was forcing from their homes. According to Schell, the dilemma was resolved by calling them "hostile civilians" at the scene of "evacuation"—strongly hinting that their forced transfer was justly called for—and then, once transferred to camps, calling them "refugees," a term that strongly suggests that these were the people fleeing their enemy. (A refugee trying to return home on his own, needless to say, became "an escapee.")

Not all of the official terminology of the period fooled people. The most conspicuous gaffes were some of the ill-fated attempts to change war-weary terms that were getting bad names for themselves. Several futile attempts were made to change "napalm"—a World War II marriage of naphthene and palmite—to new names like "napthagel" and "incendagel." As revealed recently in the *Columbia Journalism Review*, the Military Assistance Command Vietnam (MACV) put into a memo its dissatisfaction with such terms as "search and destroy," "body count," and "Hamburger Hill," asking instead for, respectively, "search and clear," "enemy deaths," and "Hill 937." The memo which was distributed to the Armed Forces Vietnam Network also ruled out "National Liberation Front" in favor of "Vietcong," and cautioned that the phrase "troops used to bait the enemy" was never to be used.

III. UNWAR II

Since the election of President Nixon, the demeaning of meaning has continued unabated into a third period. As it was in the beginning, the current official effort is to make everything—no matter how extraordinary—sound routine with the emphasis on giving the war a patina of normality, optimism, and even dullness. The effort to play things down in this current phase is generally reminiscent of the early UnWar period characterized by low-key words. It is a distinct dialect, but close enough to the first to be called UnWar II.

Late last year, for instance, Defense Secretary Melvin Laird insisted time and again that the ill-fated, out-of-the-ordinary raid to rescue POWs from North Vietnam was a routine SAR (for search and rescue) operation—a term normally used to describe rescue efforts of a much smaller size and scope. The presently popular construction, "routine, limited-duration, reinforced, protective reaction air strike," sounds more like the name of a paper given by a theoretical physicist than what it is—an air attack. "Limited air interdiction" tends to evoke a picture of a poorly-funded soil aeration program rather than heavy bombing in Laos. And in the current dialect there is no such word as "invasion." Rather it is "an incursion"—a term that makes one think of a somewhat impolite excursion.

Once again the introduction of a new dialect has been accompanied by a shift in the predominant official tense. This time most statements are made in the present ("Vietnamization is working") and the past (as in Nixon's "mission accomplished" speech to the Marines last April). The future tense is used only sparingly and then in conjunction with terms like the President's beloved promise of a "just peace" following on the heels of Vietnamization. "Just peace," which translates as "continued war without American combat troops," is as cruel a misuse of the word peace as came from President Johnson who was "waging the peace," "conducting a peace-keeping action" or saying, "Our purpose is not war but peace"—a slogan minted in mid-1966 when U.S. bombers were hitting Haiphong and Hanoi.

It took years, but at last the words and phrases of Vietlish began to falter. Gallup's pollsters found last March that seven out of ten Americans believed the Administration was veiling facts about the war. Probably the quotation from the war which will be longest remembered is that of the unnamed American major who said of the village of Bentre, "It became necessary to destroy the town to save it."

Many of the words and terms of the war are by now so completely debunked and abused that if they were not so laden with tragedy they would be funny. Among them: "pacification," "light at the end of the tunnel," "body count," "free-fire zone," "hearts and minds of the people," "suspected Vietcong target," "kill ratio," "target of opportunity," "quantification," and "search and destroy"—the last a term that even the most sluggish GI and junior high school student understands really means to "destroy and then search."

The semantic lesson of Vietnam is not that in the final analysis words began to fail those who coined them, but that they succeeded so well for so long. Obfuscating terminology buys time and continues to do so today. This is the time during which the cat-and-mouse game of verbal coinage and debunking occurs. Despite claims to the contrary, the war is still very much on and no doubt more terms will be coined for the periods ahead. For instance, yesterday's "advisers" may be tomorrow's "instructors," "support staff," or "technicians." And while "protective reaction" is still doing its job—as evidenced by the fact that so many newspapers repeat it without so much as a set of quotation marks—some publications have caught on, and its time may be drawing nigh. What will come in its place? Perhaps it is time for a revival of President Johnson's pet, "positive response," to cover such attacks, or perhaps it will be something new like "withdrawal-affiliated sortie."

Even though the language of the Vietnam War is wearing thin and requiring more frequent changes to keep us off balance, other life and death terms remain generally unchallenged. "Atomic device," which sounds like the name for a power plant, still passes for "thermonuclear weapon." People have long-since stopped flinching when they hear "Defense Department," even though that agency does more and more of its business away from home. The ever-so comforting term "national security" gets applied without public outcry to far-flung outrages such as invoking it as a reason for keeping American reporters out of Laos or for opposing publication of the Pentagon Papers.

The time has come for a citizen militia of verbal vigilantes who know the difference between a war and a "just peace" and who in their own speech apply the principles of the truth in packaging laws. With notable exceptions, the two groups in the best position to call verbal bluffs and reveal word-pollution have, regrettably, not done so. First, the press has too often babbled in official jargon or used its own weasel words to tell us what is happening. For instance, it has been only recently that more than a few periodicals have started calling war-related lies "lies" instead of "elements in the credibility gap," or "evidence of lack of candor." Second, the nation's professional linguists and semanticists seem to have decided to examine the martial language of today from the safer vantage of a decade or so hence. A search of current journals in these fields reveals that the terminology and slang of World War II have just recently become acceptable for scholarly analysis.

The best way to clear the air is to begin translating official Pentagonese and Vietlish into concise, de-euphemized English as was recently done when Senator Birch Bayh of Indiana boiled down the Administration's Vietnam policy to its essence: "It is bombing four countries, and has invaded two, in order to withdraw from one."

SUGGESTIONS FOR DISCUSSION AND WRITING

1. What does the author mean by "Humpty Dumptian semantics"? In what ways does he see such a use of language to be consistent with unwritten official policy?

2. What does the term "anti-personnel device" appear to mean? What does it actually mean? Is the term accurate and appropriate? Why or why not? If not, can you suggest an adequate substitute?

3. Read again the quotation from George Orwell in paragraph 6 of Part 2, noting that it was first published in 1946. Does there seem to be any substantial difference between the situation Orwell was describing then and the one described in this article? See if you can find some current equivalents or can in any other way relate Orwell's passage to contemporary situations.

4. It has been argued that the use of euphemism and other techniques of language criticized in this article is necessary not only to make the conditions and situations they describe more acceptable, but to make them bearable. How would you respond to this argument?

5. The author concludes with a call for a "citizen militia of verbal vigilantes" whose jobs would apparently be to expose the kinds of abuse and misuse of language described here. Do the terms "militia" and "vigilante" seem appropriate terms? Would you favor organizing such a group? Why or why not? If you would, who should belong to it, and how might it function?

6

Ronald Gross

ON LANGUAGE POLLUTION

Several authors represented in this book use the word "pollution" to describe the condition of American English today. Here, Ronald Gross, a free-lance writer and editor, probes into the causes and consequences of language pollution, a problem that he notes is greatly intensified by our mass media of communication. In the process, he considers some leading analyses of language pollution, examines the concept itself and its underlying assumptions, and suggests some techniques to detect and alleviate language pollution.

The language we use, like the air we breathe, the water we drink, and the food we eat, is increasingly polluted. The Niagara of words which barrages us every moment of our waking lives distorts and demeans our capacity to think clearly, feel truly, and act humanely. The language around us is not alive and human, but mechanical and dead. It no longer speaks to us with the voice of a real man—a man who was born, is living, and will one day die. Rather, it speaks with the inhuman screech or clatter or glossiness of the machine, in which one cog communicates with other cogs in the language of the machine of which they are both merely parts.

Such a situation is dangerous. Language is the nervous system of a society, the means by which a people learns what's going on and reacts appropriately. If an animal's nervous system does not transmit sensations and stimuli, the animal atrophies. If a nation's language decays, the nation declines. (Ezra Pound, *ABC of Reading*)

The language pollution which began as a droll concomitant of

Reprinted from *Etc.*, Vol. 26, No. 2, by permission of the International Society for General Semantics.

advertising and the media—the constant conditioning through appeals to the most trivial and petty motives and fears—has now invaded the nation's most serious discourses. Issues of war and peace, justice and sanity are debated in meaningless slogans: law and order, peace with justice, etc. John Kenneth Galbraith points this out in *The New Industrial State* and Mario Pei has noted the comparability of salesmanship and propaganda:

> The language of commercial advertising is superlatively a form of propaganda, designed to sell the idea of and desirability of the product the sponsor wants to sell. Nevertheless, such is the force of habit that one seldom hears *commercial* and *propaganda* in the same breath.

The manipulative use of language, honed to razor sharpness on Madison Avenue, is increasingly wielded for more portentous advocacy. The demeaning of meaning characteristic of the relatively trivial, consumer side of our society begins to pervade the nation's graver discourse.

We have witnessed several recent examples. The phrase "Black Power" shot through the society like a rampaging firecracker, deriving its electric potency from the fact that no one knew exactly what it meant. All the more powerful for that reason, it permitted people to project into it their inchoate aspirations and unarticulated fears.

Similarly, we debate the Vietnam war in language which is, as often noted, inadequate to the complexities and urgencies of reality. The credibility gap, the escalation of language corresponding to each escalation of the war, the "Newspeak" about "pacification programs" and "democratic government"—all testify to a pollution which has turned discussion of this issue into a dispiriting cacophony of harangues.

No wonder, then, that our public language itself becomes suspect. The Orwellian nightmare of Newspeak—a language manipulated to manipulate its users—haunts cultural criticism today, but with a difference. Conscious manipulation is not the issue so much as an impersonal degeneration in the use of language through the forces unleashed by contemporary technological and social conditions.

It is the technology of mass communications which makes today's language pollution quite different from the traditional tricks of rhetoric and special pleading which we learned about in school and college. The media have turned up the volume, multiplied the exposures, reiterated the impact, and enlarged the strategies. Today fifteen hundred messages bombard us each day. They hit us again and again. They reinforce each other in whole patterns of thought and feeling.

Professor Neil Postman of New York University has described the cumulative impact:

> As in the case of air and water pollution, the menace of language pollution increases in direct proportion to the increase in the volume of garbage. There have always been men who have used language as a means of concealing, deceiving, and expressing their ignorance, just as men have always urinated in fresh streams. A stream can tolerate, absorb, even convert to good uses a certain amount of waste. So can the semantic environment. But beyond a given bulk, garbage creates an ecological imbalance. The built-in survival strategies of the environment are overcome. It sickens and becomes useless.

Clearly, this kind of pollution requires more than the critical thinking we were taught in school. It goes beyond mere use of slogans and oversimplifications and errors in logic. That is the value of McLuhan: to make us realize that the media environment itself constitutes a new threat to sanity.

Semanticists have pioneered in diagnosing and prescribing for this condition. They have been abetted from time to time by allies from the field of literary studies. One thinks of F. R. Leavis, Daniel Boorstein, Benjamin DeMott, and Walker Gibson.

At present, however, the semanticist's concern with the language environment is being augmented by an unprecedented interest in this topic on the part of some leading literary and social critics. Indeed, it would not be excessive to say that the theme of language pollution is becoming a principal concern of cultural criticism today.

My purpose here is to consider some leading analyses of language pollution, to examine and criticize the concept itself and the underlying assumption of a relationship between a people's language and its national character and destiny, and to suggest some of the techniques needed to detect and alleviate language pollution.

In two essays included in his much-acclaimed recent book, *Language and Silence*, George Steiner describes several ways in which, in his view, "A language shows that it has in it the germ of dissolution."

> Actions of the mind that were once spontaneous become mechanical, frozen habits (dead metaphors, stock similes, slogans). Words grow longer and more ambiguous. Instead of style, there is rhetoric. Instead of precise common usage, there is jargon. Foreign roots and borrowings are no longer absorbed into the blood stream of the native tongue. They are merely swallowed and remain an alien intrusion. All these technical failures accumulate to the essential failure: the language no longer sharpens thought but blurs it. Instead of charging every expression with the greatest available energy and directness, it loosens and disperses the intensity of feeling. . . . In short, the language is no longer lived; it is merely spoken.

However, Steiner swiftly proceeds to the point of considering language as an independent living organism which can be poisoned or killed. He argues that pornographic writings, for example, "leave language poorer," and that Fascist rhetoric and inhuman actions "settle in the marrow of language. . . ." The German language, he concludes, "was not innocent of the horrors of Nazism. . . . Nazism found in the language precisely what it needed to give voice to its savagery."

The trouble is, one can probably find the symptoms which Steiner points to in any language at any time. For example, Dennis Bloodworth, writing in *The New York Times Magazine* on "China Is Like the Chinese Language," portrayed the Chinese language as peculiarly conducive to thinking which is "narrow and mechanical." Citing such symptoms as word-magic, stereotypes, clichés, puns, sloganeering, the big lie, and guilt by association, Bloodworth argued that these work on the Chinese "like pile drivers, pounding their simple messages further and further into [their] skulls." But Bloodworth made no mention of the pervasiveness of precisely similar slogans in *our* language environment: the moronic and deranged commercials and political slogans which pound at us. What would a Chinese make of the Dodge Rebellion, Marlboro Country, and It's What's Up Front that Counts?

Bloodworth puts down the Chinese language as "essentially feminine . . . dealing in concrete forms, so that abstracts cannot be properly expressed. There is no word for size: the Chinese say 'big-small.' " But, as Ezra Pound once pointed out, this concreteness prevents a Chinese from getting mired in meaningless abstractions. "In Europe," Pound wrote,

> if you ask a man to define anything, his definition always moves away from the simple things that he knows perfectly well, and recedes into an unknown region, that is a region of remoter and progressively remoter abstraction. Thus if you ask him what red is, he says it is a "colour." If you ask him what a colour is, he tells you it is a vibration or a refraction of light, or a division of the spectrum. And if you ask him what a vibration is, he tells you it is a mode of energy. . . .

A Chinese, Pound points out, would have started with the pictograms of a rose, iron rust, cherry, and flamingo. Semanticist, Stuart Chase, alluding to this quality of the Chinese language, predicted that China would prove far less susceptible than Western nations to the ideological abstractions of revolutionary Marxism. That was a bit too simple; but so are Mr. Bloodworth's generalizations.

Succumbing to inhumane and uncritical modes of thinking and speaking are, then, perennial human failings, not attributes of particular languages. What Steiner and Bloodworth are describing can better be considered as a congeries of language styles, rather than as a "pollution" inhering in the language itself. The dead language of wornout metaphors and similes, slogans, slithery ambiguities, rhetoric, and jargon can be found dominating certain enclaves of any society. Such linguistic vices may afflict individuals; they may characterize certain occupations and professions considered as a whole; or they may indeed become so prevalent in a nation's vital political communications that they may be said to affect the society's political destiny at a particular moment in time—though here it is healthy to keep in mind how rare it is that any one aspect, no matter how dramatic, truly determines a large historical development. Even in cases like this last, however, it is more accurate to discuss certain modes of expression, habits of language usage, semantic compulsions, and the like, than to proceed as Steiner does to the stage where the language is considered an organic unity in itself, of which particular linguistic acts are mere examples.

The theory and practice of semantics suggest that the focus of inquiry should be shifted to a more concrete level. Instead of focusing on language as such, conceived as a totality, an independent organism, a unitary object of reflection, attention should be given to more manageable categories which can be more precisely observed, described, and discussed, and which will permit certain distinctions to be made which escape notice when we look at a language as a whole. Indeed, it seems a little presumptuous and obscurantist to indulge in harangues about the German language or the Chinese language. How, exactly, does one go about observing an entire language, reporting one's observations so that they can be verified by others, responding to criticism of one's interpretation of the data, and refining one's conclusions on the basis of the evidence of other equally competent observers?

George Orwell pointed a more fruitful way in his essay on *Politics and the English Language* (1946). Orwell is quite specific in describing and labeling the language habits which were debasing the tongue, but affirms throughout that

the process is reversible. Modern English, especially written English, is full of bad habits which spread by imitation and which can be avoided if one is willing to take the necessary trouble. If one gets rid of these habits one can think more clearly, and to think clearly is a necessary first step towards political regeneration: so that the fight against bad English is not frivolous and is not the exclusive concern of professional writers.

The habits which Orwell anatomizes are staleness of imagery and lack of precision, the latter permitted through the prevalence of jargon, bombast, pretentious diction, latinisms, pseudo-science terminology, foreign words, the passive voice, and the use of meaningless abstractions, among which he included Fascism, democracy, socialism, freedom, patriotic, realistic, and justice. ("The whole tendency of modern prose is away from concreteness.")

These faults are not accidental, in Orwell's view. They are integral to political discourse in our time, when "it is broadly true that political writing is bad writing." The underlying reason is that political speaking and writing "are largely the defense of the indefensible. . . . Thus political language has to consist largely of euphemism, question-begging and sheer cloudy vagueness." Orwell's prophetic strain becomes uncannily exact as he describes one such example. Writing in 1946:

> Defenseless villages are bombarded from the air, the inhabitants driven out into the countryside, the cattle machine-gunned, the huts set on fire with incendiary bullets: this is called *pacification*. Millions of peasants are robbed of their farms and set trudging along the roads with no more than they can carry: this is called *transfer of population*. . . . Such phraseology is needed if one wants to name things without calling up mental pictures of them. (emphasis in original)

Fraudulence and bad faith between governors and governed thus come to our attention in the first instance through language. Someone writes those words, someone speaks them and prints them. A sudden faltering in leadership can be discerned, as such moments, in the very texture of public language.

Orwell ends with a muted call to arms. While the general

tone or spirit of a language may be beyond the control of the individuals who use it, still it is possible for us to school ourselves in more conscientious and honest composition. He even provides six rules to follow to "change one's own habits, and from time to time . . . if one jeers loudly enough, send some worn-out and useless phrase . . . into the dustbin where it belongs."

For the most part, writers have not carried on the work Orwell started in this essay, in the "Newspeak" appendix to *1984*, and other places: the task of maintaining surveillance over language on behalf of their fellow citizens. This seems, on reflection, an odd lapse. Surely those who know the most and care the most about language, who are aware of and committed to the life of language as the distinctly human mode of existence, seem best suited, indeed morally constrained, to uphold the integrity of the word not only inherently, in their art, but also in more mundane ways.

Interestingly enough it is the most avant garde and formalist writers who seem most aware of this. For example, Eugene Gomringer, Swiss-German source of the international Concrete Poetry movement, has said: "It is only possible to speak of an organic function for poetry in terms of the given linguistic situation." (We might add: semantic situation, psycho-linquistic situation, *media* situation, *communications* situation.)

Let's consider for a moment what poetry, as the queen of the literary arts, really is. "Poets are the unacknowledged legislators of the world." The pretension seems absurd in our society, with the low estate of poetry. But Shelley, who said that, and others, like Plato, who would have understood what he meant, were not thinking of poetry in the diminished sense we do: the books in the library under the label "Poetry." For them, the locus of poetry in a society was language being used with utmost potency, where words and images conveyed through language are creating and disseminating the dominant ideals, aspirations, and fears. Applying that to this society, we will look for poetry where men's minds and hearts are being shaped by verbal symbols.

It at once becomes apparent that this society is dominated by poetry: there is more poetry in the average issue of *Life* magazine than the man of the thirteenth century experienced in a year. But it is the poetry of the media, the poetry of those ad writers whom semanticist S. I. Hayakawa calls the laureates of a consumer society. And suddenly the seemingly outrageous Shelleyan pretension is not only true, but a truism: the hidden-persuaders cliché. Of course the wielders of words through the media are the unacknowledged legislators of how our fellow countrymen think, feel, act. As Alan Watts has noted, this is the most unmaterialistic society going; Americans are constantly eating the menu instead of the food. Language is the original and still the most pervasive psychedelic technology in human society, the primal mind-expanding and mind-manifesting agent for human beings. We are entirely hung up on verbal symbols, poetic abstractions, and concretions—what Ron Tavel calls the lie of the land.

What is the responsibility of the writer or other professional communicator in a time of communications overkill? I suggest that his responsibilities stem from his professional role itself, from those things he knows best because he works with them every day. Just as an automobile worker knows and can judge the quality of manufactured goods, and a construction worker can appraise the value of a house, so the writer or professional communicator knows certain things in his bones—things which can enable him to function better as a citizen and as a human being. What are some of these things?

He knows that the spoken or written word is the most malleable and exploitable of human products. A turn of the pen, a stroke on the typewriter keys, a word spoken into a microphone—all are equally easy to create whether they are true or not, whether they are destined to make for a little progress or a little more confusion in the world. He is more aware than most people that the ideas in our heads, the fears and hopes in our hearts, all come largely not from our personal experience but from what we have seen and heard and read in the media which are all around us.

In short, he knows that messages sent and received are not just incidental diversions but the very stuff of which our lives' quality is composed. He knows, therefore, that concern with the language and communications system of the nation is not a peripheral concern, but a fundamental one. He will, in turn, find himself more than casually aware of the importance of those institutions and organizations and individuals who are working to make communications in America more fruitful. He will sympathize with and possibly support actively such efforts by organizations like the League of Women Voters, Consumers Union, federal and state agencies encouraging constructive use of communications media, TV stations and newspapers which attempt to provide full, fair, and in-depth reporting of the news, individual efforts like the Underground Press and Nat Hentoff's now-defunct "Review of the Press," special programs like the Public Television Network, the Children's Television Laboratory, and WBAI, and the widest possible range of opinion-expression, including tolerance and even encouragement of magazines, publishers, and broadcasters.

Have the leading writers led the way in this endeavor? Sometimes some of them have: Orwell, Boorstein, DeMott, Leavis, Steiner, Burke, McLuhan. Most recently, Pete Hamill in a year-end front-page column in the *Village Voice*, called for "an absolute cleaning up of language as a first step in regaining our national and personal sanity. Among the terms which Hamill wants retired are militant, groovy, imperialists, up tight, white power structure, piece of the action, pig, participatory democracy and guerrilla (followed by words like theater, politics, journalism, painting, etc.).

In my own book, *Pop Poems*, I tried to take a first step in bringing the language environment into poetry. By using no language of my own, but only material taken directly from the media, I tried to show what each of the basic human experiences—love, hate, birth, death, ecstasy, pain—becomes when transformed into pop language. By snapping this language into sharp focus, turning the continuous undertone up full blast for a moment, I hoped to make readers really see and hear it with a shock of recognition.

But most writers have not interested themselves in the language environment. Mostly they have worked personally toward a verbal discourse unsullied by the language of the media—but also ineffective in revealing, counter-attacking, or redeeming that language.

On rare occasions a gifted literary man focuses sharply on this problem, and we get a dazzling example of how rewarding such criticism can be. Kenneth Burke in *The Nation*, for example, has probed the process of identification by which citizens become implicated in the policies and acts of their government. "We need to pause occasionally," Burke writes,

> and ponder the bepuzzlements of "identification" as they affect our sense of citizenship. My only claim is that by peering into this term "identification" somewhat persistently, we find that it reveals notable risks and dangers, which must be recognized if our democracy is to function at its best.

But Burke, significantly, does not confine his work to "peering into this term"; his essay is not a philosophical analysis. Rather, it is a concrete description of how certain language habits generate identification and embody its dangers:

> But surely first prize for the vagaries and vagueness of identification must go to that tiny first-person plural pronoun, "we." Until a few years ago, when the Dodgers won a ball game, all Brooklyn proudly proclaimed that "we" had won. Now this purely private company is in Los Angeles, operating on a quite different identification. Or "we" as a nation advance funds to foreign countries from which "we" as private corporations receive this money back in payment for exports. By this ambiguity of identification, as a *nation* we become "idealists" while some of our *nationals* are involved in transactions that are, to say the least, quite realistic. Or whenever "we" fight a war, the range of identifications under the one head extends from men in combat to gamblers in war stocks. Yes, the marvels and mysteries of identification come to an ultimate focus in that scarcely noticeable, workaday pronoun, "we."

I have not yet mentioned the title of Burke's essay: "Responsibilities of National Greatness." His thesis is that among our duties as citizens is an obligation to disenchant ourselves from our own delusory language habits.

> "A people that grows accustomed to sloppy writing," wrote Ezra Pound, is a people in process of losing grip on its empire and on itself. . . . Your legislator can't legislate for the public good, your commander can't command, your populace (if you be a democratic country) can't instruct its "representatives," save by language. . . . The man of understanding can no more sit quiet and resigned while his country lets its literature decay . . . than a good doctor could sit quiet and contended while some ignorant child was infecting itself with tuberculosis under the impression that it was merely eating jam tarts.

Despair of the word is the pervasive reaction today. Persuaded that communication between the generations, classes, races, etc. is impossible, activists mount demonstrations while the more passive-aggressive sorts use acid to chuck "the language bag." McLuhan's doctrine, that the contents of the media are of little importance compared to their visceral effects, is fervently embraced. Discouraged humanists like Steiner even argue that "we are passing out of an historical era of verbal primacy—out of the classic period of literate expression—into a phase of decayed language, of 'post-linguistic' forms (mathematics, symbolic notation, and perhaps partial silence)."

Yet perhaps we may yet decline to despair over the word and, rather, work to redeem it.

Language, after all, can discern and move to correct its own defects. Silence—whether the private silence of mystical transcendence, the public silence of totalitarian stasis, or the paradoxically noisome silence of a repressed, unheard class rising in rebellion—has no such redemptive power.

The job of the critic of language today calls for diligence as well as intelligence. Wholesale denunciations of the state of the tongue are of limited usefulness. It is more courageous to call one prominent man a liar than to proclaim that the entire language is become debased. Not language, but *this man's words:* not the whole tongue, but *this party's evasions and obfuscations* must become the targets. This is unremitting, unpretentious work, to be undertaken by many hands whose impact will only be collective.

Semanticists should be glad to share it with others, taking as their distinctive task, perhaps, that of pointing out the damaging effects of bad language *on* language, and affirming that our lives, insofar as they achieve public meaning, achieve it through language, and that irresponsible and inhumane uses of language impair our capacity to think and feel the world as it really is.

SUGGESTIONS FOR DISCUSSION AND WRITING

1. *The author states that "it would not be excessive to say that the theme of language pollution is becoming a principal concern of cultural criticism today." Apart from your reading in this text, where have you encountered such discussions? Who else have you known to express concern? On the basis of your experience, do you agree with the author?*

2. *The term "language pollution" is used quite often in this text. What is the appeal of the metaphor "pollution" in this context? Do you consider it appropriate? Effective? Why or why not?*

3. *The author mentions "the poetry of the media" and "the poetry of ad writers." He specifically cites* Life *magazine as a source. Examine a recent issue of* Life *or another publication to see what poetic language you can discover. Where does it occur? How is it used and for what purposes? (Do not confine your study to the advertisements.)*

4. *According to the author, philosopher Alan Watts has said that "Americans are constantly eating the menu instead of the food." (See Watts' essay) What does he mean? Test the validity of this claim by examining the language used in the menus of some local restaurants.*

5. *In his concluding paragraph, the author says that "Wholesale*

denunciations of the state of the tongue are of limited usefulness. It is more courageous to call one prominent man a liar
than to proclaim that the entire language is become debased."
In light of these statements, review the readings in this section
of the book and decide if any are "wholesale denunciations."
Are any "courageous"? (Is "courageous" the best word to use
in this context?) Do you agree with the author's statements?
Support your answer.

2

HANGUPS, TABOOS, COMMUNICATION GAPS:

THE USE AND ABUSE OF LANGUAGE

"Wow!"
"Groovy!"
"That's where it's at, baby!"
"Out of sight!"
"Spaces me way out!"
"It's my rap, man!"
"I mean it's really something else!"
"You think it's a trick bag?"
"Naw, no jive in that, man!"
"Really where it's at!"

7

William Zinsser

IS IT AN O.K. WORD, USEWISE?

The question of what constitutes "correct" English—or if indeed there is such a thing—has social implications far beyond the immediate linguistic issues. For usage is one of the more popular aspects of language study as well as one of the more controversial, and even people with little knowledge of language freely express their views on the subject—ranging from a total acceptance of all understandable communications to a strict insistence on established standards of "correctness." How, then, does a publisher setting out to prepare a dictionary determine what is an acceptable new word or construction? One way is to employ a panel made up of people respected for their own use of language —people like free-lance writer William Zinsser, a self-described "word nut and language buff," who discusses here some of the questions raised by a usage panel on which he served.

Will I accept the verb "to host"? Or "escalate" or "finalize" or "enthuse"? Do I approve of nouns posing as adjectives: "health reasons" or "disaster proportions"? How do I feel about "it's me"? Will I allow "like" to be used as a conjunction—like so many people do? Will I give my O.K. to "mighty," as in "mighty fine"? Will I give my O.K. to "O.K."?

I've been getting these questions in the mail for four years now, and so have 103 other men and women, a group of people —mostly writers, poets, editors and teachers—who care about the language and try to use it well. We are the "usage panel" formed in 1965 by a new dictionary—the American Heritage Dictionary of the English Language—to appraise the new words

Life, August 29, 1969. Copyright © 1969 by William K. Zinsser. Reprinted by permission of William K. Zinsser.

and dubious constructions that have come knocking at the door. Which should be ushered in, which thrown out?

Now the Dictionary has been born and we can see what we decided. Some of our written comments, in fact, were recently made public, proving that our passions often ran high. "Good God, no! Never!" cried Barbara W. Tuchman, asked about the verb "to author." Scholarship hath no fury like that of a language purist confronted with sludge, and I share Miss Tuchman's vow that "author" shall never be authorized, just as I agree with Lewis Mumford that the adverb "good" should be "left as the exclusive property of Hemingway" and with Gerald Carson that "normalcy" should be "permitted only to admirers of the late Warren G. Harding."

But a usage panel is only doing half its job if it merely keeps the language from becoming sloppy. Any boob can rule that the suffix "wise," as in "taxwise," is boobwise, or that being "rather unique" is no more possible than being rather pregnant. The other half of the job is to help the language grow by welcoming any newcomer that will bring strength or color.

Therefore I was glad to see in the Dictionary that 97% of us voted to accept "dropout," which is clean and vivid, but only 47% would accept "senior citizen," which is pretentious and patronizing, typical of the pudgy new intruders from the land of sociology, where a clod is an underachiever and a slum is a depressed socioeconomic area. I'm glad we accepted "escalate," the kind of verbal contraption which I ordinarily dislike but which the Vietnam war has given a precise military meaning, complete with overtones of blunder.

I'm glad we took into full membership all sorts of robust words that were formerly degraded as colloquial: adjectives like "rambunctious," verbs like "stall" and "trigger" and "rile," nouns like "shambles" and "trek," the latter approved by 78% to mean any difficult trip, as in "the commuter's daily trek to Manhattan." Originally, it was a Cape Dutch word applied to the Boers' harsh journey by ox wagon. But who is to say that the Manhattan commuter's daily trek is any less arduous, or made on trains that are much better than an ox wagon? Not us. This is the virtue of having a usage panel and tabulating its opinions in the dictionary: it puts our differences on display as well as our agreements, leaving the reader to be his own final guide. Thus our 95% vote against "myself," as in "He invited Mary and myself to dinner," condemned as "prissy," "horrible" and a "genteelism," ought to warn off anyone who doesn't want to be prissy, horrible and genteel. As Red Smith put it, "Myself" is the refuge of idiots taught early that 'me' is a dirty word."

On the other hand, only 66% of us rejected "to contact," and only half opposed the split infinitive and the verbs "to fault" and "to bus." So nobody can really fault you if you decide to willingly contact your school board and have them bus your children to another town. Our apparent rule of thumb was stated by Theodore M. Bernstein: "We should apply the test of convenience and necessity—does the word fill a real need?"

All this merely proves what any lexicographer knows—that the laws of usage are relative, bending with the taste of the lawmaker. Katherine Anne Porter calls "O.K." a "detestable vulgarity" and claims that she has never spoken the word in her life, whereas I will freely admit that I have spoken the word "O.K." "Most," as in "most everyone," was derided as "cute farmer talk" by Isaac Asimov and embraced as a "good English idiom" by Virgil Thomson. "Regime," meaning any administration, drew the approval of most everyone on the panel except Jacques Barzun, who said it was a technical term, "you blasted non-historians!" I personally railed against the bloated noun "personality," as in a "TV personality," but now I wonder if it isn't the only word for that vast new breed of people who are famous for being famous—and, quite possibly, for nothing else. What does Art Linkletter, for instance, really *do*? Or Zsa Zsa Gabor?

In the end it comes down to one question: what is "correct" usage? We have no King to establish the King's English; we only have the President's English—which we don't want. Webster, long a defender of the faith, rolled the waters in 1961 with its Third Edition, which argued that almost anything goes if somebody uses it, noting that "ain't" is "used orally in most parts of the U.S. by many cultivated speakers."

Just where Webster cultivated those speakers I ain't sure.

Nevertheless it's true that the spoken language is always looser than the written language, and the American Heritage Dictionary properly put its questions to us in both forms. Often we gladly allowed an oral idiom which we forbade in print as too informal, fully realizing, however, that "the pen must at length comply with the tongue," as Samuel Johnson said, and that today's garbage may be gold tomorrow. Usewise, some of it just can't be finalized.

On the whole our panel turned out to be liberal in accepting new words and phrases, but conservative in grammar. We strictly upheld most of the classic distinctions ("can" and "may," "fewer" and "less," etc.) and decried the classic errors, insisting that "flaunt" still doesn't mean "flout," or "infer" mean "imply," that "fortuitous" still means "accidental" and "disinterested" means "impartial," no matter how many people use them wrong. Here we were motivated by our love of the language's beautiful precision. Like any craftsmen, we enjoy using exact tools and hate to see them maltreated. "Simple illiteracy," Dwight Macdonald said, "is no basis for linguistic evolution."

"I choose always the grammatical form unless it sounds affected," explained Marianne Moore, and that, finally, is where we took our stand. We are not pedants, so hung up on correctness that we don't want the language to keep refreshing itself with phrases like "hung up." That doesn't mean, however, that we have to accept every horror that comes along, like "hopefully." Prayerfully these usages can be kept out, but fearfully many of them won't.

SUGGESTIONS FOR DISCUSSION AND WRITING

1. What does the term "usage" mean? What is meant by "correct" usage? What is the difference between "usage" and "grammar"?

2. Do you feel that a usage panel such as the one mentioned in this essay is a sound way to determine the acceptability of a given word or expression? Why or why not? If your answer is no, what would you suggest as an alternative, if any?

3. If you believe that a panel is a good way to decide questions of usage, who should be on the panel? (See the list of members in the American Heritage Dictionary for one example—the composition of the panel mentioned in this essay.)

4. The author says that a usage panel should keep the language from becoming sloppy and help it to grow by welcoming any new words that will bring strength and color to it. What does he seem to mean by "sloppy," by "strength," and by "color"? Can you provide words and expressions to illustrate the meaning of each of these words as used by the author?

5. The usage panel upheld a number of distinctions between words mentioned in paragraph 12. Explain those distinctions. Should they be preserved? Why or why not? The panel opposed certain "classic errors" listed in the same paragraph. Explain the errors involved in the use of these pairs of words. Do you support the panel's decisions? Why or why not?

8

The Editors of *Newsweek*

UP TIGHT ABOUT HANG-UPS

If the editors of Newsweek *who prepared the following essay and many of the other people quoted in it had their way, a substantial number of currently fashionable expressions would be considerably less fashionable. For these editors and their allies argue that although our language is constantly being revitalized by new words and phrases, "the square world" takes them over from the innovators and wears them out with overuse.*

Walter Muir Whitehill, an author and the director of the august Athenaeum library in Boston, couldn't believe what he saw on the annual report from Colonial Williamsburg, Inc., which administers the restored village of Williamsburg, Va. "The title of the report," reports Whitehill, "was 'Williamsburg Tells It Like It Was.'"

Groovy. Beautiful. Out of sight. The jargon of the alienated, the oppressed, the discontented is becoming the idiom of Middle —nay, Colonial—America. Television writers babble like acid-heads; newspaper columnists sound like black militants; and advertising copywriters echo the slogans of the teeny-boppers. "Turn on, before you turn in," read one advertisement in The New York Times last week, "with your own fun-at-home steam bath." "People used to want to grow up," notes Times column-ist Russell Baker, dourly. "Now they just want to sound young."

The mainstream of language, of course, is always being re-freshed by new sources of words and phrases, and only the most doctrinaire purist would argue that lively lingo should be banned from straight usage. *"Hang-up* is good, it replaces psychiatric text-book talk," says Chicago Daily News columnist Mike

Royko. Adds writer and press critic Ben Bagdikian: "I think *The Man* expresses very succinctly the idea of the person of authority. It is a private language, a secret sort of handclasp." NBC commentator David Brinkley says he likes the term *up tight* better than earlier, less expressive terms such as tensed up.

Overkill: But what happens is that the innovators—blacks, young people and, as the sociologists would put it, other "out groups"—find that their cabalistic expressions are taken over by the square world and spoken and written to death. Journalists, too, overkill with jargon and pretentious usages because they come quickly to mind and substitute for thinking. Unfortunately, interment doesn't come fast enough. A chrestomathy of current phrases that a representative group of lovers of English offer up for burial:

"*Tell it like it is,*" volunteers literary critic Philip Rahv. "It is the supreme cliché of the year. Certainly, the person saying it doesn't know what really 'is'. Who does? What an arrogant statement, a ridiculous request." British writer Katherine Whitehorn can do without *with-it* and *so-called*—"it doesn't mean the object is misnamed, just that the user doesn't like it."

Bergen Evans, professor of English at Northwestern University and a leading member of the permissive school of language, hopes he will never have to be confronted with the term *confrontation*.

Robert Manning, editor of The Atlantic, picked up a newspaper and focused on the phrase *sort of* as an expression he considers "useless, ambiguous and grating." Manning is disturbed also by the proliferation of obscenity. "I wish the problem would go away," says Manning. "The words won't. In some pieces they are essential to convey the point. But in others they are being used more and more for shock purposes only."

Louis Lyons, former curator of the Nieman Foundation at Harvard, and James Boylan, editor of the Columbia Journalism Review, are exacerbated by *you know*—which both say they hear much too often over radio and TV. "What does it mean," asks Lyons. "What do I know? What is that expression? A nervous tic? A lack of vocabulary?"

Both Bagdikian and Baker believe that the value of *Establish-*

ment has been debased. "It would be all right to keep the Establishment members," Baker says, "if we got rid of the word."

Washington newsmen are annoyed most by officialese. "The first expression that I want to go is *viable*," says Art Buchwald. "It dates back to the Kennedy Administration and it just isn't very viable any more." But he also objects to some of the phrases that Mr. Nixon has introduced. "In every speech," says Buchwald, "he throws in a line that goes: 'I want to make this perfectly clear' or 'I want to say this candidly'." Adds Russell Baker: "Republicans go in for Latin stems and roots a lot. We're bound to hear a lot about *definitization* and *implementation*."

The problem has become an English one as well as an American one. William Davis, the new editor of Punch, says he "would like to dispose of—*crisis, taking into consideration, in the final analysis, within the framework of, at this time, other things being equal* and *alive and well and living in*." Adds Bill Grundy, press critic for the weekly Spectator: "I could do without *participation; charisma* has lost its charisma for me: let's eliminate *teach-ins, sit-ins, live-ins* and any other bloody ins; and I'm sick of *in depth,* which usually means in length."

Newsweek would like to recommend early retirement for *it's what's happening, where it's at, up against the wall, doing (my, your, his, her) thing, generation gap, name of the game, piece of the action, relevant, commitment, culturally deprived, disadvantaged, value judgment* and *meaningful relationship* (instead of campus sex).

But Art Buchwald deserves to pronounce the final, meaningful, relevant, viable judgment: "Another thing I'd like to see go," he says, "is stories about words that are in or out."

SUGGESTIONS FOR DISCUSSION AND WRITING

1. This article states that the language of the alienated and the oppressed is becoming the language of Middle America. Do you see any evidence that this contention is true? (It might be helpful to look through some recent newspapers and magazines and to listen to some radio and television discussion programs or talk shows.)

2. According to the article, blacks, young people and other "out groups" find that their expressions are "taken over by the square world and spoken and written to death." How could such a takeover weaken the language for those who first used it?

3. Examine the current terms and phrases that are mentioned in this article. Then select any that you think make a particularly important contribution to our language, and explain what that contribution is and why the terms or phrases should be retained.

4. Spend some time listening to informal conversation to determine who uses the expression "you know" and how it is used.

5. Paragraph 7 notes that one magazine editor is disturbed by a proliferation of obscenity in current language. Do you agree that there is a proliferation? If so, do you see it as a problem? Support your answers. Do you agree that obscenity is sometimes essential to convey a point? Do you agree that obscenity is used "more and more for shock purposes only"? Support your answers. (Before working with this item, you may want to read the articles on obscenity by Bens and Rothwell which conclude this section.)

9

Valerie Carnes

THE LANGUAGE OF NOWSPEAK

"It is time at last," says Valerie Carnes in this essay, "for a long look at the language of the current youth movement." The name that she gives it is Nowspeak—"the language of the Movement, the youth under thirty and their over-thirty sympathizers." In this extensive analysis of Nowspeak, Ms. Carnes traces its origins, outlines its essential features, and assesses its significance. (Deleted from this reprinting is a nine-page glossary of Nowspeak, which can be found with the original essay in Carnes and Carnes, The New Humanities: Culture, Crisis, Change, *Holt, Rinehart and Winston, 1972.) Ms. Carnes teaches English at Roosevelt University, Chicago.*

Now that much of the sound and fury over hippies, yippies, flower power, student power, Berkeley, Chicago, and Columbia has begun to die away, and pot, acid, and speed have become as much household words as the name of Spiro T. Agnew it is time at last for a long look at the language of the current youth movement. For at least one thing becomes increasingly clear as the underground begins to surface: the much-celebrated generation gap of the sixties was—and still *is*—largely a linguistic gap existing between standard English and Nowspeak, the language of the Movement, the youth under thirty and their over-thirty sympathizers.

To accept even the mildest form of the linguistic relativity thesis entails the admission that one's world view is to some extent relative to his language system. Clearly the world view of a twenty-one-year-old radical whose universe is built around large categories labeled "pigs," "heads," "the System," and "the Revolution" will manifest itself quite differently from that of his Establishment counterpart who still operates in terms of more conventional classes: "liberals," "conservatives," "Commie rats," "anarchists," "Democrats," "Republicans." The very existence of the language that I have christened Nowspeak affirms the existence of a large and active youth Underground. It also institutionalizes the subculture of Beatles and Stones and Fugs and Ché Guevara-ism, of "Hair" and Tarot cards, witches and warlocks, acid and grass, and gives it in the public eye a local habitation and a name. Hippies, hipsters, beats, pushers, and heads have been part of the Scene for a very long time—since the 1920s, in fact; it is their group names that remind Peter Schrag's Forgotten Americans of these embarassing Presences in a stolidly sentimental and conformist culture.

Thus for Movement and Establishment alike the language becomes symbolic. It does not only "stand for" or "point to" the subculture: it *is* the subculture. This fact should remind us of Paul Tillich's useful distinction between a sign and a symbol: the sign, he says, points the way to the thing, but the symbol participates in it. Nowspeak is a symbol of the life-style of the emerging subculture and also serves as the System's plumber's-manual guide to that life-style. It is symbolic in this sense both for those who use it and those who do not. Users align themselves against non-users. Nowspeaking youth draw a sense of solidarity and community from the language that represents their chosen style while the Establishment feels itself to be the nation's annointed people in part because it still speaks standard English. Non-users, presenting their case in conventional pig-American-ese, argue that Movement lingo is mindless, non-expressive, illiterate, obscene, and meaningless, while the other side argues with equal fervor that all the assertions and experiences of youth are incapable of verbal expression. As one girl recently put it, "If you've been there, you'll know it, and you don't need to talk about it." In the opening bars of *Their Satanic Majesties* the Stones urge their listeners to "open your heads, let the pictures come." Indeed, one of the hidden premises of Nowspeak is the assumption that there are many classes of experience which cannot and should not be verbalized. The act of verbalization is itself a dodge, a corruption of the experience, a "sell-out" or "cop-out" from the pure moment of sensation. I am well aware of the irony implicit in this study. This is not an essay on the language of the youth culture but instead on abstractions from that language as it is spoken, transposed onto the printed page. The most important characteristic of the language is that it is spoken, not written, and is therefore in a constant state of flux. Yet paradoxically the very nonverbal nature of the language is symbolic of the world view it both influences and reflects—anti-rational, action-oriented, visual, tactile, highly sensuous, primitive, ritualistic, colorful, emotive, solipsistic, and so always the language of the present moment the immediate Scene, the place where the action is, or was—in short, the language of Now.

The primary source of Nowspeak is of course the language of other American bohemian movements. Nineteen-twenties bohemianism—Parisian expatriates, winos, Braque, Picasso, Hemingway, Stein and her beloved Alice B. Toklas, the rash of "little" magazines, and Zelda and Scott, those lovely lost children of Prohibition playing in the fountains at the Plaza—established the standard bohemian style and attitude: a sadly romantic, fatalistic, cosmopolitan, nonconforming, and lost generation of street-cafe and attic subcultures, writing poetry out of a golden alcoholic haze. Came the 1930s, and hipsters, jazz musicians, and an authentic hard-core drug underground began unwittingly to build the language that the young rebels of today's suburbia still speak. Jazz usages yielded such important terms as *action* (a general term for whatever is happening at the time), *bad* (for something very good, especially a woman), *blast* (get high), *bomb* (a failure), *bread* (money), *bug* (to annoy or disturb), *bust* (arrest), *cat* (any human being, especially a swinger), *chick* (a girl), *come down* (from a high), *cool* (ignore, snub, become less intense about a person or thing), *cut out* (leave), *dig* (understand or comprehend, in an emotional sense), *fag* (homosexual), *far out* (very advanced, ahead of its time), *funky* (basic, earthy, down-home), *groove* (a predilection or enjoyable thing), *head* (drug user), *lay* or *lay on* (to give or say), *make it* (have success), *put on* (to make fun of or ridicule without letting the victim know), *scene* (particular place or atmosphere), *stoned* (high or drunk), *turn on* (to get someone high on pot or to interest someone in a specific thing) and *wild* (remarkable). A high percentage of these terms still are in Nowspeak usage today.

Underworld language, which has found its way into Nowspeak, dates back to the time when the entire drug scene was largely confined to the fringes of society—the ghetto, the bohemian settlements, the underworld—and drug users were more or less forced by economic and social exigencies to live a life of petty crime. From this indigenous subculture come the standard slang terms referring to drug use: *cap* (drug capsule), *head* (user of drugs), *H, horse, shit, smack, duji* (heroin); *Mary Jane, MJ, pot, tea, grass, boo* (marijuana); *coke, snow, snowbird* (cocaine and its users). Most of these words are prepsychedelia and therefore refer to the more conventional drugs that were standard bohemian and ghetto fare from the twenties and thirties into the fifties and sixties—hashish, marijuana, heroin, cocaine, opium, benzedrine. Also from that nebulous area where underworld jargon coalesces with black ghetto talk come words dealing with the relations of the drug user and petty criminal with the police: *hit* (to be arrested), *bust* (to make an arrest, often for illegal drug use, as in "He got busted for possession last night"), *heat, fuzz,* or *the Man* (police), *uptight* and *strung out* (in desperate financial straits, usually as the result of intensive or prolonged drug use). One interesting term with underworld connotations is *straight.* A common word in homosexual and criminal society, it was first used to mean not with the particular "in" crowd in question (hence, heterosexual in one case, non-criminal in the other). Later the meaning became generalized so that the word now can refer to anyone who is not "with" a particular scene; hence, conventional, ordinary, not in the know, not "hip," generally "out of it." A more recent variant is more specific and less derogatory; it means "temporarily off drugs, clean for the moment," as in "Once I was straight for three days."

"Soultalk," the language of urban ghetto blacks, has become an increasingly important element in the vocabulary of the Nowspeaker, probably because of the heightened social consciousness of the Movement and its intense identification with minority groups of all kinds. Black "hip" and "soul" talk has added to Nowspeak such important words as *man* (generalized term of address, as in "Man, you're blowing my mind"), *ball* (to have sexual intercourse), *the Man* (the police; more generally, any Establishment figure, preferably white, in a position of power), *mother* (short for motherfucker, a term of derision and often hatred), *cat* (any male human being, especially a hip one), *hip* (with it, cool, in the know, under control), *hipster* (hip cat), *shit* (drugs in general), *tell it* or *tell it, man, lis'en at him, nigger* (in a soulful affectionate sense, not a condescending or derogatory one, as in "He's the baddest nigger I ever saw"), *something else* (pronounced *sum'pn else*), *police* (pronounced *po-lice*), *stuff* (heroin or the vagina), *bag* (originally, in the thirties, graft paid to the po-lice; now, a person's vocation, hobby, fancy, whimsy, or caprice, as in "that's your bag, man"), *strung out, uptight, cop* (originally an abbreviation for copulation, but by 1955 a synonym for the verb "to get," especially in relation to pot, hard drugs, hot goods, pistols), *boss* (something extraordinarily good or great, later replaced by *groovy, tough, beautiful,* and *out of sight*), *kill 'em* (for "give 'em hell," not as an expression of malice or violence). Other classics that often overlap into underworld and "beat" diction of the fifties and that have by now wandered into Nowspeak include *solid, cool, jive* (as noun), *jive-ass, thing, swing,* and *swinging* (the sixties added *swinger*), *pimp, dirt, freak, heat, right on* (term of approbation), *piece, sheet* (a jail record), *squat, square, stash, lay, mire, gone, smooth, joint, blow, play, shot, hassle, chick, junkie, bitch* (girl), *tight* (friendly), *O. D.* (overdose), *soul, soulfood, gig.*

Perhaps the single most important contribution of the black hipster is the word *baby* (pronounced "bay-buh," *a la* Janis Joplin), used in address to another, highly masculine, black male. Claude Brown offers this explanation of the elusive term in *Manchild in the Promised Land:*

The first time I heard the expression "baby" used by one cat to address another was up at Warwick in 1951. Gus Jackson used it. The term had a hip ring to it, a real colored ring. The first time I heard it I knew right away I had to start using it. It was like saying, "Man, look at me, I've got masculinity to spare." It was saying at the same time to the world, "I'm one of the hippest cats, one of the most uninhibited cats on the scene. I can say 'baby' to another cat, and he can say 'baby' to me, and we can say it with strength in our voices." If you could say it, this meant that you really had to be sure of yourself, sure of your masculinity. . . . The real hip thing about the "baby" term was it was something that only colored cats could say the way it was supposed to be said. . . .

Haight-Ashbury summer of 1967, with the subsequent growth of the youth Underground and the more amorphous Movement, popularized and brought to the surface dozens of terms like these that had once been indigenous black soultalk in the thirties, forties, fifties, and early sixties, then found their way into the vocabularies of the children of affluent upper-middle-class WASP society. That the drug culture itself followed precisely the same pattern, out of the ghetto and into suburbia, is significant, for it suggests that the daily life-style of the Harlemite hipster and pusher was transformed into a middle-class elitist cult tinged with mystical overtones largely by the use of a bona fide drug-and-underworld language.

The hipster who came into prominence in the thirties and forties and finally sprang full-blown from the media in the fifties and sixties was a young male, often black, who was "hip" (originally, "hep" to the beat), extraordinarily aware, in the know, especially about jazz, drugs, and the street scene. The word "hippie," which came into national prominence in 1967, was being used in Harlem in the early 1950s to describe the uptown white who played at being a black hipster. Robert George Reisner's *The Jazz Titans* (1960) defines a "hippie" as a young person who is trying to put on hip airs but doesn't quite make it—thus, one who may be overly hip. Malcolm X's *Autobiography* recalls a similar incident: "A few of the white men around Harlem, younger ones whom we called 'hippies,' acted more Negro than Negroes. This particular one talked more 'hip' talk than we did" (p. 94).

Beat language of the fifties drew on all these sources—soul-talk, jazz, drug, underworld and homosexual slang, hipster and hippie language. It incorporated all of these and yet, paradoxically, was unlike any of them. Norman Podhoretz in an early essay, "The Know-Nothing Bohemians," comments on the "urban, cosmopolitan bias" of twenties' bohemianism, whose ideals were "intelligence, cultivation, spiritual refinement." By contrast bohemianism in the thirties, with its abundance of card-carrying Communists and Marxists, was colored by political radicalism, intellectual seriousness, and social reform. Podhoretz succinctly sums up the difference between earlier and later bohemianisms. The 1950s "beat" ethos, he comments, was hostile to civilization, worshipped primitivism, instinct, energy, "blood," was "cool" but mystical, irrational, spontaneous, anti-language, anti-analytical, and fascinated perennially, like Ginsberg's "angel-headed hipsters" and Kerouac's Dharma bums, with violence, drugs, Dada, surrealism, wine, and madness. Interestingly enough, the word "beatnik" was media-created: its genesis coincided with the furor over the Russian satellite Sputnik, and thus were the beats subtly and erroneously identified with Communist tendencies. The word "beat" itself referred at least in part to the ubiquitous jazz beat that was so much a part of the fifties Scene; it also meant, according to Kerouac, "beatified" or "beatific," suggesting a kind of frantic hip holiness in the beat stance. For the uninitiated it also meant disgust with middle-class philistinism and provinciality, utter disgust and exhaustion with the straight scene.

Beat language, like the Nowspeak of the sixties, was relatively simple. Adjectives were pared down to an eloquent few: *great* (greatest), *tremendous, crazy, mad, wild, groovy*. Nouns and verbs were simple and expressive: *bread* (money), *crash* (to sleep, from an old Hell's Angels' term that means "to die"; may also be used to refer to a temporary residence or sleeping space, as in "He's running a crash pad for pot heads"), *joint* (a marijuana cigarette), *roach* (the butt end of a joint), *pad* (place of residence, as in "Duke, they blowin' pot like mad up at Mildred's pad," from the R. Crumb cartoon, "The Adventures of Fritz"). Slang terms for drugs also were common beat usage, perhaps as a means of avoiding the fuzz: *MJ, pot, tea, grass, H, horse, shit, O, smack* and so on.

A merger between the beat culture and the folk song and the various war–civil rights–free-speech protests of the early sixties brought the Movement as it then existed out of Greenwich Village and the Haight onto the college campuses and coffee shops and into the media. The Berkeley Free Speech Movement (FSM) institutionalized and sanctioned the use of four-letter words as an authentic gesture of protest; civil rights demonstrations publicized words like *sit-in, demonstration, nonviolence, passive resistance,* SNCC, CORE, NAACP, *civil disobedience* and *God is on our side* (both phrases from Thoreau's famous tract), *happening, love-in,* and *riot*. The folk-singing phase of the movement, centering around sad-eyed lady of the lowlands Joan Baez and early pre-electronic Dylan, was the aesthetic equivalent of social and political nonviolence. In it was the ageless lure of wild cold woods and wind and salty sea, snow-white doves and long black veils, cruel ladies and love-sick knights, and forlorn maidens haunted by restless ghosts. It was poignant, sad, archaic, funny, and full of a simple moral outrage at war and racism; yet it was also cruel with a kind of barbarous innocence, the savage tenderness of the most ruthless of the Scottish Child ballads. And of course since beauty hurts Mr. Vinyl it could not and did not last. Although folk singing added few new words as such to the growing lexicon of Nowspeak, it introduced a down-home earthy lowdown shackdown niggerbaby blues plainness of style that set the cultural stage for the earliest of hippie life-styles.

In the mid-sixties the long-standing feud of British Mods and Rockers culminated in the cultural victory of Mod and so introduced a newly self-conscious element into the indigenous American youth cult. Magically the Scene shifted from Newport to Carnaby Street and Baez and Dylan were replaced overnight by Justin and Twiggy. Boutiques mushroomed in the most Establishment of department stores and funky sleazy minifashions, bell-bottoms, elephant pants, wide belts, boots, vinyl skirts, picture matches, fans, Tiffany paper lanterns, op, pop, the Liverpool sound. Victoriana, discothéques, light shows, go-go girls, vinyl hamburgers, and burgeoning Campbell soup cans spelled out the new message in dayglo colors: COME ALIVE, YOU'RE IN THE PEPSI GENERATION. Limp-haired and limpid-eyed Lolitas, chock full of vitamin pills and orange juice, put on granny glasses, French yé-yé knits, and little white vinyl boots. Boys adopted the Teddy Boy look and tried vainly to resemble John Lennon. The style of the hour was J. C. Penney transcendental-ized by Quant and Courreges, and the media responded fittingly with a shiny new slickspeak: "where it's at," "the action genera-tion," "the Now people," "the Pepsi generation," "the Beautiful People," "camp art," "happenings" (which included such ques-tionable activities as smashing grand pianos with hammers while, in the background, thirteen radios blared *forte fortissimo* and painted go-go girls did action paintings on the side). Some of this jargonese was simulated British slang (girls were "birds" or "model girls," thanks to Twiggy and Mary Quant), and if they wore *minis* or *micro-minis*, they were *kooky, kinky,* and had "the knack" (after a British art film of that name). It was the heyday of the microcosm, the diminutive, a mod mod mod Lilliputian world for all the Little People. Everything from the poor-boy skinny-rib sweater to Vesuvius erupting was "fun," "crazy," "super," "marvellous," "fantastic" or "groovy." Clothes were fun things. Shoes were to fall in love with. Makeup was super stuff. Discothéques were fun places. Arnel was when. Yé-yé. Yeah. Yeah. Yeah.

Hippie summer of 1967, heralded by the Human Be-In in San Francisco and by the haunting imperative issuing from every jukebox across the nation, instructing the new generation to wear a flower in its collective hair, saw the first full-scale sur-facing of the new-style Underground of the sixties. By August of 1967 every major magazine from *Playboy* to the *Saturday Evening Post* was preparing its own lead article on the hippie phenomenon, complete with full-color photographs of lush para-disal landscapes where lank golden girls ran barefoot forever through the Kodachrome grass, their long manes tumbling in the wind, light shows and artlessly painted bodies gyrating in time to invisible acid rock bands, gaunt gurus wordlessly holy on acid, celluloid flowers, newspaper posters, head shops, Diggers, Hell's Angels. Leary and Ginsberg leading mantras, and bespectacled bearded boys with beads and bells and Digger hats and bloodshot eyes that seemed to see beyond the world they never made to some better secret cloud—cuckoo-land green with the sweet aroma of burning grass. The ceremony of innocence had begun, and from everywhere the summer hippies converged on the Haight. When they arrived they found a prefabricated culture waiting for them: buttons, a ready-made dress style, head shops full of groovy merchandise, records, drugs, crash pads, free stores, free food, free love, free rock and an instant name, "hippies." To go along with all this there was, not surprisingly, a language. With very minor variations it was 1920s bohemian, thirties hipster-drug-soultalk out of fifties beat by way of folk-protest-rock-yeah-yeah-mod-yé-yé, and all systematized and solidified by the ever-present media. The hippies' chief contribution to Nowspeak was in the area of drug euphemisms. Many of these were the old reliables of the twenties and thirties resurrected for the occasion: *pot, tea, boo, horse, O, joint, roach, grass, fix, connection, stash.* Others were relatively new, having sprung up like the holy mushrooms of Mexico in response to the new and popular psychedelics or "head" drugs: *hallucinogenic, buzz, flash, crash, LSD, acid, STP, speed, crystals, downer, bummer, freak-out, freaked out, freak* (as noun: acid freak, print freak, speed freak, motorcycle freak), *head, breakthrough* (also a military and scientific term), *trip, trip out, doing one's own thing, bag, groove.* Many words used to describe the effects of the psychedelics were phrases taken over from descriptions of the state of alcoholic inebriation: *high* (in a state of euphoria achieved by drugs or alcohol; as a noun, the state itself, or more generally, an overall sense of joy or well-being, as in "When I was on a high I thought I would found this groovy scene, see, 'Teen-age Evangelism'"), *stoned* (excessively high on drugs, "I want to save that for later when we're stoned") and so on.

Significantly, many "In" phrases at the time were implicit mechanical metaphors like Timothy Leary's famous injunction to "tune in, turn on, drop out"—figures of speech that are all drawn, implicitly or explicitly, from radio or television. "Turned on," used as an adjective, meaning high or under the influence of drugs or, more generally, receptive to drugs or to experience of any kind, especially that of an unconventional nature, illustrates the tendency of such words to broaden their range of possible meanings. (We already have noted that early jazz usage limited the "turn-on" to drugs and Charlie Parker's horn.) Another electronic-mechanical metaphor is the word *vibe*, short for *vibrations*. Like *turned on* it also has a more generalized meaning than merely the implicit mechanical metaphor: it may refer to the atmosphere or spirit of a scene or person, or to the cosmic forces present in a particular setting. Thus a person, scene, event, or general situation is said to send out *good vibes* or *bad vibes*, depending on the speaker's reaction. Witches and warlocks were much prized on the Haight-Ashbury scene in 1967 for their ability to psych out good vibes. The term thus suggests a coalescence of electronic and cosmic-mystic metaphors of popular occultism. Mysticism and the occult also added *guru, yoga, meditation* (one was said to be "on meditation"—an obvious transfer of the drug metaphor to a nondrug experience), *sadhana* (Hindu equivalent of one's own thing), *karma* (destiny), *horoscope, zodiac, warlock, witch, sitar, mantra, hare krishna, maharishi, swami, mandala, veda, Gita, om*, and the elusive *vibe*.

It is difficult to overestimate the importance of the hippie subculture that began in 1967. It gave disaffected American youth, disillusioned by an ugly and senseless war and by a growing credibility gap, a rallying point and a locus of their new self-image. It also gave rise to a whole horde of movements that were and still are only tangentially related to hippiedom, but somehow still acquire guilt or innocence by association: SDS, student power, antiwar protest groups, YIPPIE (Youth International Party), the Chicago demonstrations of 1968, disturbances at Columbia, Harvard, Cornell, and San Francisco State, the Woodstock music festival, and the People's Park episode in Berkeley, 1969. Out of each of these small movements has arisen a set of chants, slogans, words, and phrases that for one reason or another caught on and became part of the language system: "all power to the people," "up against the wall, mofo," "into the streets," "down with pigs," "student power," "zap the world with love," "chicks up front," "give a flower to a cop," "Ho, Ho, Ho Chi Minh," "Hey, hey, LBJ," "Right on!" Specific events have also added to this new idiom. Thus Abbie Hoffman in a passage from *Rights in Conflict* describes the origin of the two terms *pig* (cop) and *Yippie* (Youth International Party member), which became the semantic poles of the Chicago riots in the summer of 1968: "There we were, all stoned, rolling around the floor . . . yippie! . . . Somebody says oink and that's it, pig, it's a natural, man, we gotta win" (p. 29).

As the passage above illustrates, much of the language was an authentic response to an immediate situation; some of it, however, was media-created or was given national prominence by the media: *name of the game, the generation gap, the credibility gap, where the action is, never trust anyone over thirty, the In Crowd, the Now Generation, the new morality, where it's at, the flower children, flower power* (this one attached to a photograph of a pig-hippie confrontation in San Francisco where the hippies zapped the barrels of the cops' guns with flowers), *charisma, tell it like it is* (possibly a corruption of the black "tell it" or "tell it, man"), *the Beautiful People* (originally a *Vogue-Bazaar* jet-set term transferred to the under-thirty crowd sometime during that eventful summer of 1967). Buttons contributed their share of slogans, too: "Save water, shower with a friend," "War is harmful to children and other living things," "Draft beer, not students," "Reality is a crutch," and "Frodo lives" and "Welcome to the Middle Earth," an in-signal for Tolkien lovers everywhere. Pop psychiatry and sociology contributed *confrontation, meaningful relationship* (*Newsweek*, 3, February 1969, calls this one a substitute for "campus sex"), *hang-up* (any psychological problem; also, any intense or consuming interest in anything), *strung out, relate, relevant, irrelevant* (said to be true of all academic pursuits), *therapy, shrink* (a psychiatrist, as in Arlo Guthrie's "Shrink, I wanna kill"), "group" (for group therapy), *group dynamics, T-group* (sensitivity-training session); *communicate, communication, nude therapy, body language, life-style, crisis, dialogue* (*or meaningful dialogue*) and *commitment.* . . .

Like any language system, Nowspeak has its own value system built into it. The language serves several purposes at once: it is a code to freak out the ever-present Establishment, it solidifies the feeling of community among this tenuously-bound subculture and assures its members that the Underground, the Movement—even the Revolution—really do exist, even if it's only in your head, and finally, it polarizes present-day society into linguistic camps and thence into social and political camps that follow from these linguistic sets. It is no great revelation to anyone that the world looks quite different to a young man who thinks of everything from cutting his hair to negotiating with the college administration in terms of "selling out to the System" than it looks to his father, who is scarcely aware that there is a System, much less that he is himself a part of it. A common geographical space and roughly coincident chronology is practically all that the two share: their politics, morality, aims, ideology, aesthetics—in short, their culture—are quite different, and the difference often starts and ends with the variance in languages. Ludwig Wittgenstein has hypothesized that the words that are used to describe aesthetic judgments play a very complicated but very definite role in the culture of a period. To describe their use or to describe what you mean by a cultured taste, you have to describe a whole culture. Since an entirely different cultural game with different rules is played in different ages, fully to describe a set of aesthetic rules means to describe the culture of a period. The fact that the Nowspeaker's highest accolades are "groovy," "wild," "beautiful!" "out of sight," and "naturally spaced" as opposed to his father's or professor's "very intelligent," "cultivated," "sensible," "successful" or "well-rounded" means something far more significant than merely the choice of one word over another: it means a totally new aesthetics and hence a whole new value system for the subculture.

Part of the point of the new aesthetic, of course, is that it is moving toward a non-verbal orientation. Contentless courses, meditation, yoga, chanting, drugs, T-groups, nude therapy, action painting, onstage nudity, touch therapy, group gropes, guerilla theatre in the streets, seances, satanism, be-ins, body language, dancing, rock festivals, proclamations of the Age of Aquarius and everywhere action, action, action—all these signs of the times are indications that McLuhan's retribalized youth are trying desperately to develop ways of communicating with something other than words. It is not only the old politics, the old imperialism, the old morality, the old society that is under attack; it is rationality and language itself. To present the Now people with carefully-worded logical arguments against their world view is only to compound the irony. Words are a large part of what their revolt is about. If language is a tool of the Establishment, then to present a linguistic argument to the Now people is already to have sold out to the System.

But the wheel of civilization has not yet turned full circle, and we are living literally in a transitional age between the old culture when intelligence was verbal almost by definition and the new nonverbal total-experience aesthetic. It is possible, then, to make one further step beyond our examination of the language and say that from an analysis of Nowspeak we can draw a number of valid inferences about the culture that it describes: its latent but intense romanticism, its folkishness and tribal qualities, its highly emotive nature, its solipsism, its "this-here-now-ness" and orientation toward the present existential moment, its connotative and reductive aspects. Let us see how this is so.

Perhaps the most striking quality of Nowspeak is that it is a highly romantic language, designed to mirror what all romanticisms ultimately mirror: the revolutionary transvaluation of all values. Thus the verbs of Nowspeak express action in onomatopoeic, slangy, quick and brittle phrases exploding like small balloons over the heads of some giant Superman or Phantom: *cop out, zap, zonk, sell out, bust, tune in, hit, flip, crash, groove.* They are comic-book and cartoon-time verbs for a TV generation. Among the most-quoted quotes of the Movement is the saying of Mao Tse-Tung, "Act first, then think, then act, then think, then act." Nowspeak is an action language for an action generation naturally "spaced" on the power of the moment. Print is irrelevant, hopelessly linear and static; it doesn't move, doesn't swing, groove, jiggle, gyrate, rock, or roll. Worst of all, it can't keep up with the Scene, can't go where it's at or where it's just been. Only with pure spontaneous action can things not fall apart and the center hold just a little longer.

Nowspeak nouns express a world view that is divided, like the world of the ancient Manicheans, into the powers of light and the powers of darkness, the Beautiful People and the System. The powers of darkness are identified with authority, uptightness, non-grooving, stodginess, and age: *the Man, the Establishment, pigs, sell-outs, game-players, uncools, hang-ups, fascists.* The powers of light in Nowspeak become *the New Left, the Movement,* the "good people," the In Crowd, the Underground, the Scene, the Age of Aquarius. Adjectives express superlative approval ("Beautiful!" "Wild!" "Freaky!") or describe emotional excesses of disapproval ("fascist pigs!" "You're uptight, man, you're blowing my mind, don't hassle me," "That's a heavy scene, man," "Oh no, you don't want grim, man; you want grim, you go to Chicago"). The vast and amorphous movement that gave birth to Nowspeak shows the same characteristics as nineteenth-century English, French, and German romanticisms: energy, boldness of thought, emphasis on creativity, the adulation of the new, the cult of personalities and the hero of the surface, stress on spontaneity and freedom of expression, anti-mechanistic and anti-scientific tendencies, supernaturalism, strangeness, a glorification of all sensory experience, the exaltation of wild freaky individualism, noncomformity, social responsibility, and the cult of sensibility. Nowspeak reflects to a greater or lesser degree all these romantic tendencies. The words as we have seen are highly emotive, intensional rather than extensional, connotative rather than denotative, expressive rather than emotionally neutral; and their impact is fully realized only by the "cool head" community of participants in this new cult of sensibility. Words furnish a kind of verbal shorthand to communicate to others who are also hip to the Scene: they know, for example, that *happening* refers to an event that's a trip of some kind for its participants and implies the excitement of something meaningful going on with a possibility of wonder and surprise; that you can get a *contact high,* or vicarious buzz, from interacting with someone who's up on drugs; that to *turn on* means to come alive and carries with it the implication that ordinary straight society creates people who are not alive and must be switched on to exist in any real sense. They also realize that *where it's at* refers to the whole physical or psychological locus of real and significant activity going on at some place and time, as opposed to the ritual and sham of the Establishment scene, and are hip to the implicit theatrical overtones of *Scene* itself: it suggests the whole of a setting and the action occurring with it—the physical setting plus mood (vibes) plus people (the theatrical analogue is set plus props plus staging plus actors plus script plus promoters *ad infinitum*). But there is no way that the straight world can know all these things unless it too switches on, psychs out the vibes, and goes.

All Western romanticisms are Edenic in impulse and origin, for all presuppose the fact of the Fall, symbolically if not literally, and all affirm the necessity of returning to the primordial Garden before the intrusion of the serpent machine. There are accurate and often chilling parallels to be drawn between the present youth cult in the United States and similar nineteenth- and early twentieth-century European cults with their fierce Rousseauism, their revolutionary cries for liberty, fraternity, equality, their *Sturm und Drang*, Pantisocracies, lyrical ballads, Satanism, Gothicism, *Volkgeists* and *Wanderlust*. The life-style of the young in twentieth-century America is also romantic, tribalized, and folkish, comprised of one part beat-academic–plain-style–Susan-Sontag–bricks-and-boards–white–washed–walls–authentic-products of cottage-industry–Chianti-drinking–yogurt-growing ethos; one part light-show–Quant-by-quant–psychotic-acid-freak-rock-stoned media-bag; and two parts idealized peasant and tribal ethos—hence the long hair, the fierce tribal loyalties, the barefoot hippie girls drifting artlessly through endless meadows of the mind, beards, mustaches, sideburns, dashikis, tatty raccoon coats, caftans, beads, bells, buttons, sandals (always the sign of the bohemian in Weejun'd America), Afros, Digger hats, minis, maxis, boots, and Indian headbands. Marshall McLuhan in a recent *Playboy* interview (March 1969) comments perceptively on what he calls the retribalization of American youth: "Our teenage generation is already becoming part of a jungle clan. . . . Sexual freedom is as natural to newly tribalized youth as drugs. . . . LSD and related hallucinogenic drugs . . . breed a highly tribal and communally oriented subculture, so it's understandable why the retribalized young take to drugs like a duck to water." The natural-man, tribal, folkish, Edenic aspect of the youth cult figures heavily in its language. There is a freer use of sexual, anal and other "taboo" terms and four-letter words: the language is simpler, the vocabulary is cut to a bare minimum, and there are many coined words, themselves authentic products of the Movement. Adjectives and nouns that denote approval are terms that express the ability to lose one's inhibitions, to move in a natural, uninhibited un-hung-up manner, to go where the action is and move with it, to put oneself in touch with cosmic rhythms—in short, to psych out the scene, feel its vibes, and then groove with it.

As we have seen, Nowspeak relies heavily on connotative power rather than denotative meaning for its impact. . . . Nowspeak at its worst can be a slick, vague, repetitive, and frustrating Hipspeak that smacks of the hard sell and fast deal quite as much as of the new morality and aesthetic. At its best, however, it is gutsy, emotive, colorful, and highly expressive of a whole range of thought and action that conventional English simply cannot express. Webster's offers us no exact equivalent for "pig" or "uptight" or "sell-out" or for the depth of ridicule and contempt that the terms convey, nor for the wildly enthusiastic approbation that lies behind "out of sight!" "spaced!" "freaky!" or "beautiful!" A friend of mine, recently turned twenty, spent a frustrating half-hour trying to describe to a gathering of cool heads the experiences of a recent acid trip and finally lapsed into "Oh, wow! If you only knew . . . like wild! freaky scene, man, just this freaky scene. . . . Oh, wow . . . spaced out . . . like you know, stoned . . . if you just knew, I mean, if you only knew." More intimate acquaintance with the dictionary would not have helped him communicate the incommunicable, for the experiences he was describing lie, for the moment at least, far beyond the pale of ordinary Sally-Dick-and-Jane reality. No wonder, then, that Nowspeak is against reason, against interpretation, against language itself: how else could it survive? Similarly for the use of taboo words, for it is a means of expressing utter disdain for ticky-tacky Establishment values to use obscenity in describing some of its more hallowed members and institutions.

If we think of the movement as McLuhan does in terms of a return to a romanticized primitive tribal ethos, we must also recognize that this language serves as an in-group sign, the verbal equivalent of a secret handclasp, a password that simultaneously gives solidarity to the inner circle and freaks out and excludes non-users, the ubiquitous Establishment. This use of language reminds us of Kenneth Burke's theory of language as gesture, for Nowspeak is indeed a sort of symbolic nose-thumbing at the Establishment—a complex and fun way of saying "Screw you" in a linguistic set that only the initiates know. Nowspeak is the code that the System must break, and as such it unites the various branches of the nebulous movement with an often specious sense of community. Nowspeak appears deceptively simple; actually, it is quite complex and involves many subtleties of syntax and style. Since it is spoken, not written, it is transmitted and its conventions established by word-of-mouth communication. The only sure way to establish current usage is to be in constant contact with speakers, for the language changes daily and today's In phrase is liable to be tomorrow's tired-out cliché. A written version of the language is at best only an approximation of its spoken form. Youth-oriented magazines such as *Cavalier, Ramparts,* and *Evergreen* realize this and effect in their writing style a skillful synthesis between ordinary English and authentic Nowspeak by repeating key words in contexts that indicate the cultural sympathies of the editors. Dust jackets, theatre marquees, and record jackets also let the young audience know by verbal sleight-of-mouth that the designer or producer was "where it was at" when the artifact in question was produced. By succumbing to the hip sell and buying the product the young consumer is invited to join the cool community where he, too, can be Norman Mailer-ed, Maxwell Taylor-ed *ad nauseum.*

By nature Nowspeak is sensation-oriented rather than experience-oriented, solipsistic rather than chronological or historical. While typical standard English sentence structure is chronological ("It was raining," "They left with us on Tuesday," "He used to drop by for drinks on Wednesday nights"), Nowspeak is non-chronological, non-temporal, a language of, for, and about the present moment. It is a process language designed to express the shifts, the swift reversals, the kaleidoscopic flux, the insecurities and ephemera of an electric kool-aid acid world. Like the Hopi Indian's tongue, Nowspeak is designed to tell us only that "it is summering," not that "it is summer": witness the number of words that describe ongoing or continuing action (*happening, Scene, where it's at, swinging*). Thus the language is geared toward making what the American philosopher Charles Hartshorne has called "this-here-now" statements about immediate actions and present states of being. To listen to the Now people rapping or to read an underground newspaper is to live briefly in the historical present. Few if any of the verbs are in the past tense, and most of the sentences are short, simple declarative statements directed less toward imparting information than toward creating a mood or emotion. Most of the statements are action-directed imperatives ("screw in the streets," "kill the pigs," "stop the trial") or exclamatory-declarative statements with a pithy, down-home epigrammatic brevity about them ("All power to the people," "This is a racist culture," "The streets belong to the people"). Daniel J. Boorstin, writing for the October 1968 *Esquire*, calls the Movement "the social expression of a movement from Experience to Sensation"—the shift from cumulative and communicable observation of or acquaintance with facts and events to simple awareness of perception which by definition is personal, private, highly confined, and essentially incommunicable. "What history is to the person in quest of experience," he writes, "a 'happening' is to the person in quest of sensation. For a 'happening' is something totally discrete. It adds to our sensations without increasing our experience." Perhaps we can see in the sensation-orientation, the "this-here-now"–ness of Nowspeak and its speakers a popularization of pseudo-Whiteheadian process metaphysics. This new pop philosophy mirrors the shift in contemporary world view from traditional substance-attribute metaphysics to a *weltanschauung* where things fall apart, the center cannot hold, movies-within-films-within-metaflicks are cinematic commonplaces, and today's pop idol is tomorrow's Nowhere Man. Once-credible reality was shattered with the dreamy lyricism of early grass and acid rock ("Strawberry fields forever") and now like Humpty-Dumpty's egg, the pieces of this cosmic Chinese puzzle cannot be put back together. Nowspeak reflects all these things: for a fragmented and incoherent time it offers us a pastiche-lingo whose silences and ellipses are more eloquent than its words.

Nowspeak, like most subculture languages, is more incantation than analysis or definition and thus relies heavily on word connotation rather than denotation. We already have noted the proper names that have charisma and evocative power. Certain other words and phrases also have it: "The Revolution," "power (supply: black, student, flower)," "the System," "the Movement," "kill pigs," "do your own thing." Men have died for less clearly defined terms than these. Nat Hentoff in the April 1969 *Evergreen* tells the story of a recent meeting of young liberal teachers in New York that quickly degenerated into a name-calling contest on the word "racist." The fact that the word was left undefined during the meeting was irrelevant. The evocative power of the word was enough. The important thing about words like the Movement and the Establishment is not that anyone can point to referents for them, but that they are sufficient in emotional force to generate their own new myths as they gather the tribes about them. For the Nowspeaker, as for Lewis Carroll's Humpty Dumpty, the word can mean anything that pleases the speaker at the time: for example, the word *uptight*, which seems to change meanings with the seasons. Claude Brown in "The Language of Soul" (*Esquire*, April 1968) remarks that the word came into use about 1953 in Harlem and meant being in financial straits. In time, it came to be popular with junkies to describe their perpetual condition of needing money for the next fix. In the early sixties when "uptight" was first making its way into under-thirty jargon, a younger generation of people in black urban communities of the East revived the word with new meaning: "everything is cool, under control, going my way." For the Nowspeaker "uptight" may be either a term of approbation ("everything is proceeding according to plan," "I have it all psyched out," "I'm cool, I'm hip") or of derision (as an equivalent to "square," "uncool," "not with it"). Once again, it is not the denotative power of the word that counts (*uptight* may denote two completely antithetical states, depending on its usage); it is the connotation of the word, the manner of uttering it, the occasion, the context, and the emotive force that determines the word's meaning in a given situation.

Stanley Kripner's paper before the International Society of General Semantics in August 1968 suggested that what the youthful user of "head drugs" learns from his earliest drug experiences is no very specific knowledge or information: instead he learns a new semantic set proper to the occasion ("spaced out," "groovy," "freak out," "high," "crash," "turned on"). To put the matter in good linguistic terminology, we might say that the Nowspeaker often mistakes the map for the territory; he speaks intensionally rather than extensionally, evocatively and incantatorially instead of analytically and rationally. Both in popular and a McLuhanesque sense of the word, Nowspeak is a "cool" language—indefinable, vague, often imprecise, requiring rigorous audience participation to fill in the holes in the content. Thus for the Nowspeaker the medium is quite literally the message.

Like George Orwell's famous Newspeak, Nowspeak is essentially a reductive language intended to facilitate rather than stimulate thought by limiting the possible alternatives that can be articulated within the language set. Designed for instant speech, minimum thought, and instant replay, it is built around an implicit two-value logic that denies or disregards the possibility of compromise or alternative systems. It is easy for America's retribalized youth to think in terms of these neat polar opposites—pig and Yippie (the poles of the 1968 Chicago confrontation), New Left and Establishment, System and Revolution —for it provides a comfortable means of instantly categorizing all the possible experiences that one might have. For the Nowspeaker the world is all black or white with no redeeming shade of grey in between. Black is beautiful and white is a sell-out. The student is a nigger. All power to the people, death to pigs. Down with the System; up, up, and away with the Beautiful People. Reason is bad, feeling is good. Act, think, act, think, then act, act, act. Nietzsche's prophetic transvaluation of all values has at last come to pass. The lack of a middle ground, a middle term somewhere between the extremes of total conformity and total assault on the culture, makes it impossible for Nowspeak to reflect with accuracy any world other than one drawn in the starkest of blacks and whites. There is, for example, no such animal as "pig-hippie" for that would be an animal as anomalous and absurd as Suzanne Langer's "rabbit-dog." One must be one or the other, never both at once. Thus, for all its dayglo colors, its newspaper taxis and marshmallow people, plasticene ponies and insanity's horse adorning the skies, the world of Nowspeak is a strangely sinister, almost medieval world, a battlefield where the children of light and the sons of darkness, the Now Generation and the Oldthinkers, play out the psychedelic *psychomachia* to the finish. The lines were drawn long ago with deadly clarity, and it may be too late to turn back the clock. As Gore Vidal reminds us in the final essay of *Sex, Death and Money*, the wheel of civilization is once more beginning to turn and most of us can only watch in morbid fascination as the flower kids in this strangest of all Children's Crusades are pied-piped away by the idol of the hour.

Yet the case for language may not be totally lost. It may well be this polarizing tendency of Nowspeak that will spell its end as the ruling subculture jargon. All philosophical systems have built into them certain basic assumptions that substantially limit the types of statements possible within each system. The same can be said of languages, for the verbal set of any culture (or subculture) determines to a great extent the limits of its possible assertions, its knowledge, its ideology, its perceptions, and hence its achievements. Like the heroine of Vilgot Sjöman's *I Am Curious (Yellow)* we all are feeling the need to smash our tidy op art cardboard archives with all the groovy letters and slogans and In words pasted all over the slick surface, and to find a new box with new labels for our collective files. Already hip young journalists, politicians, students, teachers, playwrights, poets, and critics are beginning to chafe at the restrictions of a language designed for incantation and slogans rather than for thoughtful analysis and action. Nat Hentoff's *Evergreen* article speaks of the New Left's "prison of words," and, after analysis of such phrases as Herbert Marcuse's "discriminative tolerance," Hentoff concludes that it is a polite euphemism for "elitist authoritarianism"; that "all power to all people" means not what it seems to say, but rather implies the implicitly snobbish view, "all power to me and everyone else who believes exactly as I do." For the first time perhaps in this decade we are beginning to look behind the words to the things and ideas, to search out hidden paradoxes ("All power to all people," and "America is a nation of fascist pigs," for example, are slogans as compatible as "Buddha is and is not"—and about equally meaningful).

Nowspeak has served its function and served it well and faithfully. Despite obvious limitations of its own, it has freed standard Americanese from the impoverishment of Webster's, Madison Avenue, pop psychiatry, military-industrial jargon, academese, and koffee-klatch-and-pizza-late-late-show TV. It has introduced a colorful, freaky, rhythmic, whimsical, gutsy, outrageous, "sexy, childish, irreligious and mad" element into a language that was giving signs of languishing in its prime. It has elevated the jargon of the hipster, the black, the drug pusher, bohemian, beat, hippie, and general rebel with or without a cause to the status of legitimate usage and has infused instant glamour and expressiveness into the speech of millions (both the *New York Times* and David Brinkley have noted a special affinity for *uptight*). In a very real sense, Nowspeak is itself the pop poetry of the new age just as rock is its lyric voice. Yet in an equally real sense the greatest strength of Nowspeak lies in its power and need to be superseded. C. D. Burns put it this way in an essay called "The Sense of the Horizon" (1933):

> The experience of any moment has its horizons. Today's experience, which is not tomorrow's, has in it some hints and implications which are tomorrow on the horizon of today. . . . However wide it may be, that common world also has its horizon; and on that horizon new experiences are always appearing.

That Nowspeak's horizon is Now is significant: that is at once its lifeblood and its death knell. Already the neon lights have burnt out on Carnaby Street, the Beatles have gone their separate ways, the Haight stands emptied of its brilliant frisking flower children, the orchard gone to ashes, and the dry leaves swirl like fallen Lucifer's host in the People's Park. Sergeant Pepper's buried; he will not come out of his grave. The summer people have taken to the streets, and the old hippies have fled into the mountains, feeling some new wind brewing in them as they breathe. And which of us knows what rough beast of a newer Nowspeak, its hour come 'round at last, slouches toward San Francisco to be born?

SUGGESTIONS FOR DISCUSSION AND WRITING

1. According to this essay, the so-called generation gap is actually a linguistic gap. Are you convinced that this is the case? Write an essay developing your view on this issue.

2. Examine the contributions to Nowspeak made by one of the sources mentioned in the essay—such as earlier bohemian movements, underworld language, or soul talk, and prepare a report on your findings.

3. Do you agree that advertising has made extensive use of Nowspeak? Survey some recent advertisements to determine just how extensive that use may be. See if you can ascertain how and why such language is used.

4. The author says that Nowspeak at its best is "gutsy, emotive, colorful, and highly expressive of a whole range of thought and action that conventional English simply cannot express." Choose some appropriate terms or phrases and explain how they might bear out this statement.

5. The conclusion of this essay affirms the author's beliefs that Nowspeak has made an important contribution to our language, but its period is passing. Take one of the contributions she credits Nowspeak with and write a paper explaining what that contribution was and how it was made. Or write a paper showing how some aspects of Nowspeak either is or is not going out of style.

10

John H. Bens

TABOO OR NOT TABOO

One of the most controversial issues of English usage is verbal obscenity. Indeed, sensitivity to "four-letter words" has led to widespread taboos—prohibitions against the use of such language on the grounds that it is offensive to society at large. But regardless of our attitudes about this language, it does, in fact, exist; and its power to affect people is attested to by every effort we make to ignore its existence. In this essay, John Bens of Merritt College, Oakland, California, deals frankly with the issue of verbal obscenity. Although initially presented to fellow teachers of English, his discussion should concern all students of language, for obscenity is, as Bens points out, one of the linguistic realities with which all of us live.

A colleague told me an amusing and sad story concerning a taboo of language. Years ago at college, one of his professors lectured for an hour on the dishonesty of certain dictionary editors who omitted a word from the dictionary because of moral objections. One's personal morality must never get in the way of scholarship, he thundered. When the period was over, a student raised his hand and asked, "But sir, what was the word?" The professor flushed and faltered. "I don't know," he said, "if . . . if I can tell you in mixed company." Medical doctors as late as the nineteenth century were expected to examine and treat pregnant women with the patient completely clothed. At the birth the doctor reached under the bedclothes to deliver the child and to preserve the mother's and his own modesty.

Unlike the professor and the doctors, I will not observe the

From *College Composition and Communication*, October 1971. Copyright 1971 by the National Council of Teachers of English. Reprinted by permission of the publisher and John Bens.

taboos. I will be using the offending words. The presentation will not be painless. The "other-worldliness" of teachers, particularly English teachers, is part of American folklore, Edward Sagarin in his excellent book *The Anatomy of Dirty Words* (published 1962) writes, "It was the American campaign against the word *cock* that caused Amos Bronson Alcox to change his name, and one might conjecture whether spinster schoolteachers and prudish librarians would have permitted *Little Women* and *Little Men* to become classics for young people of America had they been authored by his daughter under the name Louisa May Alcox." Sagarin points out that the desire to avoid a word that might call attention to the penis caused nineteenth-century America to say rooster rather than cock, to say weathervane rather than weathercock, to say haystack rather than haycock.

Prudery, of course, isn't limited to teachers. In his book *Mrs. Grundy* (subtitled *Studies in English Prudery*), published in America in 1964, Peter Fryer writes, "The great Roman orator, Cicero, advised his friends not to say 'little pavements' by adding a diminutive to *pavimenta*, for the word so formed, *pavimentula*, would suggest *mentula*, which meant 'penis.'" License plates in America and Great Britain are closely censored to make sure the letter combinations neither offend nor sexually excite the populace. Gershon Legman in his *now* readily available collection of essays *Love and Death* (published after unbelievable difficulties in 1949) comments on the result of prudery. "Words, thoughts, ideas—all are punned upon, hinted at, symbolized, turned upside-down and acrosticked, acted out in idiotic mummery, and finally, for the benefit of the dullest, are lettered out in kindergarten style. Thus Shakespeare's 'Her very C's, her U's, 'n' her T's' (*Twelfth Night*, 11.v.88), the meaning of which puzzles professors so much, audiences so little. When genius must stoop to the nursery subterfuge of spelling its tabooed word out, nothing is to be expected of lesser craftsmen in resisting the censorship of sex." The word, Shakespeare's word lettered out in kindergarten style, was *cunt*. Webster's Third Edition defines *cunt* as pudenda or the female regarded as sexual object. The poet Robert Graves tells of a soldier shot in the buttocks who was asked by a lady hospital visitor where he had been wounded and replied, "I'm sorry, Ma'am, I don't know. I never learned Latin."

The English teacher's trade is communication and language is the tool. My maternal grandmother was an extremely outspoken and salty lady. When her children got too prim and proper, too prudish, she would say to them, "If you deny the tools, give up the trade." The laboratory technician who says, "That specimen is too terrible, I can't look at it"; the doctor who says, "That illness, that wound, I can't work on it"; the psychiatrist who says, "You're too terrible. I can't deal with your problem," we would call unprofessional. But again, and again, and again we turn our backs on the language of reality, hiding from and urging our students to hide from life.

A conversation outside an English class at Merritt College triggered this paper. The topic—taboo words—of course goes back many years. When Adam and Eve left the Garden of Eden, Adam is supposed to have remarked to Eve, "Well, everything is in a state of transition." Denying this state of transition has, over the years, come to be the job of the Establishment. Apparently believing that as much of Paradise as could be restored has been restored, the Establishment digs in. Whatever insures the security or the status quo of Demiparadise is good, and whatever threatens the security or status quo is bad. Two bulwarks of our Eden or Demiparadise, and of any society I suppose, are procreation and elimination—the creating of life and the disposal of the lifeless. So awful, in the sense of inspiring dread or deep reverence, are these two bulwarks within our Eden that taboos have grown up around them. Reference to them can be made by certain sacred groups—medical people and mothers. So awful, in the sense of disagreeable, offensive, objectionable, are these two bulwarks that reference to them by the uncredentialed is outside the pale of polite society. Medical people employ scientific terms. (Examined by a proctologist some weeks ago a friend of mine asked the doctor, "A OK?" Like Queen Victoria, the doctor was not amused.) Mothers usually employ euphemisms or disphemisms. That last term was new to me until I did a bit of homework for this paper. A euphemism insures our comfort; a dysphemism insures our discomfort. A euphemism for masturbation is "playing with one's self." A dysphemism for masturbation is "self abuse" or "the solitary sin." Except for mothers and doctors, everyone in our Eden is supposed to pretend neither procreation nor elimination exists. The taboos must be strictly observed. That the words *fuck* and *shit* were at one time acceptable in English has nothing to do with the fact that if tabooed words are said, printed, thought, or pictured, our Demiparadise is lost. Historic fact be damned. Paradise! Love it or leave it!

Of late there seems to be a revolt in Paradise. I have been away from teaching for two years, but before I left both my students and I knew the rules and tended to observe them. In the fall of 1969 I returned to teaching and a change was apparent. Shatteringly, I no longer could think of myself as a successful teacher. In the fall quarter of 1969 I had the idea I was auditioning for a part, that there was a hell of a good universe next door, and that I was delaying my students' departure. There was so much *sotto voce* swearing in one English class that I invited discussion of the words I was hearing. Giggling, embarrassment, and silence was the response. After class a black student—intelligent, militant, and with a marvelous sense of humor—volunteered that he'd had difficulty in the military service because of language. The term *motherfucker* was almost as regular in this student's speech as are *beauty* and *truth* in the speech of the English teacher. The sergeant objected to the term *motherfucker* and regularly handed out punishment to the soldier. "What about that term *son of a bitch* that you're always using," the soldier challenged. "There's nothing wrong with *son of a bitch*," said the sergeant. "Well, there's nothing wrong with *motherfucker*," said the soldier. The punishment of extra duty continued. Sergeants don't debate.

Many English teachers don't debate or, rather, they avoid debate by avoiding hearing or seeing the taboo words. Cursing, profanity, obscenity—whether in a piece of literature or used spontaneously or by design by a student—simply doesn't exist. A popular bit of graffitti when I was in college was "English teachers do not have to go to the toilet." A variant of the avoidance technique was used by a teacher of English as a foreign language in Japan in 1958. The young American woman was teaching a

lesson on the e sound at a seminar for Japanese teachers of English. A student, one of the Japanese, wrote rhyming words on the blackboard while the other teachers took notes. LUCK, STRUCK, MUCK, BUCK . . . "Great God," Edith, our American friend thought, "it's going to happen any moment," and it did. She averted her eyes. And then the oral drill began. To hear *that* word from those lips, the lips of Madame Butterfly, thirty Madame Butterflies. RUCK, STLUCK, MUCK. . . . Edith was on her feet. She walked to the front of the room and simply erased the offending word. "No," she said. Simply, "No," and returned to her seat. In 1958 that solution seemed obvious and correct.

Today the offending word is not so easily erased. "Does she or doesn't she?" asks an advertisement for a hair dye. Noonday Press has just published *The Life and Loves of Mr. Jiveass Nigger*. The movie, *Putney Swope*, is advertised by a non-picture of the finger of scorn. All the books that formerly were smuggled into the country are available locally. In a recent textbook contract I have seen, the publisher disclaims all responsibility should suits charging obscenity be brought because of the textbook. The Magnolia Thunder Pussy is an icecream parlor in Oakland, California. At a dinner party recently an extremely quiet, extremely liberal, and extremely purposeful older woman told a joke that necessitated her saying *fucking* several times. When the joke was over and the laughter had quieted, her husband observed, "Two years ago Marie thought that word was a city in China." The films of today are tomorrow's TV fare.

Lines, however, are being drawn. Stenographers transcribing the space conversation of one of the astronaut teams deleted offending words in the transcription. The *San Francisco Chronicle* reports the firing of a local disk jockey for playing the song, "I'm Not Getting Any Nooky." The effect on high school students from reading *The Dictionary of American Slang*, *Dutchman*, and *Soul on Ice*, is of concern to political powers in Sacramento.

Undoubtedly I'm being facetious about and unfair to those who favor a stricter observance of the taboos than do I. I'll attempt to undo the wrong. Reviewing a drama textbook for a publisher last year, I was surprised to see the play *Command*

Decision in the table of contents. The play was copyrighted in 1946 and dealt with the beginnings of precision bombing by our airforce in World War II. In *Representative American Plays* (7th Edition, copyright 1957) by Arthur Hobsin Quinn, Professor Quinn says in his introduction, "[*Command Decision*] proves that the language of men at war does not have to be overloaded with profanity or obscenity, which disfigures so much of writing today, that these are really interruptions or mere punctuation in the narrative and have no artistic value." *Life* magazine would probably concur. Sagarin, in his work, quotes *Life* regarding four-letter words and *From Here to Eternity*: "This particular brand of 'realism' is phony, anyhow. Four-letter words in print, especially when they occur with the clamorous repetition of *From Here to Eternity*, take on an emphasis and a total significance which they do not have in the actual life and language of the soldier. There, as anyone who has been in or around armies knows, they are blurred and minimized by the frequency of their use. Printing magnifies them, and the result is a misleading falseness which is the opposite of valid realism." I would like to come back to the Quinn and *Life* magazine points of view at the close of my paper.

Today if avoiding or ignoring taboo words in the classroom is impossible, what to do? Forbidding their use is a grand way of opening discussion with a bang! Easing into the discussion might be easier on both instructor and students. Some of the materials that I have used with some success, materials that touch on taboos, cushion the sensitive. Aubrey Menen, whose father was Indian and his mother Irish, tells in his autobiographical *Dead Man in the Silver Market* of being taken half way round the world, from London to India, when he was thirteen to visit his paternal grandmother. Menen writes about her: "She rarely spoke to anyone who was not of her own social station and she received them formally: that is to say, with her breasts completely bare. Even in her time women were growing lax about this custom in Malabar. But my grandmother insisted on it. She thought that married women who wore blouses and pretty *saris* were Jezebels; in her view, a wife who dressed herself above her waist could only be aiming at adultery." The position of English women in society couldn't be discussed in Menen's grandmother's house, for she permitted no lewd talk in her presence. The socially approved in one country can be the obscenity in another. Many of my students were overseas in the military and know of customs that might be forbidden or frowned on in America. They can tell, too, of words, gestures, and behavior of their own that caused consternation abroad. The short story "Sun and Shadow" by Ray Bradbury is more graphic than the Menen material. In the Bradbury story a Mexican man named Ricardo takes offense when American photographers and models attempt to take fashion pictures in his village. They treat the village and its inhabitants as though they were cardboard cutouts meant to provide picturesque background for the high fashion models. When reason, when logic proves futile—the foreigners won't and can't understand—Ricardo finally stops the picture taking by standing in camera range and dropping his pants. The nakedness is obscene to the photographer and models. "Was that picturesque enough?" Ricardo asks. A dog urinates against a wall and Ricardo says to the photographer, "Quick, quick. Get a picture before the sun dries it." Nakedness, urine, naturalness—but the photographer thought it unnatural (i.e., obscene).

A lifetime of observing taboos makes explicit discussion about taboo words difficult for some instructors. For many students, in my experience, the discussion is almost impossible. The difficulty can be made an advantage. In what situations *wouldn't* the student be surprised to hear the words? In the male world of the locker room, in the military, in situations where one's prowess, particularly one's physical prowess of bravery may be tested, the magic (i.e., taboo, obscene) words are brought out of hiding. Bright, militant women in a class might raise the question whether taboo words are denied them because the words are so bad and women are so good, or because the words are so good (beneficent male magic) and women, in the badness or inferiority of their presence alone, negate the magic.

A situation demanding bravery and physical prowess on the part of some (many? most?) young people today, both male and female, is the revolt from the Demiparadise of the Establishment.

In a phonograph album called "Freak Out" the Mothers of Invention sing, "Plastic America walk on by the schools that do not teach. Plastic America walk on by the minds you do not reach." They sing that the long-haired freaks (i.e., the young) are in revolt and will not fight in wars, nor be bought by the supermarkets and hardware stores, nor drugged by the liquor stores. Four years ago this album was released, didn't sell and was recalled. Today it is a best seller. The young with their spotlight are merciless. They feel that the school has been the incubator for an establishment that wouldn't examine itself against the values it proclaimed to the world. To aid the youth—not to put them down, nor to wage war on them—the school could create an atmosphere in which youth will turn the same brilliant light, the same blunt honesty, on themselves and their revolt. How ironic if today's youth becomes as wretched, uptight, and obscene tomorrow, as they think today's establishment is.

Might the school aid youth in examining their current use of taboo words? Youth could be helped to see that the obscene words seem to serve two purposes in the revolt. The words are available to all the troops (saying them is proof of bravery and liberation); and the words wound and infuriate the establishment. Sitting in on a class several weeks ago I must have heard the word *fuck* at least forty times and *shit* about as many. The Establishment was the subject of discussion. I asked the instructor if other obscene words were ever made use of. Apparently they weren't. I wondered if the words were thought of as proof of loyalty and militancy, a pledge of allegiance, as it were. I suggested she ask the students to explore the worlds of obscenity they were neglecting. To ask themselves why the neglect. To ask themselves, when the shibboleths of the establishment are torn down, must new shibboleths be set up. A society in which everyone does his own thing could include no shibboleths.

The revolt of the young is presented dramatically in a new pictorial essay book entitled *America In Crisis* (published in 1969). One picture shows a young protestor in Chicago holding a sign reading "The elections don't mean shit." My students won't initiate discussion of the photograph. The students must be helped to question. A class discussion of the sign, let alone of the girl who was holding it, might provoke the following: Elections are a shibboleth by which the Establishment maintains itself in power, perpetuating inequity and hypocrisy. *Shit*, a taboo word to the Establishment, is perhaps one of the few magic words strong enough to attack the inequity and hypocrisy that has wrapped itself in the flag of the word "elections." The very intelligent, black, militant student I mentioned earlier could well have devised that effective sign. In his English class I showed a film on Mahatma Gandhi and my student responded, "Gandhi was out of his rabbit ass mind." Much of the militant philosophy is, I think, to be found in his one sentence dismissal of the film and Gandhi. To fail to analyze the sentence because of the taboo word *ass* will, I'm afraid, make asses of us all.

Psychiatrist Renatus Hartogs in his book *Four Letter Word Games* (published 1967) talks of the necessity of the modern shaman, today's "black humorist," the Lenny Bruces who violate our taboos for us because we want them violated but are afraid to violate them ourselves. Hartogs talks of "scouring obscenity," scrubbing tradition until tradition is reshaped into new values. The very words that Professor Quinn and *Life* magazine objected to as unartistic, as the opposite of valid realism, that we as teachers have avoided acknowledging for generations, are awful words—awful because they are disagreeable, objectionable, and unpleasant and awful in that they inspire profound and reverential fear. They are words that touch the matrix of our lives.

SUGGESTIONS FOR DISCUSSION AND WRITING

1. *The author warns us in his second paragraph that in this essay he will not observe the taboos but will use the offending words. Does his warning adequately prepare you for what follows? Does his use of taboo words seem less shocking than their use might be in another context? Why or why not?*

2. *Taboo words obviously shock or offend many people. What might some of the reasons be? What is your own reaction to such words? Do you find any of them offensive? If so, what are those words and what is offensive about them?*

3. *The author raises the possibility that the words "fuck" and "shit" may be used by many people "as proof of loyalty and militancy, a pledge of allegiance, as it were." Can you support or refute this contention?*

4. *What is the most obscene word that you know? What makes it obscene? That is, why do you consider it obscene? Have you ever used the word? If so, under what circumstances and for what purposes?*

5. *Are taboo words used in any of your classes? If so, who uses them and for what reasons? Do you find instructors or others who will discuss "four-letter words" but will not use the actual words? Are they being hypocritical? Should taboo words be discussed in the college classroom? Support your answer.*

11

J. Dan Rothwell

VERBAL OBSCENITY: TIME FOR SECOND THOUGHTS

The preceding essay urges that we face the fact of verbal obscenity as the first step in learning to cope with it. In this one, J. Dan Rothwell both faces it and copes with it Grounding his discussion in rhetorical scholarship, he analyzes the uses and effects of verbal obscenity, and through the example of his own essay concludes that "Hoping it will go away will not make it so. It is time to accept verbal obscenity as a significant rhetorical device and help discover appropriate responses to its use." Mr. Rothwell teaches Speech at Fort Hays Kansas State College.

Classical and contemporary rhetorical theory uniformly rejects the use of verbal obscenity as a legitimate rhetorical strategy. Aristotle, although not specifically singling out obscenity, denounces "meanness" in language as inappropriate.[1] Cicero admonishes those whose style is not "agreeable, savoring of erudition and liberal knowledge, worthy of admiration, [and] polished . . ."[2] Quintilian speaks of "*propriety* in the use of words." His unqualified dictum is to avoid language that is "obscene, unseemly, or mean."[3]

The overwhelming majority of more recent rhetoricians have seemed to share the views of the writers of antiquity on the matter of verbal obscenity Most contemporary theorists seem to be-

From *Western Speech*, Fall 1971. Reprinted by permission of *Western Speech* and J. Dan Rothwell.

[1] Aristotle, *Rhetoric*, trans. W. Rhys Roberts (New York, 1954), 1404b. 3–4.

[2] Cicero, *De Oratore*, trans. J. S. Watson (Philadelphia, 1897), III. xxv.

[3] Quintilian, *Institutio Oratoria*, trans. H. E. Butler (New York, 1922), VIII. ii. 1.

lieve that obscenity requires no further explication. A few, however, venture to make brief comments regarding the advisability
of employing verbal obscenity as a rhetorical strategy. Brigance
stipulates that "crude words won't serve people who think and
act, feel and talk, on problems of the civilized world."[4] Eisenson
and Boase make this observation: "There are some words which
we do not speak in polite society; there are other words which we
do not speak with propriety in mixed company . . . In brief, even
in our highly civilized society some words are considered *taboo*."[5]
Capp leaves no doubt concerning his viewpoint: "Off-color
words, obscenity, and profanity should not be used at all."[6] Andersch, Staats, and Bostrom, in concurring with Capp's unequivocal position, argue that "Swearing, particularly, has no place in
anyone's language. . . . These words are generally offensive and
cannot be considered appropriate for any occasion."[7] Ironically,
thoughtful study of verbal obscenity is predominantly treated
as a taboo, a subject unworthy of scholarly exploration.

Despite consensus on the point among rhetorical scholars,
verbal obscenity persists and, in fact, is a principal rhetorical
strategy of the so-called New Left. Walker's definitive study of
the Democratic National Convention held in Chicago in 1968
is replete with examples of verbal obscenity utilized by the
youthful agitators.[8] (Printing explicit, uncensored examples of
obscenity is a relatively recent phenomenon.) Black Panthers
Eldridge Cleaver, Bobby Seale, and H. Rap Brown liberally
sprinkle their speeches with obscenity. Vietnam veterans marched
on the nation's capitol in April of this year shouting obscenities
in their anti-war protest. Obscenity has been employed frequently by campus demonstrators for the last several years.
Moral indignation against the use of foul language has not

---

[4] William Norwood Brigance, *Speech: Its Techniques and Disciplines in a Free Society*, 2nd ed. (New York, 1961), p. 299.

[5] Jon Eisenson and Paul H. Boase, *Basic Speech*, 2nd ed. (New York, 1964), p. 188.

[6] Glenn R. Capp, *How to Communicate Orally* (Englewood Cliffs, N.J., 1961), p. 220.

[7] Elizabeth G. Andersch, Lorin C. Staats, and Robert N. Bostrum, *Communication in Everyday Use*, 3rd ed. (New York, 1969), pp. 134–35.

[8] Daniel Walker, *Rights in Conflict* (New York, 1968), pp. 235–80.

lessened its frequency, nor does it appear to be a useful justification for virtually ignoring its impact upon the rhetorical scene. The inadequacy of rhetorical theory in this realm of persuasion is emphasized by Scott and Smith: "The managerial advice implicit in current theories of debate and discussion scarcely contemplates the possibility that respectable people should confront disruption of reasonable or customary actions, *obscenity* [italic mine], threats of violence, and the like."[9]

Despite the moral repugnance of verbal obscenity, the frequency with which it is utilized justifies a closer and more thorough analysis of this rhetorical strategy than it has thus far received. Although a few excellent articles have been published recently on confrontation and agitational rhetoric, verbal obscenity has been uniformly lumped together with widely varying rhetorical strategies and tactics of militants. Little attention has been focused upon verbal obscenity in an effort to explore its principal purposes and profound effects. It is the intent of this article to pursue that end, concentrating primarily upon the use of verbal obscenity as a rhetorical strategy.

For the purpose of clarification, verbal obscenity is defined as a type of swearing that utilizes indecent words and phrases. Such "indecent" terms fall into essentially four categories: (1) copulative terms such as "fuck," (2) excretory terms such as "shit" and "piss," (3) terms related to the human genitals such as "cunt" and "cock," and (4) terms related to sexual irregularities such as "bastard" and "bitch." These words are generally considered obscent because of their application and the negative connotations associated with them. Terms such as "damn" and "hell" are general swearwords not usually considered indecent in either their meaning or application. They may add strength, however, to obscene words when used as adjectives.

PRINCIPAL PURPOSES OF VERBAL OBSCENITY

CREATE ATTENTION. The social unacceptability of verbal obscenity relegates its use as a rhetorical strategy to minorities

[9] Robert L. Scott and Donald K. Smith, "The Rhetoric of Confrontation," *Quarterly Journal of Speech*, 55 (1969), 8.

in our society. Most people castigate those who dare to speak obscenities in the public forum, despite the fact that a substantial portion of the "Silent Majority" seem to have little aversion to private cursing. Montagu makes this very point: "Because swearing is socially condemned, there are many who publicly join in its denunciation but privately take a somewhat different view of it."[10]

It is a rather obvious fact that the press has launched many otherwise unnoticed individuals and dissident groups into national prominence. Without press coverage, groups such as the S.D.S. and Black Panthers would have remained relatively obscure to the average American. While it is true that violent or disruptive acts are largely responsible for the substantial interest by the press in these groups, verbal obscenity has likewise proved catalytic in drawing attention to militants. This kind of shock rhetoric is outrageous to the majority of Americans, who find it inconceivable that foul language could be utilized so blatantly in public. McEdwards, in her article on agitative rhetoric, explains that the agitator needs to "gain attention by using strong, passionate language—language whose connotations evoke an immediate emotional response in the listener."[11] Verbal obscenity provides the most jolting, evocative stimulus to society; the style of dissent is outrageousness. Anything less can be easily dismissed. A milder form of verbal abuse may prove to be equally effective in gaining attention, but this in no way negates the fact that obscenity draws attention to itself as well as to those using it. Although this may not be a unique function of verbal obscenity, it is nevertheless its initial purpose.

DISCREDIT. Hoffer, in his study of the anatomy of mass movements, indirectly gives a strong rationale for the use of verbal obscenity: "Mass movements do not usually rise until the prevailing order has been discredited. The discrediting is . . . the deliberate work of men of words with a grievance."[12] Assuming

---

[10] Ashley Montagu, *The Anatomy of Swearing* (New York, 1967), p. 2.
[11] Mary G. McEdwards, "Agitative Rhetoric: Its Nature and Effect," in *The Rhetoric of Our Times*, ed. J. Jeffery Auer (New York, 1969), p. 9.
[12] Eric Hoffer, *The True Believer* (New York, 1951), p. 129.

mass support is a goal of today's agitators, one of their primary functions must be to discredit the existing institutions and leadership.

Verbal obscenity is, by definition, antithetical to the "establishment." Society brands four-letter words as taboo. Obscenity, therefore, expresses a profound contempt for society's standards, a revolt against authority, and an irreverence for things sacred. The "system" must be defiled because, in the mind of the agitator, it is this system that perpetuates racism, poverty, and a multitude of other injustices. There is a strong sentiment among militants for an "honest" rhetoric, devoid of sham and pretense, especially in, to their minds, an atmosphere of euphemistic platitudes aimed at hiding the naked truth. "Law and order" and "states' rights" are masks for injustices in the eyes of the agitators. The indiscriminate napalming of defenseless villagers in Vietnam is part of our "pacification" program. The invective employed by Spiro Agnew against the agitators is excused as "positive polarization." Obscenity is the style of dissent because the enemy has created the taboo. Rap Brown explains this phenomenon in his autobiography: "If white folks say gray suits are fashionable, you go buy a pink one. If they say america [sic] is great, you say america ain't shit. Chairman Mao says, 'Whatever the enemy supports, we oppose. Whatever the enemy opposes, we support,' "[13] Civility is an instrument of the *status quo*; verbal obscenity is a symbol of rebellion against the power structure. Agitators seek profound change, and profanity offers a profound change from the accepted style of dissent.

In this way, verbal obscenity is unique as a form of agitative rhetoric. The emphasis is not simply upon "telling it like it is" but upon telling it *exactly* like it is. It may be enough for agitators to describe the police as "pigs," but how do they adequately describe racism, poverty, and the Vietnam War? To the agitator these are the real obscenities. Bobby Seale once explained his penchant for the four-letter word with the terse comment that "the filthiest word I know is 'kill' and this is what other men have

[13] H. Rap Brown, *Die Nigger Die!* (New York, 1969), p. 55.

done to the Negro for years."[14] Indecent descriptions of the draft and the Vietnam War are frequently dismissed by agitators with the curt reply, "We are not obscene; Vietnam is obscene." In this sense, verbal obscenity is uniquely suited to the crime. It expresses best the feelings of outrage against society's complicity in these obscene injustices. Verbal obscenity represents the antithesis of civility and decorum which, according to the agitator, have disguised the profane truth.

PROVOKE. One of the principal functions of verbal obscenity is to provoke violent confrontations. Verbal obscenity at the Chicago Democratic National Convention was clearly intended to provoke a violent encounter between law enforcement officers and the demonstrators.[15] This nation has frequently witnessed students. during campus protests, inviting police retaliation by numerous methods, including the use of obscenity. Although this strategy may appear self-defeating, there is a reasonable explanation for this apparent insanity.

Even though physical acts of violence, such as throwing bricks and bottles at police, may successfully provoke violent retaliation, verbal obscenity is the most effective rhetorical method available to agitators for inciting a violent response. As psychologist Arnold H. Buss explains, obscenity "represents the most intense verbal aggression."[16] Although it is in some ways understandable that police retaliate in the face of such severe verbal abuse, that retaliation, nevertheless, tends to prove the point of view of the agitators. The violent reactions of the power structure to these insults "proves" that policemen are really "pigs." As Cleaver states, "So if you shoot me down today, if you drag me back to prison today, Fuck You! You're a Pig!"[17] Obscenity encourages violence and may indirectly marshal support for the agitators not because obscenity is condoned, but

[14] Quoted by Mary Ellen Leary, "The Uproar Over Cleaver," *New Republic*, 30 Nov. 1968, p. 23.

[15] John Waite Bowers and Donovan J. Ochs, *The Rhetoric of Agitation and Control* (Reading, Mass., 1971), p. 70.

[16] Arnold H. Buss, *The Psychology of Aggression* (New York, 1961), p. 7.

[17] Speech delivered by Eldridge Cleaver at Sacramento State College, October 2, 1968.

because repressive tactics are deplored. Loss of restraint by police provides a kind of symbolic victory. The focus may change from the obscenity, which provokes violence, to the violent response itself.

Unfortunately, strong evidence indicates that the police are easily provoked by radicals. A study of the police by *Fortune* magazine concludes that "Most policemen view young radicals from middle-class backgrounds with especially intense moral repugnance."[18] Psychiatrist John P. Spiegel, Director of the Lemberg Center for the Study of Violence, agrees: "Militant youths and black militants are perceived [by police] not only as un-American, but also non-human. Ruled out of the human race, they become non-persons and therefore deserving of intense attack, as one would attack a rattlesnake."[19] This "intense moral repugnance" makes verbal obscenity an especially suitable rhetorical strategy for provoking police retaliation. Obscene language is morally repugnant. When demonstrators employ this kind of rhetoric they reinforce the preconceived notions of law enforcement officers regarding the "non-human" status of militants. Verbal obscenity can only increase the already substantial hostility harbored by police towards agitators in general. The susceptibility of law enforcement officers to provocation is summed up by Rodney Stark, who, under a grant from the Ford Foundation, did a careful study of the behavior of the police during campus demonstrations. He concludes that "the police can almost certainly be counted on to mishandle their assignment and turn all the suspicion and hostility of students into blinding anger."[20] Thus, verbal obscenity can be the most effective rhetorical weapon in the agitators' arsenal for the purpose of provoking violent confrontation.

IDENTIFICATION. A fourth function of verbal obscenity is the creation of strong interpersonal identification. Several examples

---

[18] A. James Reichley, "The Way to Cool the Police Rebellion," *Fortune*, Dec. 1968, p. 111.

[19] Quoted by Rodney Stark, "Protest + Police = Riot," in *Black Power and Student Rebellion*, ed. James McEvoy and Abraham Miller (Belmont, Calif., 1969), p. 172.

[20] *Ibid.*, p. 178.

come to mind in support of this observation. A national Gallup Poll conducted in 1969 reveals that 46 per cent of black Americans believe the local police "are harmful to Negro rights," an increase of 13 per cent from 1966.[21] In light of this fact, the Black Panthers' obscene vilification of police apparently expresses the private feelings of many black Americans. Although they may not approve of the Panther terminology, they may admire those who have the courage and audacity to insult policemen. Donald McCullom, former head of the Civil Rights Coordinating Committee in Oakland, supports this point: "The Black Panthers are simply articulating what the black community feels."[22] An unidentified black professional leader in California substantiates the point regarding identification between the black community and the Panthers when he says, "This violence and this filthy talk isn't my bag. . . . But, man, it make me PROUD they stand up."[23] The provocative language of the Panthers may result in identification with oppressed blacks, because the Panthers have the courage to say in public what some will only express in private.

Identification among young ghetto blacks, primarily males, also results from a verbal skill game called the "dozens" or "sounding." Anthropologist Roger Abrahams explains the function of obscenity: "The contest often begins with a simple curse, like 'Fuck you,' which may elicit the conventional response, 'Fuck your mother.' At this point the decision will be made whether to play or not."[24] Subject matter is concerned with topics that the young blacks are sensitive about. One's sexual prowess often provides the focus of attention while one's imagination is the only limitation on both story-line and language. In the most involved versions of the "dozens," insults are often framed in rhyme with obscenities interspersed throughout. Abrahams provides an example:

[21] "How Attitudes Have Changed," *Newsweek*, 30 June 1968, p. 19.
[22] Quoted by Leary, p. 24.
[23] Quoted by *ibid*.
[24] Roger Abrahams, "Patterns of Performance in the British West Indies," in *Afro-American Anthropology, Contemporary Perspectives*, ed. Norman E. Whitten, Jr., and John F. Szwed (New York, 1970), p. 165.

I fucked your mother on an electric wire.
I made her pussy rise higher and higher.

I fucked your mother between two cans.
Up jumped a baby and hollered, "Superman."[25]

In this example the opponent's mother is the object of deroga-
tion claiming sexual wantonness, a frequent occurrence in playing the "dozens."[26] Thus the term "motherfucker" occupies a
prominent place in the vocabulary of the young ghetto black.

The purpose of the "dozens" is essentially self-assertive. By
humiliating his opponent the black youth establishes an *ethos*
within the community, a reputation among other blacks. The
process of self-identity is developed by such verbal contests. The
growing awareness, especially of sexual matters, among adoles-
cent blacks is expressed in games like the "dozens." At the same
time, according to Abrahams, "sounding" is a method of assert-
ing one's masculinity: "To say 'I fucked your mother' is not only
to say that womanly weakness is ridiculous, but that the teller's
virility has been exercised. At the same time he has prepared a
defense for himself against incest, homosexuality, or any other
forbidden sexual motive. In this way the youths prepare themselves for the hypermasculine world of the gang."[27]

An additional function of this verbal skill game is the release
of aggression through verbal insults rather than physical violence.
This will be discussed in more detail in the following section. It
also relates to identification, however, from the standpoint that
rhetorical ability is highly valued among young blacks. In one
sense it is more highly prized than physical strength. The status
of a participant in the "dozens" is greatly diminished if he has to
resort to fighting as an answer to a verbal attack.[28]

Obscenity provides the players with a stronger arsenal of
insults. Cleaver elaborates on this point: "We could talk about
'you dirty mother-intercourser.' We could say that. But it doesn't

[25] Roger D. Abrahams, *Deep Down in the Jungle* (Hatboro, Pa., 1964),
p. 52.
[26] *Ibid.*
[27] *Ibid.*, p. 57.
[28] Thomas Kochman, "Toward an Ethnography of Black American
Speech Behavior," in Whitten and Szwed. p. 159.

have the impact, it doesn't have the little pungent punch . . ."[29]
Thus, obscenity is helpful in goading an opponent into "blowing
his cool." The "best talkers" are admired for their verbal agility;
the unskilled are humiliated. Brown, for instance, received the
honorific nickname "Rap" for his ability in such verbal contests
as the "dozens."[30]

Verbal obscenity may also be a planned rhetorical strategy to
create identification between agitators and potential allies. The
years 1965–67 are about the time when black militants expelled
white radicals from the battle against racism. The advent of
Black Power ushered in the concepts of self-help and black initia-
tive in the struggle for equality. The civil rights movement took
a more militant tone. Coalition with whites was no longer a central part of the "new" civil rights movement. Black agitators
became suspicious of white radicals, who often seemed more
concerned with the Vietnam War than racism. The frequent use
of verbal obscenity by white militants, therefore, may be an
attempt to dispel the suspicions of blacks concerning the intentions and resolve of white radicals. Eugene Goodheart, Professor
of Literature at M.I.T. states: "The *machismo* and ghetto energy
of their language suggest that these white radicals are expiating
for their expulsion—trying to prove to their mistrustful black
brothers that they too can think black."[31] White radicals hope
to identify with blacks through language as well as action.

PROVIDE CATHARSIS. Verbal obscenity provides one other
essential function to the user. It is cathartic. Although almost any
emotionally charged word can provide catharsis, especially more
intensely abusive terms such as "pig" and "fascist," the highly
emotional nature of obscenity generates a purgative feeling
within the individual who employs such language when delivered
with its characteristic gusto and vitality. Either knowingly or
unwittingly the rhetorical agent seeks a release of his pent-up
frustrations in aggressive language, which may be only a pre-

[29] Speech delivered by Eldridge Cleaver at Sacramento State College,
October 2, 1968.
[30] Brown, p. 27.
[31] Eugene Goodheart, "The Rhetoric of Violence," *Nation*, 6 Apr. 1970.
p. 399.

lude to physical violence. Whether a person selects obscene or merely abusive language is a personal choice, but for some individuals there is a greater likelihood that verbal obscenity will be utilized as a panacea for seemingly unbearable inner frustration as hostility increases. Political scientist Allan Kornberg and sociologist Joel Smith, both of Duke University, provide conjecture on this phenomenon in their 1969 prognosis of future disorders on their own campus: "Although even the most active white students (but not black) until recently have largely refrained from employing the viler insults and obscenities used by activists at other college campuses . . . [i]t is not inconceivable, were there to be another more serious clash in which police were called by the administration . . . that such obscene expletives would be employed . . ."[32] While some students probably do not set out to provoke violent confrontations with authorities during campus demonstrations, their anger may overwhelm their sense of judgment and result in their use of verbal obscenity for its psychologically medicinal quality. This, in turn, could prove to be a provocative act, but it may have begun as a mere release of intense frustration and passion.

The "dozens" is another example of the cathartic function of verbal obscenity. Frustration is indigenous to a ghetto existence. The characteristically foul nature of the language of the "dozens" serves as a safety valve for the ghetto dweller. In fact, one of the primary purposes of this verbal game is to release aggression through intense verbal insults.[33] While blacks, within the confines of their ghetto environment, may consider terms such as "motherfucker" more abusive than obscene when used in playing the "dozens," such obscenities are directly related to the degree of abuse intended. As Cleaver once again explains, "motherfucker" is intended to be a *profound* [italics mine] putdown."[34] Verval aggression, therefore, is a surrogate for physical aggression. The black man finds relief from his anger

---

[32] Allan Kornberg and Joel Smith, " 'It Ain't Over Yet': Activism in a Southern University," in McEvoy and Miller, p. 113.

[33] Abrahams, *Deep Down in the Jungle*, p. 58.

[34] Speech delivered by Eldridge Cleaver at Sacramento State College, October 2, 1968.

and frustration within the confines of a game of abuse. The use of obscenity, consequently, has a therapeutic value in this context.

The cathartic quality of obscenity may be affected by how frequently and in what fashion the terms are used. Montagu cites a good example from an uncertain source, possibly of Australian origin: "I was walking along on this fucking fine morning, fucking sun fucking shining away, little country fucking lane, and I meets up with this fucking girl. Fucking lovely she was, so we gets into fucking conversation and I takes her over a fucking gate into a fucking field and we has sexual intercourse."[35] The frequency of the obscene term and its almost casual use reduce the cathartic effect of a normally evocative word. The objective sense of the word is also, quite obviously, lost.

EFFECTS OF VERBAL OBSCENITY

GENERAL PRINCIPLES. There are three primary factors, in addition to the specific purposes already discussed, that significantly alter the effects of verbal obscenity. These must be explored briefly prior to an evaluation of the actual effects of verbal obscenity.

The first important factor is *who* employs the obscenity. The degree of shock and outrage resulting from the use of verbal obscenity will be determined largely by the individual rhetorical agent. For example, a longshoreman is not expected to use polite phraseology, especially when angry, but a priest is always expected to use dignified language commensurate with his role in society. If a priest utilizes verbal obscenity for any reason, it is viewed by most as a desecration of his religious office. Society's sense of outrage and righteous anger would most probably lead to severe punitive action against the priest.

Women have long been considered the "gentler" sex. They are expected to act like "ladies," which excludes the use of obscenity for any reason, despite the fact that "gentlemen" have been afforded the luxury of four speech and dirty jokes among themselves for centuries. Perhaps it is this curious double stan-

[35] Quoted by Montagu, p. 314.

dard that has produced such rage among law enforcement officers when faced with verbal obscenity by female demonstrators. Guardsmen during the Kent State University confrontation were particularly incensed by this phenomenon. According to Michener, "To hear obscenities in common usage from girls who could have been their sisters produced a psychic shock which ran deep. To many of the Guardsmen, these girls had removed themselves from any special category of 'women and children'."[36]

A second factor which significantly alters the perception of the repugnance of verbal obscenity is *where* it is employed. As previously mentioned, indecent language is more outrageous when used in public, especially certain places. A church is obviously off limits for such language. The state of Kansas has a stricture against the use of obscenity by faculty members on university property. Courts of law, restaurants, in fact almost all public places, with the possible exceptions of taverns and public restrooms, are considered inappropriate forums for verbal obscenity. Nevertheless, while we frequently mask our true feelings in public for the sake of decorum, one's private home or automobile serves as a sufficient shelter for verbal obscenity. Fast provides an excellent example of verbal obscenity performed in the safety of the private automobile: "In a car, when our body zones are extended, we often feel free to drop the masks, and if someone cuts in front of us or tailgates us, we may loose tides of profanity that are shocking in their out-of-proportion emotions. . . . But here is a situation where we are generally invisible and the need to mask is gone. Our reactions can be all the greater because of this."[37] Once again verbal obscenity performs a therapeutic service, but the catharsis achieved in this example is distinctly relegated to a private forum where it is more acceptable to remove the behavioral mask.

A third factor significantly affecting the response to verbal obscenity is *how* the indecent terms are used. To call someone a "bastard" will frequently invite reprisal. Yet the term sometimes expresses admiration and affection as in the statement,

[36] James A. Michener, "Kent State: What Happened and Why," *Reader's Digest*, Apr. 1971, p. 232.

[37] Julius Fast, *Body Language* (New York, 1971), p. 55.

"The poor bastard never had a chance," or "He was a bastard with the girls." The term "motherfucker" is another case in point. Among blacks in particular, this normally obscene word can be used as an honorific term. One of the most complimentary things that can be said of a man is that he is a "mean motherfucker" or a "tough motherfucker."[38]

No word, therefore, isolated from the rhetorical situation, is obscene. It becomes indecent from the context in which it is used. The purpose for which obscenity is used, who uses it, where it is used, and how it is employed all function as determinants of the acceptability of such terms.

OBSERVABLE RESULTS. Although it is difficult to measure accurately the effects of verbal obscenity—many other devices are intermingled by the agitator to create attention, discredit, provoke, create identification, and provide catharsis—certain results are apparent, nevertheless. The principal effect of verbal obscenity is polarization, which emanates from the social disapproval of this type of language as discussed previously. The results of this polarization are sometimes profound and diverse. Few people are capable of remaining apathetic to the use of verbal obscenity by anyone, much less agitators. Consequently, the agitator wins at least a superficial, if not a consequential, victory by forcing the majority into separate and opposing camps preparing for battle. This is one of the purposes of confrontation rhetoric.[39] It is important that the agitator know his allies and his foes.

Polarization created by verbal obscenity produces several additional effects. The most obvious effect is the clouding of issues and an emphasis upon the obscenities themselves. Ronald Dellums, black congressman from Berkeley, makes this very point in reference to the Black Panthers: "White reaction to the Panthers is hung up on words—militancy, violence, revolution, black. Even the obscenities. People are so involved with the language

---

[38] Abrahams, *Deep Down in the Jungle*, p. 261.
[39] Irving Howe. "The New 'Confrontation Politics' Is a Dangerous Game," in *The Rhetoric of Revolution*, ed. Christopher Katope and Paul Zolbrod (New York, 1970), p. 197.

they ignore what is being said."[40] While verbal obscenity creates attention, it may draw attention merely to the profanity, itself, rather than to issues like police brutality and racism.

Polarization precipitated by verbal obscenity also produces an aggressive response. Buss explains the basis for this: "When an anger stimulus is presented to a recipient, it elicits an anger reaction and a tendency to counterattack."[41] This "anger reaction" may take two forms, counter-obscenity and physical violence. The Chicago Democratic National Convention witnessed a number of incidents where police openly provoked protesters with equally hostile profanity.[42] Counter-obscenity, however, may be only the first step. Agitators on several occasions have elicited the desired response from the police and National Guard. The beating of agitators, and in many instances innocent bystanders, during the Chicago Convention resulted in a "police riot."[43] Bowers and Ochs, in their detailed study of protest movements, make this observation regarding the provocative role obscenity played on that occasion: "The tactic that probably prompted the 'police riot,' the violent suppression witnessed by millions on television, was the use of obscenity. . . . That the obscenity was instrumental in producing violent confrontation is clear from post-confrontation statements by city officials."[44]

The brutal response to verbal obscenity, however, may not be limited to mere beatings. The tragic deaths of four Kent State University students in May, 1970, can be at least partly attributed to the profanity used by Kent State students. Michener, in his reconstruction of the Kent State confrontations, concludes, "Worse, in a way, than the missiles were the epithets. A steady barrage of verbal filth, curses and fatal challenges came down upon the Guard, whose masks did not prevent them from hearing what they were being called."[45] The end result was probably more than most of the agitators expected, but it clearly indicates the danger inherent in such a rhetorical strategy.

---

[40] Quoted by Leary, p. 24.
[41] Buss, p. 12.
[42] Walker, pp. 237–53.
[43] Ibid., pp. 5 ff.
[44] Bowers and Ochs, pp. 69–71.
[45] Michener, p. 240.

While agitators may be successful in provoking a violent response, they cannot always claim an actual victory in the resulting polarization. A Gallup Poll taken after the Chicago confrontation showed 55 per cent of Americans in agreement with the police tactics and 31 per cent opposed.[46] Michener's study of Kent State shows strong approval of National Guard actions by the majority of Kent citizens, and strong disapproval by students of Kent State.[47] One ultimately must ask the question, "Is the use of verbal obscenity worth the price?" The agitator is frequently successful in provoking police to act violently and "prove" to many that they are truly "pigs." Yet obscenity also alienates a great portion, often a majority, of Americans from the cause of the agitator. Verbal obscenity may also result in the shedding of innocent blood, such as occurred at Kent State; in this context, if agitators can claim victory at all, it is only a qualified one.

CONCLUSION

When Voltaire spoke his famous words defending a person's right to say that which he deplored, he probably did not envision the use of verbal obscenity. The ultimate question, however, is not the freedom of foul speech, but how best to respond to verbal obscenity. Despite its moral repugnance, it will not disappear simply because it is disliked by most.

Neither denunciation nor suppression of its use is an adequate response to the fact of verbal obscenity; the students of rhetoric must seek to understand the purposes and effects of this rhetorical strategy. Despite centuries of negative criticism, verbal obscenity has become a more frequent rhetorical device. It is successful in creating attention, in discrediting an enemy, in provoking violence, in fostering identification, and in providing catharsis. Its effects are governed by a variety of circumstances which need to be understood more fully. It has precipitated a police riot, brutal beatings, and even death. Hoping it will go away will not make it so. It is time to accept verbal obscenity as

[46] Stark, p. 177.
[47] Michener, pp. 261–71.

a significant rhetorical device and help discover appropriate responses to its use.

SUGGESTIONS FOR DISCUSSION AND WRITING

1. *As we know from this essay, both classical and contemporary rhetoricians reject the use of verbal obscenity as a legitimate rhetorical strategy. Do you agree with them? Why or why not? Under what circumstances is obscenity acceptable to you? When is it not acceptable? Explain the reasons behind your answers.*

2. *The author points out that many people who publicly condemn swearing or obscenity use such language themselves in private. Have you known people to do so? Is there any such difference between your own public and private use of language? If there is, can you justify the difference?*

3. *Can you add any purposes for verbal obscenity to those named by the author? Examine a situation in which extensive obscenity occurs, and see if you can determine the purposes of that obscenity.*

4. *Are males more likely than females to use obscenity? Does obscenity seem to you to be more appropriate for males? Is there any relationship between the use of obscenity and the qualities that make one a gentleman or a lady?*

5. *This essay recognizes verbal obscenity as a fact of life and the author sees the crucial problem in this matter as how to respond to it. Do you agree that this is the major problem, or do you see it to be something else? What suggestions can you offer to help people respond to verbal obscenity?*

3

UP AGAINST THE WALL:
RHETORIC AND REVOLUTION

Drawing by Saxon; © 1968 The New Yorker Magazine, Inc.

"If I am elected, I promise to get things moving again. Like there are a lot of groovy things that ought to be done about like self-determination and the way the power structure makes rules that affect all kinds of things it has become too stagnant to dig, and with your support, together we can make this country groovy again."

12

Tom Hayden

LANGUAGE BECOMES CRIMINAL

As the last three essays in the previous section make clear, the cultural conflicts emerging out of our language are by no means limited to the niceties of English usage. Never before in the history of American politics has language played such a crucial and controversial role as in the past several years. In this selection, a leading figure in the New Left political movement, Tom Hayden, recounts the way in which language became a central issue of not only political but legal controversy in the trial that arose out of the violence surrounding the 1968 Democratic National Convention. Reprinted from Mr. Hayden's book on that trial, the selection is taken from his discussion of the fundamental cultural conflicts that he saw reflected in the confrontation between "The Establishment" and "The Movement" in Chicago.

A third example of the cultural conflict revolved around language. The government's case was a massive structure of obscene and provocative language attributed to us by police informers, language which the jury was supposed to imagine coming from our mouths as they stared at us across the courtroom. Some of the language was pure invention; most of it was a twisting of words which once had been used by us. Through the testimony over language, we came to the essence of the supposed "communication gap" between the generations.

The language of the establishment is mutilated by hypocrisy. When "love" is used in advertising, "peace" in foreign policy, "freedom" in private enterprise, then these words have been

From *Trial* by Tom Hayden. Copyright © 1970 by Tom Hayden. First appeared (sic) in *Ramparts*, July 1970. Reprinted by permission of Holt, Rinehart and Winston, Inc.

stolen from their humanist origins, and new words become vital
for the identity of people seeking to remake themselves and society. Negroes become "black," blacks become "Panthers," the
oppressors become "pigs." Often the only words with emotional
content are those which cannot be spoken or published in the
"legitimate" world: fuck, motherfucker, shit and other "obscenities." New words are needed to express feelings: right on, cool,
outta sight, freaky. New language becomes a weapon of the
movement because it is mysterious, threatening to conventional
power: "We're gonna off the pig"; "We're gonna freak the
delegates."

Clearly, some rhetoric of the Left is wooden, inflated, irrelevant; crippling to the mind and an obstacle to communication.
If we were interested in mild improvements to the system, perhaps we would use the prevailing language of the system. But
one of the first tasks of those creating a new society is that of
creating a new and distinct identity. This identity cannot be fully
conscious at first, but as a movement grows, through years or
generations, it contains its own body of experience, its styles and
habits, and a common language becomes part of the new identity.
The old language is depleted. In order to dream, to invoke anger
or love, new language becomes necessary. Music and dance are
forms of communication partly because they are directly expressive of feelings for which there is as yet no language.

(Part of the emphasis on "obscenity" was of course through
deliberate courtroom deceit by police witnesses who acted
"ashamed" to repeat our words in the presence of the jury. But
the deceit may have reflected a reality. Many policemen are vulgar with prostitutes, black prisoners and fellow officers, but
"pure" towards their families, priests and judges. One Chicago
psychiatrist told us of several cases where police wives filed for
divorce because their husbands would not even make love with
them. They seem to regard women as either virgins or whores.
This split life reflects a fear of "permissiveness" that is very
much present when the police smash heads. They do it with the
horrible excitement of children squashing bugs.)

Filtered through the mind of the police agent, language becomes criminal. The agent is looking for evidence; in fact, he

has a vested interest in discovering evidence, and begins with the assumption of guilt. Any reference to violence or blood, by an automatic mechanism in the police mind, means offensive attacks on constituted authorities. Our `language thus becomes evidence of our criminality because it shows us to be outside the system. Perhaps our language would be acceptable if it were divorced from practice. Obscenity always has been allowed as part of free speech; it is the fact that our language is part of our action that is criminal. A jury of our peers would truly have been necessary for our language to have been judged, or even understood. Or at the very least, our middle-aged jury should have heard the expert testimony of someone who could partly bridge the communication gap.

Example: In July 1968 I gave a speech about the Vietnam war, most of which was an analysis of how the bombing halt and the peace talks were designed to undercut the antiwar movement. Towards the end I said that we in this country might have to shed our blood, just as the Vietnamese have shed theirs, if we were really serious about identifying with their suffering. I said further that the U.S. was violating its own laws in order to carry on the war and that it would be necessary for the protest movement to disregard the conventional rules of the game if it wanted to be effective. The FBI informer present at that meeting was from suburban New Jersey and was paid $10 plus expenses for attending meetings. He originally became an informer, he testified, at the request of a neighbor, an FBI agent, while they were chatting at a Little League ballfield. Through the ears of this agent, my speech was "the most inflammatory speech I've ever heard in my life." He testified (sincerely, I'm sure) that I had called for "shedding blood" and "breaking rules" in Chicago.

Example: Police agent Tobin was following Rennie Davis on August 27, the first night the Chicago demonstrators stayed all night in front of the Conrad Hilton. At that time, Rennie had an impromptu sidewalk meeting with the deputy police superintendent, during which they agreed that people would be allowed in the park after the 11 P.M. curfew. Tobin testified that Rennie made a defiant speech 15 minutes after their meeting to the effect that "the park is ours, stay in the park." Unfortunately for officer Tobin, his own grand jury testimony had Rennie saying, "we *have* the park." The slightest change of words had completely altered their substance.

Example: The government thought it highly incriminating when Norman Mailer testified that Jerry Rubin told him the presence of thousands of young longhairs in Chicago would "intimidate the Establishment." On cross-examination, Mailer retracted the word "intimidate," declaring it was impossible to recall words exactly; that Jerry probably wouldn't use a word like that, he would say something like "freak out." Mailer admitted that "intimidate" was more a word to his own liking because he had a bullying personality. "Words are nothing if not their nuance," he told the judge.

Len Weinglass stated the issue perfectly in his summation by quoting a passage from Matthew:

Think not that I am come to send peace on earth
I came not to send peace, but a sword
For I am come to set man against his father
And the daughter against her mother
And a man's foes shall be they of his own household

As Len pointed out, a Chicago-style undercover agent listening to this Biblical declaration probably would be left with the impression that Matthew had advocated the use of a sword against fathers and mothers. In fact, Christ's very existence—the idea he embodied—was sufficient to provoke the Establishment into violent over-reaction.

.   .   .

SUGGESTIONS FOR DISCUSSION AND WRITING

1. What is the communication gap bewteen generations referred to in the first paragraph? What does the author see as its

causes? Do you agree or disagree with his assessment of the situation? See if you can find evidence to support your position from any of the other selections that you have read in this book.

2. The author charges that "The language of the establishment is mutilated by hypocrisy." Support or refute this charge.

3. According to the author, a new language is needed to create a new identity and a new society. Re-examine the reasons that he gives for the creation of this new language and evaluate each of them in light of your previous reading in this volume.

4. Study the author's comments on obscenity and determine whether or not his ideas on the subject are consistent with those expressed in the essays by Bens and Rothwell in the previous section.

5. Novelist Norman Mailer is quoted by the author as saying that "Words are nothing if not their naunce." What does he mean by that statement?

13

Mark Rudd

SYMBOLS OF THE REVOLUTION

The ability to use language has always been one of the keys to success in politics. During the past few years, we have seen some groups select a style of language just as deliberately as they would choose any other tactic to wage their political battles. The shot heard round the academic world was Mark Rudd's use of "bullshit" in response to a discussion between Columbia University faculty and students during the campus disturbances of Spring 1968. In this selection, the author explains the reasoning behind a verbal strategy aimed at driving opponents "up against the ivy wall." Mark Rudd was one of the leaders of the student groups that spearheaded the strike at Columbia.

During the course of the Columbia strike a whole set of symbols and slogans inevitably emerged. It is difficult for someone who wasn't there, or more accurately, for someone who's not part of the New Left to understand these symbols and their significance. Red flags, red armbands, "Up against the wall, motherfucker," communes, all became integral parts of the strike, helped to define the strike.

Up Against the Wall, Motherfucker!

Perhaps nothing upset our enemies more than this slogan. To them it seemed to show the extent to which we had broken with their norms, how far we had sunk to brutality, hatred, and obscenity. Great! *The New York Times* put forward three interpretations of the slogan, the only one of which I remember is the

"Symbols of the Revolution" by Mark Rudd. From *Up Against The Ivy Wall*, by Jerry L. Avorn and members of the staff of the *Columbia Daily Spectator*. Copyright © 1968 by Members of the Board Associates. Reprinted by permission of Atheneum Publishers.

one which had to do with putting the administration up against the wall before a firing squad—apparently our fascistic "final solution." The truth is almost as bad; the slogan defined Grayson Kirk, David Truman, the Trustees, many of the faculty, the cops as our enemies. Liberal solutions, "restructuring," partial understandings, compromise are not allowed anymore. The essence of the matter is that we are out for social and political revolution, nothing less. This, of course, puts the administration of Columbia University in somewhat of a bind: if they accede to any of our demands they will be the first representatives of the ruling class to have fallen under a motley mop of student rebels. Secondly, they will only be whetting our insatiable appetites. Better to beat us down: 1,100 busted, hundreds to be thrown out of school.

"Up against the wall, motherfucker" defines the terms. It puts the administration and the interests they represent on one side, leftist students and the interests of humanity on the other. Those undecided in the middle are forced to choose sides. The great victory of the strike was that so many joined our side and so few supported the administration (the few hundred or so in the "Majority Coalition" were the most isolated and pathetic people on campus). The "organized" left on campus has been small—perhaps 150 were active in SDS, in that—but the number who identified with the left, with opposition to the war and to racism now, the whole structure of capitalism, grow to immense proportions.

"Up against the wall, motherfucker" has had a long odyssey. It originated in the ghetto, with the cops using it when they stop and search or bust people. Columbia strikers, to their mixed reaction, found the cops really do use it. LeRoi Jones got two years in jail for using it in a poem:

The magic words are
Up against the wall, motherfucker,
This is a stick-up.

(Of course, when quoted in *The New York Times*, the poem contained the word "mother-blank.") An SDS chapter on the lower East side, a group organizing hippies, winos, drop-outs, neighborhood people with a program of revolutionary politics and life-style, adopted the slogan as its name. We picked it up in our chapter, using it for the title of one edition of our newspaper, the edition which appeared on April 22, 1968, the day before the demonstrations began. In that paper appeared an open letter to Grayson Kirk in which I defined our goal as socialism, and Kirk and the ruling class as our enemies. The letter ended with the quote from LeRoi Jones. From there, the slogan became a natural for the strike, ranging in use from graffitti to shouts of the entire Math commune against the police.

We co-opted the word "motherfucker" from the ghetto much as we adopted the struggle of blacks and the other oppressed as our own. When young people start calling those in power, the people whose places we're being trained to fill, "Motherfucker" you know the structure of authority is breaking down. We recognize that our own quest for freedom puts us against "the man" just as black people and Vietnamese fight him. The war comes home.

The obscenity, too, helped define our struggle. Finally, we could say in public what we had been saying among ourselves. We could use our own language, much more expressive than the repressed language of Grayson Kirk. When I told a meeting of the Ad Hoc Faculty Group that the talks we were having with them were bullshit, I expressed myself thoroughly, naturally. The reaction to the style was stronger than the reaction to the content. All forms of authority, traditional "respect" (you show respect, obviously, by not using your own language), had broken down. The norms of repression and domination, maintaining the hierarchical structure of the classroom and the society, were swept aside. The revolution frightened some, broke others, freed many.

SUGGESTIONS FOR DISCUSSION AND WRITING

1. The term "motherfucker" is highly offensive to many people. What do you think some of the reasons are that they find it so offensive? Does it offend you? Why or why not?

2. Review the reasons the author gives for using the slogan "Up against the wall, motherfucker!" Then examine the discussions of the term "motherfucker" elsewhere in this volume. (See especially the essays by Rothwell and Goodheart.) In what ways do these discussions support what the author of this selection says about the term?

3. The author states that much of the language of the New Left has been taken from the ghetto. Investigate the influence of ghetto language on the language of the New Left and write a report on your findings.

4. Are the author's remarks about the New Left's use of obscenity consistent with the discussions of obscenity by Bens and Rothwell? Point out any areas of agreement or disagreement.

5. When the author used the term "bullshit" in front of a university faculty group to express his feelings about the talks between them and some students, he found that "the reaction to the style was stronger than the reaction to the content" of his expression. What does he mean? How do you define "style?" What is the relationship between style and content? Is it possible to separate them in actual usage? Do you think that in conflicts such as the one described in this essay the people who react strongly to obscenity are more concerned with style than content? Should they be? Support your answers.

14

The Editors of *Time*

VIOLENT PROTEST: A DEBASED LANGUAGE

In this essay from Time *magazine, a member of the editorial staff of that publication sees the language of protest quite differently from the authors of the two preceding selections. Concerned because some protestors have moved from verbal to violent tactics, he asserts that contempt for language is ultimately destructive of not only dialogue but rationality itself. And he argues that words, when cogently used, are still as powerful a force as ever, and urges dissenters to "assert their own dignity and maintain their tradition by upholding the ultimate value of the word."*

Words, like trees, bend with the prevailing winds. In the climate of opinion of the past few years, the word dissent has undergone a decided transformation. For most of U.S. history, it clearly meant speech—the unorthodox opinion, the challenging idea. Then, during the 1960s, civil rights protesters took to the streets to fight segregation, and the word became associated with demonstrations as much as with speech. As protests have continued to broaden and increase, dissent has come to be used to describe and defend a wide variety of physical acts, including violence toward property and even toward people.

The explanation many protesters offer for their switch from verbal to physical dissent is that no one pays attention to words alone any longer. However eloquent it has been, however imaginative its uses, language has not succeeded in eliminating racial discrimination or ending the war in Indochina. So the pro-

Reprinted by permission from *Time*, The Weekly Newsmagazine; Time Inc. 1970.

testers have resorted to what Social Psychologist Franklyn Haiman of Northwestern University calls "body rhetoric"—sit-ins, lie-ins, marches—and more and more bodies have started colliding. Such public confrontations are an expression of gathering frustration over a society that no longer seems to respond to more traditional forms of dissent.

This argument contains a measure of truth. It is also true than in many cases the massed forces of dissent—as at most of last week's rallies mourning the Kent State four—have demonstrated a commendable restraint in not letting verbal protest build into violence. The fact remains, however, that all too often these days dissent is a matter of arson and rock throwing. The reason may be that protesters have despaired of the efficacy of words before they have really mastered them. It is significant that this generation of dissenters has failed to produce a literature, or even a polemic that is likely to endure. On the contrary, it has been persistently, even proudly, nonverbal. It has emphasized a communication of feeling rather than of words. The vocabulary of protest, often weighted down with an outmoded Marxism, is relentlessly conventional and conformist. The phrases—"up against the wall," "get the pigs," "tell it like it is"—are endlessly repeated, less for their intrinsic eloquence than for their emotive and symbolic value. And that sort of thing gets tiresome; to borrow from the jargon, it "turns people off." Even the most outrageous obscenities lose their impact when they are used ad nauseam.

There is often a disconcerting inexactness about today's rhetoric of dissent. To denounce the Establishment in blanket terms makes little sense in a society composed of several establishments, each with its own ideology and set of mores—many of them surprisingly competitive. "Power to the people" is an admirable democratic slogan—except that, as used presently, what it really seems to mean is power to the leftist radicals who seek to control any revolution in America. It is verbal overkill to describe every mild demurral by whites against the most bluntly radical of black-militant demands as nothing but "racism." And the case for political dissent is weakened when almost any attempts, however peaceful, by college authorities to restore law and order on campus are automatically condemned by militant radicals as proof that the U.S. is a "fascist Amerika." Taken at face value, many protest slogans suggest that the dissenters have seriously misestimated U.S. society and its possibility for evolutionary change.

The ultimate debasement of language, of course, is violence. Except for protesters who simply want to destroy—and there are more than a few—most dissenters turn to violence in a desperate effort to communicate their profound feelings of grievance. Yet surely this is too crude a way to get their message across. A bomb, for example, lacks specificity; its meaning is as scattered as its debris. Some people may interpret such an act as a signal to pay more attention to the protester and his cause; many more are likely to read into it a need to make life a lot tougher for the protester. Violence is, essentially, a confession of ultimate inarticulateness.

Throughout history, dissent has been more effectively expressed by the word than by the weapon. The French Revolution was betrayed by the ruthless masters of the Terror who silenced all opposition with the guillotine. The enduring importance of the revolution lies, rather, in the principles enunciated on its behalf by the philosophers of the Enlightenment, who bequeathed the notion of human equality to the modern world. During its bleakest hours, the American Revolution was resuscitated not so much by brilliant military strategy as by brilliant words—those of Tom Paine in the "times that try men's souls." Even less persuasive and more recondite words can have an impact that dramatic acts do not. Wrote Lord Keynes: "Madmen in authority, who hear voices in the air, are distilling their frenzy from some academic scribbler of a few years back. I am sure that the power of vested interests is vastly exaggerated compared with the gradual encroachment of ideas."

Debasement of the language cannot be blamed on protesters alone. The news media, the advertising agencies, the Government—even President Nixon himself—have all helped flatten and attenuate the English tongue. When radicals misuse language, they are only applying the lesson they have been so well taught by their society. The lesson has been reinforced by philosophers now in fashion—Marshall McLuhan, for instance, who says that pictures are more important than words and contemplates a society of inarticulate tribal emotions based on instant sight and sound. Or Herbert Marcuse, who teaches that protesting words are as empty as air in a technological society where power is concentrated in a few hands. Such a contempt for language makes people impatient with the orderly processes of thought. No sooner is something glimpsed or considered than it is demanded. Not only is dialogue destroyed, but so is rationality, when protesters insist upon immediate capitulation to their "non-negotiable demands." This is what infants demand—and totalitarians.

Reactionary as the thought may seem, words are still as powerful a force as ever, when they are cogently used. It was, after all, language, alone that catapulted Spiro Agnew from a political nonentity to a national figure with an enthusiastic personal following. Agnew, to be sure, can be accused of appealing to the raw emotions of the body politic in his now-famous attacks on "effete snobs" and "tomentose exhibitionists." On the other hand, a protester would have a hard time telling the Vice President that mere speech is not capable of stirring people. Unwittingly, he has shown his antagonists on the left that it can still be done.

During a period of national turmoil and self-doubt, it is all the more imperative for protesters to put down their rocks and find their voices again. As a commentary on the Kent State tragedy, President Nixon's remark that "when dissent turns to violence it invites tragedy" is callously inadequate. His warning, however, carries the weight of history: in a general unleashing of violence, dissent is the first casualty. Today the nation is in considerable need of healing, as well as elevating, language; often in the past that need has been filled by protesters whose perspective on society matched their passionate commitment to its improvement. Now is the time for dissenters to assert their own dignity and maintain their tradition by upholding the ultimate value of the word.

SUGGESTIONS FOR DISCUSSION AND WRITING

1. *Examine the meaning of the word "dissent" to see whether or not it has undergone the transformation ascribed to it in this essay.*

2. *According to this essay, many protestors have switched from verbal to physical dissent because "no one pays attention to words alone any longer." Do you agree or disagree with these protestors? (You might use some of the other readings in this text to support your answer. See especially the essays by Maddocks, Carnes, Goodheart, and Corbett, and those on non-verbal communication, particularly the one by Hedgepeth.)*

3. *Obviously the author of this essay takes a different view of the language of protest from that of the authors of the previous two selections. Compare the two positions and determine which impresses you as more valid.*

4. *This essay argues that contempt for language is ultimately destructive of not only dialogue but rationality itself. Based on your other readings in this volume, do you agree or disagree? (See especially the selections by Cogley, Maddocks, Gross, and Carnes, along with the other essays in this section.)*

5. *Evaluate the charge that "There is often a disconcerting inexactness about today's rhetoric of dissent" in light of what is said about this use of language by Carnes, Hayden, and Rudd.*

15

Eugene Goodheart

THE RHETORIC OF VIOLENCE

Political protest has, as we all know, taken some new turns in recent years. Some of its directions have been mapped out in the earlier essays in this section. Here, Eugene Goodheart, who teaches English at Massachusetts Institute of Technology, explores a further development along the same lines—verbal violence, political rhetoric intended to create the effect of violence in language. In discussing his topic, the author recognizes the linguistic distortions of established authority as well as the linguistic excesses of the militants; but he argues that "The baloney of Establishment rhetoric does not justify the disease of militant rhetoric."

The operative words are "pig," "bullshit," "motherfucker." It is the language of Left militant students who find themselves "up against the wall." The "alma-mater fuckers" (Lionel Trilling's phrase) thrust the new militant rhetoric into prominence first in 1965 at Berkeley, then in 1967 at Columbia. The Columbia episode made the new rhetoric a permanent feature of the political landscape. Perhaps the most memorable moment was Mark Rudd's denunciation of a faculty meeting with the cry "bullshit." The years 1965–67 are about the time when the black militants expelled the white radicals from the fight against racism. The *machismo* and ghetto energy of their language suggest that these white radicals are expiating for their expulsion—trying to prove to their mistrustful black brothers that they too can think black. The great volume of comment about militant rhetoric ranges from indignation to amused or impassioned defense. For reasons that I hope will soon become clear, it is immensely diffi-

Reprinted with permission from *The Nation* April 6, 1970.

cult to find the right perspective and tone for writing convincingly about the phenomenon.

Unfortunately, the political and ethical issues created by radical rhetoric easily become confused with the legal question. I was recently asked by the university in which I teach to serve on a panel concerned with legal aspects of the political demonstrations that had taken place there. They had consisted for the most part of obstructive sit-ins and sloganeering. Much of the anxiety in the panel discussions concerned verbal violence, not physical violence. There was considerable evidence of threatening and abusive language, but it was clear that little of the verbal violence had spilled over into physical action. Nevertheless, the sense of outrage experienced by those who were the objects of abuse was so strong that for them verbal attack seemed the equivalent of physical violence. It became necessary to argue, as the majority of the panel (myself included) argued, that whatever one thinks of the use of words like "pig" and "motherfucker" in political protest, one should not seek redress from civil authorities. For anybody of libertarian persuasion the recourse to law in such a matter must be resisted, especially at a moment like the present, when the "law and order" argument has become immensely attractive to the general society. Moreover, implicit in the legal response to political demonstration, is the irrelevant idea of retributive justice and the feeling of self-righteousness on those administering justice—a feeling that no American can well afford.

But neither can the militants afford *their* selfrighteousness in the political debate. Indeed, the style of militant rhetoric effectively prevents debate. Or at least, the style makes it very hard to bring the issue into focus. For instance, when criticizing militant rhetoric one runs the risks of falling into a humorless solemnity. The trick perfected by the Yippies is a quick capacity for modulating from impassioned denunciation to an extravagantly farcical jeering. By hoking it up to make the whole idea of institutional authority seem absurd, the language or gesture of militancy effectively disarms its adversaries. So what if a student smokes the president's cigars or scrawls graffiti on the wall? A censorious or disapproving response only reveals the critic to be "uptight," the insinuation being that American puritanism, with its repressiveness and hypocrisy, is somehow implicated in the self-righteousness of American foreign policy.

There is truth in this perception. But the quick sliding tone of militant rhetoric is a disingenuous exercise in evading legitimate criticism or debate. If one believes, as the militants believe, that injustice is pervasive in the world and that the very life of our planet is endangered not only by military ambitions but by indifference to ecological problems, then the Dada politics of the militants is inappropriate. The problems need solutions, not publicity, whereas Dada politics is at best a comic relief from an apocalyptic situation. It is also a symptom of our catastrophic age—hysteria sublimated into farce. Norman Mailer said that the Chicago 7 were incapable of conspiracy because they were egomaniacs. It is hard to see how egomania will help us in the struggle for planetary survival.

The militants try to disarm their critics by claiming that the real violence is the institutional authority they are attacking; the real obscenity is in the killing of innocent civilians, the exploitation of ghetto blacks, the unconscionable perpetuation of poverty. Doubtless that is where the real obscenity is. But this "defense" of rhetorical violence has as much cogency as the response of the commissar to the American businessman in the Moscow Metro who wondered aloud why the trains were so infrequent: "And what about the lynchings down South?" By what logic is a lesser obscenity justified by a larger one in the camp of the enemy? Presumably by the pragmatic logic which justifies any tactic to achieve the desirable goal of ending the killing and eliminating exploitation and poverty. "Pig" and "motherfucker" are intended to provoke violence in the enemy, thus to show the world the real nature of the beast beneath the skin of civilized decorum, and thus to generate support from the inactive but sympathetic middle, which needs evidence of institutional violence in order to be "radicalized." But if "pig" and "motherfucker" are as potent as the militants imply by their devotion to this rhetoric, should they not be expected to arouse revulsion, if not violence, from the uncommitted middle? Even a violent police response to the language comes to be justified by the sentiment—well, after all even the cops are human. It remains unclear what constructive political ends are served (on radical terms) by the Manichean rhetoric.

For many militants the use of this language is not simply a matter of political expediency. There is strong sentiment in the new militancy for an honest and expressive politics. The language of politics must express itself openly, honestly, even brutally—especially in an atmosphere dominated by euphemism and outright lie. The classic defense of an uneuphemistic political rhetoric is Orwell's *Politics and the English Language* (1946):

> In our time, political speech and writing are largely the defense of the indefensible. Things like the continuance of British rule in India, the Russian purges and deportations, the dropping of the atom bombs on Japan, can indeed be defended, but only by arguments which are too brutal for most people to face, and which do not square with the professed aims of political parties. Thus political language has to consist largely of euphemism, question-begging and sheer cloudy vagueness. Defenceless villages are bombarded from the air, the inhabitants driven out into the countryside, the cattle machinegunned, the huts set on fire with incendiary bullets: this is called *pacification*. Millions of peasants are robbed of their farms and sent trudging along the roads with no more than they can carry: this is called *transfer of population or rectification of frontiers*. People are imprisoned for years without trial, or shot in the back of the neck or sent to die of scurvy in the Arctic lumber camps: this is called *elimination of unreliable elements*. Such phraseology is needed if one wants to name things without calling up mental pictures of them.

It should be noted that Orwell's corrective language is free of any suggestion of obscenity and I would suggest consequently more powerful. Simply by giving the situation its true name and by refusing to engage in melodramatic editorializing the obscenity is made transparent. The words "pigs" or "motherfucker" reveal little about cops, faculty, institutional administrations. They may reveal the emotions of the demonstrators toward their enemies, though more often than not the ritualized use of the language empties it of genuine emotion. Moreover, the language unwittingly reflects on the man who uses it rather than on the object of its use. I recall seeing a YAF student wearing a button condemning the SDS. Two swastikas replaced the esses, and from the distance it appeared as if the student were wearing a button vaunting his commitment to Nazism. There is a comparable boomerang in the militant rhetoric of insult.

One recalls the romantic sentiment and rhetoric of the civil rights movement before the split between white and black. It is customary to scorn both the sentiment and the rhetoric as naive and illusive. It is true that there were false notes in Martin Luther King's eloquence, and the abrasiveness of the new rhetoric was welcomed as a tonic. But the considerable virtue of the earlier rhetoric, for all its false notes, was that it suggested a world antithetic to the world it was attacking. The new rhetoric emulates the violence of a world it professes to despise. And the new rhetoric is unredeemed by its professed commitment to truth, because it is guilty of reverse sentimentality. It lacks the kind of conscience that Orwell proposed for honest political discourse and action.

Jason Epstein, a sophisticated defender of violent political rhetoric, sees criticism of militant rhetoric as motivated by squeamishness:

> Yet there is something squeamish in Trilling's view that the moral ideas—or fantasies as he calls them—of political dissidents in our time have merged with a violent reality. It is as if he too had come to take literally the violent political rhetoric of the moment and regarded it, as the authors of the anti-riot act, in a cruder way, had also done, as the moral equivalent of violent action, as if the moral rhetoric implicit in the occasional violent acts of political dissenters, and not the violence itself—their own and the official violence which often stimulates it—were the true object of moral or judicial scrutiny.

But this ignores the purpose of "violent political rhetoric," which is to create the *effect of violence* in language. A man who is called "pig" is supposed to feel the cruelty of the insult in his gut. No one who has actually witnessed a confrontation could possibly take Mr. Epstein's line in the matter. Indeed, when the violence of the language ceases to be experienced as violence, the language loses its effectiveness. In order to maintain credibility the militants might *logically* have to decide to throw bombs.

Apart from the matter of expediency, there is the question of the good faith of the rhetoric. The militant feeling against business as usual is part of the movement's moral strength. It is valuable for the movement to dramatize continually the moral idiocy of a society that devotes most of its energy to the making of armaments, when its very survival is in question. The coercive impulse in militancy is to force the society to untrack itself from its present disastrous course. But it is also a fact that the ideological habits of the militants constitute a sort of business as usual. The militant response can become an immoral inflexibility —an expression of unwillingness to listen to a genuine objection and to change one's mind when reality requires a change of mind.

In their critiques and actions the militants operate too often on a double standard, which makes their activity immune from the charges they level at others. Take for instance, the charge of "elitism" that is constantly leveled against all social institutions. The movement itself is elitist—its authority is the moral law, not the silent majority. The distinction that should be made is between good elitism and bad elitism, elitism based on a moral or intellectual idea rather than on mere power. On this distinction the militants are too often vulnerable, for they illicitly identify their own power drive with the moral law. Students will demand power, junior faculty will demand power, not from any reasoned argument for the morality of the demand but from an assumed identity between the power of the group and the morality of the goal. This kind of elitism is finally no different in moral quality from an elitism based on inherited privilege or on any kind of arbitrarily constituted authority.

That does not invalidate the charges which the militants level at institutional authority. Institutional authority is rarely willing to change except under strong prodding. One hardly needs to prove the frequent corruption and bad faith of institutional authority and of its civil, bland, reassuring rhetoric. The militants, it seems to me, are perfectly right in wanting the universities to be instrumental to social change—up to a point. The classic definition that the campus is a place devoted exclusively to the disinterested pursuit of thought has been effectively discredited by the presence there of technological study and of Political Science Departments that serve the interests of the Establishment. If one does technological work in the universities one should devote oneself to the rehabilitation of the cities and the elimination of poverty, rather than to military hardware and the development of counterinsurgency programs. It is the mark of intellectual vitality, indeed of disinterest, that an institution is able to redirect its energies where they will do the most good to society, even if this involves a sacrifice of the personal investment that administration and faculty have made in certain kinds of activity for ten, fifteen or twenty years. What is called academic freedom is often a mask for this personal investment. On the other hand, the view that the university must become a completely *instrumental* institution is indiscriminate and poisonous. Philosophical speculation, mathematical study, literary criticism: they constitute part of the intellectual pleasure, happiness and discipline of a humane society. Not only do they not require validation but one might suspect the health and value of a society or a political viewpoint that requires that they be validated as instruments of social change.

It has been increasingly difficult to argue for what Renata Adler calls the radical middle in the universities. The war in Vietnam goes on, the urban crisis deepens. One wants action, so the militant tries to find in language the moral equivalent of action. But the moral equivalent proves to be invective. Those in the "middle" (students and faculty) feel they must respond to the radical challenge because a truth is embedded in the behavior and language of the militants; at the same time, they cannot endure the self-righteousness, disingenuousness and obtuseness of movement people—or at least those movement people who have been stupefied by their own rhetoric. To the extent that the radical middle is present in the movement its effect is civilizing and humanizing. Unfortunately, the articulateness of those in the middle often lacks sufficient force, perhaps because their critical perspective is qualified by guilt. Not wanting to create trouble for the militants, they are often reduced to impotent silence. Polarization makes it difficult to express rational intermediate positions—and when one polarization is false and unnecessary (concerned with fabricated issues having little to do with the fundamental corruption of society) it has a noxious effect on the moral and intellectual life of the university.

I anticipate a question that may be asked by liberals as well as radical militants: why take the time even to write an article to criticize the current rhetoric, if the real obscenity in American life is the continuing war and the proposed deployment of ABM in a society that needs its major energy devoted to the elimination of pollution and poverty? The answer is that the rhetoric is part of the suicidal impulse of contemporary radicalism: it shows an ideological commitment to antagonize would-be powerful allies because they suffer from the vice of liberalism. It is misplaced purism to worry about the less than spotless credentials of a Congressman or a former Presidential adviser who is now prepared to exert himself for unilateral withdrawal from Vietnam, or who may be able to add to the votes against ABM and MIRV. Such people are not "irrelevant" to the struggle for a more decent world, though they may be irrelevant in the "revolutionary" situation that exists only in the incredible egotism of self-styled revolutionaries.

The baloney of Establishment rhetoric does not justify the disease of militant rhetoric—even if one wants to argue that the disease has been created by the system. It *has* been created by the system, but we are all victims of the system, and cannot afford the "luxury" of being involved in a symptomatic politics. Rage (real or simulated) will not prevail against this blind and greedy society. We need a politics at once radical and liberal, intelligent and passionate, and righteous without self-congratulation.

SUGGESTIONS FOR DISCUSSION AND WRITING

1. Investigate the use of the word "pig" to characterize policemen and other law enforcement officers. Where does it come from and who uses it? How is it used and why? What has been the reaction to the term by those who are called "pigs"?

2. The purpose of violent political rhetoric is, according to the author, "to create the effect of violence in language"; and, as noted here, some people who are the objects of verbal attack do regard it as equivalent to physical violence. Why do people react so strongly to such language? Discuss this matter in light of your previous reading in this volume.

3. Although the author is critical of militant rhetoric, he also points out that "There is a strong sentiment in the new militancy for an honest and expressive politics. The language of politics must express itself openly, honestly, even brutally—especially in an atmosphere dominated by euphemism and outright lie." Discuss this statement in view of your previous reading and the following essay by Corbett.

4. According to paragraph five, some who use obscenity and violence justify doing so on the grounds that American institutions are themselves guilty of obscenity and violence. How is each party using the terms? In your judgment, is there any equivalency?

5. The author concludes that "The baloney of Establishment rhetoric does not justify the disease of militant rhetoric." What are the implications of the use of the words "baloney" and "disease." Discuss their appropriateness. Do you agree with the statement? Why or why not?

16

Edward P. J. Corbett

THE RHETORIC OF THE OPEN HAND AND THE RHETORIC OF THE CLOSED FIST

As we have seen throughout this section and in some of the earlier readings as well, the nation witnessed some startling new developments in rhetorical strategy during the last half of the 1960s. Groups of militant young people intent on carrying their messages to the public at large abandoned—indeed, deliberately rejected—traditional rhetorical styles and techniques in favor of tactics rarely used before that time. In this essay originally prepared for an audience of teaching colleagues, Edward P. J. Corbett, chairman of the English Department at Ohio State University, traces the contrast between the older rhetorical modes and this new strategy. Students who wish to concentrate on the contemporary rhetorical techniques examined here may, after reading Mr. Corbett's two introductory paragraphs, skim the next seven paragraphs and then resume reading in detail.

The favorite metaphors used during the Renaissance in referring to logic and rhetoric were Zeno's analogies of the closed fist and the open hand. The closed fist symbolized the tight, spare, compressed discourse of the philosopher; the open hand symbolized the relaxed, expansive, ingratiating discourse of the orator. When, sometime after the appearance of Descartes's *Discourse on Method* in 1637, logic became more a theory of inquiry than a theory of communication, rhetoric became the rationale for both learned discourse and popular discourse, and these traditional

From *College Composition and Communication*, Dec. 1969. Copyright © 1969 by the National Council of Teachers of English. Reprinted by permission of the publisher and Edward P. J. Corbett.

metaphors came to be looked upon as describing the two varieties of communicative discourse. I see the two metaphors now as having taken on a new tenor. The open hand might be said to characterize the kind of persuasive discourse that seeks to carry its point by reasoned, sustained, conciliatory discussion of the issues. The closed fist might signify the kind of persuasive activity that seeks to carry its point by non-rationale, non-sequential, often non-verbal, frequently provocative means. The raised closed fist of the black-power militant may be emblematic of this whole new development in the strategies of persuasion in the 1960's.

The style, the tactics, the ethos of much of the activity which seeks to change attitudes and influence action have certainly changed remarkably during the troubled years of the 1960's. I should like to describe the changes I have noted, to compare these new rhetorical strategies with those that prevailed in the Renaissance when the study of rhetoric and logic reigned supreme in the schools, and to try to account for the changes that have taken place.

Book-length historical studies produced during the last thirty years or so by such scholars as T. W. Baldwin, William G. Crane, Wilbur Samuel Howell, Sister Miriam Joseph, Rosemond Tuve, and Walter J. Ong have served to acquaint teachers of the humanities with the general rationale and the specific details of the disciplines of rhetoric and logic in the English Renaissance schools. The arts of communication—rhetoric, poetics, and logic or dialectic—that were incorporated into the curriculum of the Renaissance schools of England were essentially the same disciplines that were originated by Aristotle and extended or modified by Cicero, Quintilian, and Horace and by such medieval scholars and teachers as St. Augustine, Alcuin, John of Salisbury, and Geoffrey of Vinsauf. They were rigidly codified and structured studies, taught predominantly in Latin until vernacular texts on rhetoric, logic, and poetics began appearing about the middle of the sixteenth century. Although the Renaissance humanists adopted the full panoply of persuasive strategies—the logical, the emotional, and the ethical—they certainly placed the greatest emphasis on the cognitive approach to invention. In none of the

Renaissance rhetorics do we find as much attention paid to emotional appeals as Aristotle paid in Book Two of his *Rhetoric*. It is not until the third quarter of the eighteenth century, with the appearance of George Campbell's *The Philosophy of Rhetoric*, which coincided with the growth of interest in faculty psychology, that we find increasing attention being paid to the strategies of the emotional appeal. The emphasis on the cerebral in Renaissance discourse is the natural consequence of the close union of rhetoric and dialectic in the Tudor classroom. The emotional had its chief outlet in the lyrics and dramas of the period.

The ethical appeal does not receive much explicit attention in Renaissance rhetoric, but the concern for the persuasive efficacy of the personal image of the speaker or writer is implicit in the whole educational bias of the period. One of the reasons for the popularity of Cicero and Quintilian's rhetorics with Renaissance schoolmasters, most of whom were ordained priests, was that these Roman rhetoricians placed so much emphasis on the moral formation of the aspiring pupil. They subscribed to the definition of the ideal orator as being "a *good* man skilled in speaking." The appeal of such how-to-win-friends-and-influence-people texts as Ascham's *Schoolmaster* and Castiglione's *The Courtier* was that these texts were designed to produce the man for all seasons. The Renaissance schoolmaster's efforts were directed to the education of an aristocracy, not only in the sense of education for the landed gentry but also in the Greek sense of rule by the *best* men, men characterized by those Aristotelian ideals of good sense, good will, and good moral disposition.

Another thing we must keep in mind when assessing the rationale of Renaissance rhetorical training is that Europe was just entering upon the typographical age, with all the cultural consequences which that revolution effected. It is significant, and perhaps ironic, that the two men who have written most extensively about the electronic era upon which we have now entered are two Renaissance scholars—Walter J. Ong and his former colleague Marshall McLuhan, who, as few people are aware, wrote, his doctoral dissertation on Thomas Nashe (Cambridge, 1944). Printing from movable type was barely a half century old when the Renaissance began in England, but this revolution very soon exerted a profound influence on the schooling and the mental set of the period. As Father Ong has reminded us,[1] there was a heavy oral residue in Tudor prose style throughout most of the sixteenth century, as is evidenced in the stitching-together, nonperiodic pattern of prose discourse, a pattern which was fostered by the great stress in Renaissance schools on *copia*, on commonplaces, on formulary phrases and structures. The lingering on of the oral medium is evidenced too in the scholastic disputations, in the oratorical structure recommended by the letter-writing manuals for formal epistles, and in that most oral of all the literary arts, the drama, which attained its pinnacle of glory during this period.

But the predominance of dynamic, personalizing sound soon gave way, in the academic world at least, to the frozen, silent, impersonal matrix of print. As Marshall McLuhan has been telling us, print served to detribalize man, to remove him from the group, to make him more independent, more solitary, more inner-directed. Instead of the teacher on one end of the bench and the student on the other end, we now had the student curled up in the corner with a book. Instead of the give-and-take, question-and-answer dialogue between teacher and pupil, we now had the teacher's monologue, delivered from the lectern from a hand-written or printed text and not so much *heard* by the student as he sat silently in his seat as *transcribed* by him into his notebook.

As a consequence, persuasive discourse for the next three centuries took the form mainly, not of the stop-and-go fragmentary, oral-aural dialogue that Socrates had practiced but of the sequential, structured monologue that Aristotle, Cicero, and Quintilian had given instructions about in their rhetorics. One difference of course is that whereas the classical rhetoricians were dealing with the kind of monologue that would be delivered orally before a live audience, the Renaissance rhetoricians dealt with the kind of monologue that more often than not would be delivered to an unseen audience in the visualist medium of hand-writing or print. This is not to say that persuasive discourse in

[1] "Oral Residue in Tudor Prose Style," *PMLA*, LXXX (June, 1965), 145–54.

the oral-aural medium disappeared entirely during the late Renaissance. Throughout the period, there continued to be a great deal of discourse conducted orally, in the courtrooms, the parliaments, and the classroom. But with the growing consciousness of an international community of scholars, merchants, and statesmen, the Renaissance man found that he had to manage more and more of his communication with that farflung community through the medium of the printed book or the hand-written letter.

Latin of course was the international language of communication in scholarship, commerce, and diplomacy, and that fact not only strengthened the position of Latin in the curriculum but helped to foster the growing orientation of the period to the print medium, because, as Father Ong has reminded us,[2] once Latin had ceased to be the language of the family circle, as it certainly had by the time of the Renaissance, it became a language artificially preserved and controlled by writing and by printing. And while there were some educated people during this period who could speak Latin fluently, the significant fact is that there was no one who could speak Latin who could not also write it. That proficiency was certainly not possessed by the majority of Englishmen, who could handle only the vernacular; for that majority, the vernacular was exclusively an oral medium.

And while I am speaking about language, I might make the observation that the language of traditional discourse, in classical times as well as in the Renaissance, tended to be highly formal, learned, even uncommon. It is curious that this should have been so, because rhetoric, from its beginning, was conceived of as the discipline which governed communication with a mass audience. But the whole doctrine of the schemes and tropes was founded on the notion that language would more effectively convey a message to an audience if it frequently departed from the literal meaning and the normal patterns of words. Wilbur Samuel Howell suggests a plausible reason for the development of this linguistic bias:

It is suggestive to speculate upon the cultural implications

2 "The Vernacular Matrix of the New Criticism," *The Barbarian Within* (New York, 1962), pp. 177–205.

of a rhetorical theory which equates true elegance and hence true effectiveness with a system of studied departures from the established patterns of everyday speech. Such a theory appears to be the normal concomitant of the social and political situation in which the holders of power are hereditary aristocrats who must be conciliated by the commoners if the latter are to gain privileges for themselves. In a situation like that, persuasive forms of speech would emerge as agreeable forms; and agreeable forms would be those which sound agreeable to the aristocratic holders of power. What forms could sound more agreeable to the aristocrat than those which originated in a repudiation of the speech of the lower classes? Would not such forms remind him of the superiority of his own origin and thus be a way of softening his will by the subtle inducements of flattery?[3]

Late in the seventeenth century, with the growth of parliamentary government and with the reform programs of the Royal Society, there was a revolt against this notion of a mandarin language. But even as early as the mid-sixteenth century, John Jewel, in his *Oration against Rhetoric*, delivered before the members of Corpus Christi College at Oxford, raised some serious doubts about the appropriateness and effectiveness of the ornate style of address:

> For if in speaking, we seek this (as we certainly do), that we may be understood by others with whom we deal, who can discover a better mode of speech than to speak intelligibly, simply, and clearly? What need of art? What need of childish ornaments?[4]

In a recent article on "The Rhetoric of Confrontation," Robert L. Scott and Donald K. Smith observed, "Since the time of Aristotle, academic rhetorics have been for the most part instruments of established society, presupposing the 'goods' of order, civility, reason, decorum, and civil or theocratic law."[5] We might use that quotation as a transition to the description of the

---

[3] *Logic and Rhetoric in England, 1500–1700* (Princeton, N.J., 1956), p. 117.
[4] Hoyt H. Hudson, "Jewel's Oration against Rhetoric: A Translation," *QJS*, XIV (1928), 381.
[5] *QJS*, LV (February, 1969), 7.

rhetoric of the closed fist, since it contains suggestions of how and why changes have taken place in the style and strategies of modern rhetoric. I hope, however, that this abrupt transition will not create the impression that the reasoned, highly structured, elegant manner of discourse that prevailed in the Renaissance changed suddenly into the new style of rhetoric. There were all those intermediate stages, all those contributions to the development of a "new rhetoric" made by Peter Ramus and Omer Talon, by René Descartes and the Port-Royal logicians, by Thomas Hobbes, Francis Bacon, John Locke, and David Hume, by Hugh Blair, George Campbell, and Richard Whately, by the Boylston Professors of Rhetoric at Harvard in the nineteenth century, and by Alfred Korzybski, I. A. Richards, and Kenneth Burke in the twentieth century, but time simply does not allow for a tracing out of that history here.[6]

Let us begin by acknowledging that there has been a marked revival of interest in rhetoric in the twentieth century and that there has been a conspicuous increase in rhetorical activities in this country during the 1950's and 1960's. It is Wayne Booth's judgment that "we are *quantitatively* the most rhetorical age in history—and not only in the undeniable sense that more men are living by rhetoric than ever before."[7] Let us see what some of the characteristics are of this new rhetorical activity to which I have attached the metaphor of the closed fist.

One of the more obvious characteristics of those contemporary activities that seek to change attitudes and affect action is that many of them are non-verbal. Demonstrations of all kinds—marches, boycotts, sit-in, take-overs, riots—have taken on a new currency in our time, and if they need a label, they might be called "muscular rhetoric" or "body rhetoric." They seek to convey a message, to exercise an influence, simply by massed physical presence, either static or kinetic, either organized or spon-

---

[6] See my articles, "Rhetoric and Teachers of English," *QJS*, LI (December, 1965), 375–81, and "What Is Being Revived?" *College Composition and Communication*, XVIII (October, 1967), 166–72, for a brief survey of this history.

[7] "The Revival of Rhetoric," *PMLA*, LXXX (May, 1965), quoted from *New Rhetorics*, ed. Martin Steinmann, Jr. (New York, 1967), p. 5.

taneous. The accouterments of the demonstrators are often such non-verbal symbols as flags, armbands, bizarre costumes, and occult insignia worn as pins, buttons, or neck-chains. It is remarkable too how much a part music plays in this non-verbal rhetoric, especially the music of the strummed guitar. Words, of course, do play some part in these demonstrations, but words clearly play a subsidiary role, and it is notable how fragmentary these verbal utterances are. Aside from the broadsides that issue from the mimeograph machines, written words mainly appear as slogans inscribed on posters or as graffiti painted on walls. In the oral medium, single words or phrases are chanted endlessly in unison. Of course when the ultimate confrontation comes, coherent sentences have to be resorted to, and we are back to the strategies of traditional rhetoric. But body rhetoric has set the stage for the nitty-gritty of negotiation, and in the last analysis, body rhetoric is the medium that has conveyed the main message.

The heavy reliance on non-verbal means of communication serves to confirm Marshall McLuhan's claim that the electronic media have expanded and intensified the human sensoria. Aural, visual, and tactual images have an immediacy, an intensity, a simultaneity about them that words strung out one after the other on a page can hardly achieve. Recently I visted the Electric Circus in Greenwich Village, and after an hour in that atmosphere of high-decibel music, blinking strobe lights, and throbbing floor, I understood for the first time what young people mean when they speak of a complete immersion in an experience that involves the senses of sight, hearing, touch, and even smell simultaneously. And I began to understand too why there has been a shift in educational theory recently from the cognitive approach of men like Jerome Bruner to the affective approach of men like Jean Piaget. This may be part too of what George Steiner refers to as "the retreat from the word," a retreat that he finds taking place not only in the physical and biological sciences but also in such traditionally verbal disciplines as history, economics, sociology, and logic. Unlike the writer of the Tudor, Elizabethan, and Jacobean periods who handled his language in a spirit of exuberant discovery, the writer today, Steiner maintains, "tends to use fewer and simpler words, both because mass culture has watered down the concept of literacy and because the sum of realities of which words can give a necessary and sufficient account has sharply diminished."[8] Any new rhetoric that develops will certainly have to give increasing attention to the non-verbal means of communication.

Another characteristic of the rhetoric of the closed fist is that it tends to be a group rhetoric, a gregarious rhetoric. Traditional rhetoric was designed for the solitary speaker or writer addressing a captive audience. The solitary speaker or writer held forth, as I am doing now, for an allotted time or space. Today, except for the lone martyr who immolates his draft card or himself, a good deal of rhetorical activity is conducted in groups. The mass demonstration, which we have just considered, is the best manifestation of this phenomenon. One of the vogue words today is *participatory*, and *participatory* means of course "operating as part of a group." This tendency may be a confirmation of another of McLuhan's claims, namely that far from making passive automatons of its viewers, television has retribalized men to the point of making them want to act in concert with others. And so the new passion of the young for action and for involvement, for abandoning the passive lecture-room, with its print-locked books, and mixing in the marketplace. A new sense of community and commitment flourishes today, as is evident in the popularity of the Peace Corps and the Vista and the tutoring programs. We see it too in the renascence of the dialogue, or what I call the "polylogue," forms of discourse—the interview, the panel show, the brainstorming sessions, the group dynamics, the living theater. One of the reasons why dissidents against the establishment so often resort to gregarious rhetoric is simply the realization that there is safety and strength in numbers. And in densely populated, highly complex societies, like ours, the individual is such a cipher that he thinks it presumptuous of him to demand the sustained attention of an audience, but he realizes that his anonymity acquires a powerful voice when it merges

8 "The Retreat from the Word," *Language and Silence* (New York, 1967), p. 25.

with the group. *Vox populi* can be heard in the back benches of the executive and legislative assemblies.

A third characteristic of the new rhetoric of the closed fist is that it relies more on coercive than on persuasive tactics. There was a moral dimension to the traditional persuasive process. As Yves Simon has said, "To persuade a man is to awaken in him a voluntary inclination toward a certain course of action . . . persuasion implies the operation of free choice."[9] Leland M. Griffin sees rhetorical activity become coercive rather than persuasive when it resorts to the non-rational, when it is dependent, as he puts it, on "seat of the pants" rather than on "seat of the intellect."[10] James R. Andrews refines this definition a bit when he says, "Rhetoric becomes less persuasive and more coercive to the extent that it limits the viable alternatives open to the receivers of the communication."[11] He cites as an example of coercive tactics the answer Mark Rudd gave to the many offers to negotiate made by the Columbia administration during the campus disturbances in the spring of 1968. According to the *Newsweek* account of the incident (May 6, 1968, p. 43), Mark Rudd's response was an unequivocal "bull shit." Andrew's comment is, "The choice then was between the SDS position and 'bull shit': no choice at all."

I see *choices* as the key concept of rhetoric. Accordingly, where the choices are arbitrarily pared down or eliminated, rhetoric begins to disappear. This may very well be the most ominous tendency of the new rhetoric. But I can see why the tendency has developed. Mahatma Gandhi once said, "Violence is essentially wordless, and it can begin only where thought and rational communication have broken down. Any society which is geared for violent action is by that fact systematically unreasonable." People are likely to resort to coercive, non-rational, even violent tactics to gain their ends when they feel that the normal channels of communication are ineffectual or unavailable.

[9] *Philosophy of Democratic Government* (Chicago, 1951), p. 109.

[10] "The Rhetorical Structure of the 'New Left' Movement: Part I," *QJS*, L (April, 1964), 127.

[11] "Confrontation at Columbia: A Case Study in Coercive Rhetoric," *QJS*, LV (February, 1969), 12.

It is significant that the ones who have most often resorted to these coercive tactics have been the dispossessed, the disenfranchised in our society—poor people, students, minority groups —people who do not have ready access to the established channels of communications. As *The Report of the National Advisory Commission on Civil Disorders* (New York: Bantam Books, 1968) puts it, "The frustrations of powerlessness have led some to the conviction that there is no effective alternative to violence as a means of expression and redress, as a way of 'moving the system' " (p. 205).

As I say, I can understand why some people in our society resort to gut responses, but I become apprehensive when I see people abandoning the reasonable and reasoning approach in situations where their freedom or their welfare is not at stake. I am talking about the habit, both in ordinary conversation or in formal discourse, of saying the thing that is patently untrue or grossly illogical. Mouthing untrue or invalid propositions is of course not peculiar to our age. We have all been guilty of that on occasion; I know I have. What does seem to be on the increase, however, is the deliberate disdain for, even revolt against, truth and logic among those whom we would expect to be more responsible.[12]

In a recent articles in the *AAUP Bulletin*, A. M. Tibbetts remarked,

> On most issues of importance that arise in university life, students are failing to investigate fully, clarify premises, define terms, think logically, use evidence properly, and write (or speak) precisely, truthfully, and to the point. As a consequence of these failures, many universities are moving toward the very antithesis of what they are supposed to be. They are gradually becoming places of untruth and unreason.[13]

[12] See Franklyn S. Haiman, "The Rhetoric of 1968: A Farewell to Rational Discourse," *The Ethics of Controversy: Politics and Protest* (Lawrence, Kansas, 1968), pp. 123-42. Reprinted in *Contemporary American Speeches*, ed. Wil A. Linkugel, R. R. Allen, and Richard L. Johannesen, Second Edition (Belmont, California, 1969), pp. 153–67.

[13] "To Encourage Reason on the Campus," *AAUP Bulletin*, LIV (December, 1968), 466.

Among the examples of "unreason" that Tibbets cited was one involving a very bright student in an advanced course of his, who said to him one day after a heated classroom discussion, "In not letting me, as a student, help run this university, they are taking away my civil rights." When Tibbets pressed him to define *civil rights* so that they could intelligently discuss his assertion, the student replied, "Definitions are irrelevant; I'm talking about *facts*."

Wayne Booth, Dean of the College at the University of Chicago, also notes a disturbing increase of unreason in the rhetoric of the left, right, and center. "The simple task of putting ideas together logically so that they 'track' or 'follow,'" Booth says, "doesn't seem to appeal to many of us any more." Booth cites the example of a speech that Leslie Fiedler gave at Chicago a few years ago, in which Fiedler advanced the thesis that "all the younger generation is really imitating Negro culture and that the cultural warfare between what he calls palefaces and redskins accounts for our literature today." When Booth protested to a student afterwards that Fiedler had not offered any evidence or proof to substantiate his thesis, the student replied, "But that doesn't matter, because it was so interesting."[14]

This is the kind of irrationality or non-rationality that should disturb all of us in the university community. This is not the desperate rhetoric of a disenfranchised people who have exhausted, or who do not have available, the normal channels of communication with those who can do something to alleviate their miseries. This is the aberrant rhetoric of supposedly intelligent people professionally engaged in the pursuit of truth and reason. The older rhetoricians, who devoted most of their attention in the classroom and in their texts to instruction in the strategies of the logical appeal, would be appalled at this development in contemporary rhetoric. This retreat from reason may be part of the shift to the primacy of the emotional appeal. God help us all.

The fourth characteristic, one that is closely allied to the previous mark and one that lends a particular aptness to my

[14] "'Now Don't Try to Reason with Me': Rhetoric Today, Left, Right, and Center," *The University of Chicago Magazine*, LX (November, 1967), 12.

metaphor of the closed fist, is that a good deal of contemporary rhetoric is non-conciliatory. By this I mean that whereas speakers and writers once took special pains to ingratiate themselves with their audience, today many speakers and writers seem actually to go out of their way to antagonize or alienate their audience. Aristotle regarded the ethical appeal, the image of himself that a speaker projected, as the most potent means of persuasion. Militants today seem to think that all they need to do to move an audience is "tell it like it is." It matters not that in the process the audience is shocked or angered or unsettled. Jim Corder has made this observation: "Argument often fails because speakers and writers assume that the right to speak, coupled with sincerity, inevitably endows their voices with worth." Because any position we take in an argument necessarily establishes a note of partiality, we must, Corder contends, search out those ethical arguments which can make "what is partial worth someone's time."[15]

It was Kenneth Burke who, in his *A Rhetoric of Motives*, established *identification* as the crucial strategy in the persuasive process. "Identification," Burke says, "is compensatory to division. If men were not apart from one another, there would be no need for the rhetorician to proclaim their unity." "You persuade a man," Burke goes on to say, "only insofar as you can talk his language by speech, gesture, tonality, order, image, attitude, idea, *identifying* your ways with his. . . . For the orator, following Aristotle and Cicero, will seek to display the appropriate 'signs' of character needed to earn the audience's good will."[16]

That is a lesson that many contemporary speakers or writers have not learned. Of if they have learned it, they have chosen to ignore it. A third possibility is that they are seeking to develop a new technique of ethical appeal. Maybe their thinking is that the way to move people is to speak abrasively. "The squeaking wheel gets the grease." Shouts, threats, obscenities do gain attention. Whether they elicit conviction or action from anyone

---

[15] "Ethical Argument and *Rambler No. 154*," *QJS*, LIV (December, 1968), 352.

[16] *A Grammar of Motives* and *A Rhetoric of Motives*, Meridian edition (1962), pp. 579–80.

not already committed to the speaker's point of view is another matter. There is another folk maxim to set against the one about the squeaking wheel: "You attract more flies with honey than with vinegar." The open hand has at least the chance of being grasped cordially. The closed fist just prompts another closed fist to be raised.

I have been tracing out the contrasts between an older mode of discourse which was verbal, sequential, logical, monologuist, and ingratiating and a newer style of communication which is often non-verbal, fragmentary, coercive, interlocutory, and alienating. In the course of this exposition, I suppose I have betrayed my preference. But I am really not disposed to contend that the older mode of discourse is superior on all counts for our age. Our world is changing at a faster rate than any of us realize. It is notable that the newer style of rhetoric has been adopted mainly by young people. Perhaps the generation under thirty realizes more than the rest of us just how much the world has changed, senses, if it does not realize, that we exist in a world dominated by the electronic media. I for one regard these young people as a beautiful generation—although I wish that they were not so implacably self-righteous and that along with their burning preoccupation with the present they displayed some interest in the past and some concern for the future.

Extravagant and inconsistent as his pronouncements sometimes are, Marshall McLuhan has indeed articulated the epistemological and elocutionary disposition of the present age. There are two ironies in all of this: first of all, McLuhan, the apostle of the electronic media, has propagated his message to the world largely through the medium of the printed page; secondly, we have returned to the oral-aural world in which classical rhetoric had its beginnings over 2,000 years ago. But perhaps in these two ironies we can see the opportunity for a rapprochement between the rhetoric of the open hand and the rhetoric of the closed fist.

The exponents of the older mode of discourse have been too slow to recognize the efficacy of the new techniques of communication. Who can deny that body rhetoric, for instance, has had its successes in affecting attitudes and actions in regard to such

matters as the Vietnam war, civil rights, the military-industrial
alliance, the rationale and content of the college curriculum? On
the other hand, the practitioners of the new rhetoric have been
too quick to reject the proven soundness of many of the strategies
of the older rhetoric. The younger generation may regard the
open hand as bearing too much of a resemblance to the glad
hand; they may see the civility, decorum, and orderliness of
the older mode of discourse as a facade behind which the establishment in all ages has perpetrated injustices on the have-nots.
But if there has been hypocrisy in the older rhetoric, it has been
the result of human frailty, not of an inherent weakness in that
ancient art which taught that a man was most persuasive when
he displayed himself as a man of good sense, good will, and good
moral character. In the existential mood of the times, it may seem
that reason has not governed, and cannot effectively govern, the
affairs of men. But it would be a simple task to demonstrate just
how quickly the everyday world would unravel if man, the
rational animal, were to abandon logic.

The open hand and the closed fist have the same basic skeletal
structure. If rhetoric is, as Aristotle defined it, "a discovery of
all the available means of persuasion," let us be prepared to open
and close that hand as the occasion demands. Then maybe the
hand-me-down from the dim past can lend a hand-up to us poor
mortals in this humming present.

SUGGESTIONS FOR DISCUSSION AND WRITING

1. Which do you prefer—the rhetoric of the open hand or the
   rhetoric of the closed fist, and why?
2. The author emphasizes the importance of nonverbal communication in the rhetoric of protest. Compare his ideas on this
   subject with those of the other authors in this section and
   Carnes in the previous section. He specifically mentions the

role of flags, armbands, costumes, pins, buttons, neck-chains, and music. Consider the contribution of one of these to the Movement and write a paper on that subject.

3. Examine the role of body rhetoric in the language of protest. What are its sources, its characteristic features, and its effects? (You may wish to do some reading in the section on nonverbal communication before pursuing this topic.)

4. The author says that today "Many speakers and writers seem actually to go out of their way to antagonize or alienate their audience." If you have ever observed such a situation, recount it. Give particular attention to cause and effect relationships. Do you consider this deliberate antagonism to be a useful rhetorical strategy? Why or why not?

5. Like the author of the previous selection, this one is disturbed by what he sees as the self-righteousness of young militants. What do they mean by this term and how might it be evident in the language and other communication techniques of the militants?

4

COLOR SCHEMES:

LANGUAGE AND RACE

17

John M. Haller

THE SEMANTICS OF COLOR

If, as most of the authors in this book maintain, language does indeed shape thought, then our culture is—at least in part—a product of our language, and there is a direct relationship between language and race. All the selections in this portion of the book focus on that relationship. In the first one, John M. Haller, writing in ETC. A Review of General Semantics, indicates that the colors black and white "have penetrated so deeply into our language—and our thinking—that we cannot talk without using them." And, more to the point, these colors have created in the language "a polarity charged with meaning and emotion."

The psychology of color is a special study and a profound one. From it we learn that colors have absolute values, as well as associative ones. By manipulating background colors and circumambient lighting, experimenters can produce given moods in subjects: nausea, languor, serenity, cooperativeness, irritableness, excitation. The question naturally occurs that if color can so affect behavior over the short term, may it not affect outlook and personality over the long term?

Among the arguments that may be marshaled in support of this assumption, one of the most powerful is the existence of a peculiar psychological polarity ingrained in the very heart of our language. Leaving to one side other colors whose associations are more complex and ambiguous and concentrating on white and black, we see that throughout the whole group of Indo-Germanic languages white is used in an appreciative sense and black in a pejorative sense. Since white is the color of daylight

Reprinted from *Etc.*, Vol. 26, No. 2, by permission of the International Society for General Semantics.

and black the color of night, it appears that nature herself has established the grand dichotomy between the two colors.

Those who would argue that these values are relative or acquired ones rather than absolute ones and that we have conceived our prejudices on other grounds, real or imaginary, and transferred them to the colors have the weaker side of the argument. For the truth, apparent to all, is that our spirits expand with the rising sun and wane with the setting sun. Instinctively we rejoice in the light, and instinctively we fear the darkness; these natural feelings can be reversed only by long training. If we lived under conditions of continuous illumination or continuous lack of illumination, we should doubtless have different feelings; but, the physical world being as it is, our minds are from birth predisposed to the dichotomous habit. For most of us, all things are either white or black, good or evil, right or wrong. Few ever outgrow this simple habit of thought, it being reserved for genius, as Nietzsche observed, to develop a capacity for nuance.

Since black is the color of night, it is by extension the color associated with evil, wrong-doing, fear, loathsomeness. In a sense black is negative in that it suggests emptiness or deficiency; at the same time, however, it contains the suggestion of horrible and powerful beings invisible, hence doubly fearful, lurking in the obscurity. Hell is represented as a black, gloomy pit, its darkness broken only by the fires of torment. Devils are traditionally limned in black; and, when one visits the earth on some errand, he is invariably dressed in sable. Heaven, in contrast, is a place of splendor, irradiated with light; angels are white-faced, robed in white, crowned with white halos.

Satan, awakening in his lake of fire, contemplates

The dismal situation waste and wild.
A dungeon horrible on all sides around
As one great furnace flames; yet from those flames
No light, but rather darkness visible
Served only to discover sights of woe,
Regions of sorrow, doleful shades . . .

His prison was ordained in "utter darkness," "in horrid silence."

Hell is a "Stygian darkness," a "gloom of Tartarus profound," "a dark and dreary vale," a "universe of death."

In *L'Allegro* all the evil associated with darkness is condensed in ten evocative lines.

Hence, loathed Melancholy,
Of Cerberus and blackest Midnight born,
In Stygian cave forlorn
'Mongst horrid shapes, and shrieks, and sights unholy,
Find out some uncouth cell,
Where brooding darkness spreads his jealous wings,
And the night-raven sings;
There under ebon shades and low-browed rocks,
As ragged as thy locks,
In dark Cimmerian desert ever dwell.

White is the color of purity, black the color of sin. Brides wear white, white flowers adorn the altar, white candles burn beside them. In the words of an old novel. "The bride's virginal purity contrasted with the groom's blackness of heart."

White is the color of cleanliness, black the color of dirt. Snow is white, mud black. To clean an object is to whiten it; to soil it is to stain it with black. "Immaculate" connotes whiteness cleansed of all black spots. Nurses' uniforms are white, as are cooks' hats and aprons.

White is the color of intelligence, black the color of ignorance. An intelligent man is *bright* or *brilliant*— that is, having a mind the color of white light. A stupid person is a *dimwit,* his eyes lack *luster,* his brain lacks *fire.* An informed person is *enlightened,* an ignorant person *benighted.* The intelligent individual makes *illuminating* remarks that *throw light* on the subject; he has a *lucid* mind, he *elucidates* a point and *enlightens* his auditors. The dullard is *obscure, unclear,* his meaning is *indistinct, shrouded in mists, hidden in darkness;* his thoughts are *muddied, turbid.* Southey was renowned for his *transparent style,* Hegel notorious for his density. "To see" is synonymous with "to understand"; Goethe on his death-bed cried out for *mehr Licht.*

White and black have penetrated so deeply into our language— and our thinking—that we cannot talk without using them. We *blacken* a man's reputation, *whitewash* a political mistake. A den is a *black sink of iniquity*, war is a *black crime against humanity*, Englishmen were stuffed into the *Black Hole of Calcutta*. The loss of a football game is a *black day* for the Navy; to anticipate such a loss is to *look on the black side* of things. To fail to mow one's lawn is to receive a *black mark* in the community. We are *black-balled* at the club, *blackmailed* by our onetime friends, and *blacklisted* by our enemies.

Concealed in Latin and Greek roots, black and white continue both to influence our mode of thinking and to reveal our natural prepossessions. To suffer from *melancholy* is to have *black bile*. To *denigrate* a person is to say *black* things about him. To take *umbrage* is to feel resentment at being *denigrated*. When we speak *candidly*, we speak honestly—that is, *whitely*. When we say that pageant was *splendid* or the costume *resplendent*, we mean that it shone, like white light.

This peculiar, built-in value relationship is of course exploited by racist. According to anthropologist Carleton Coon (*The Living Races of Man*), virtually all cultures in all parts of the world regard, and seem always to have regarded, white skin as desirable and black skin as undesirable. Aaron's dramatic cry, "Is black so base a hue?" received no answer in the play (*Titus Andronicus*) and receives none today. To swim against the current is always difficult, and those individuals who endeavor to point out that skin color has, or should have, nothing to do with physical, mental, and moral qualities find themselves struggling against a linguistic current as insidious as it is powerful. Defensive attempts by African Négritude cultists to reverse the color relationship remain unconvincing, however admirable ethically. Attacking white as a pale, washed-out, diluted color, deficient in all vital qualities, they sing the praises of blackness. "Black is a beautiful color," they chant, "black is the color of the earth, the color of strength." Some African tribes represent the devil as *white*; the Togo poet Dr. Raphael Armattoe visualizes God as black: "Our God is black, the black of eternal blackness, with large voluptuous lips."

Examples could be multiplied, but the point has been made. To indicate the existence in our language of a white-black polarity charged with meaning and emotion, sometimes conscious, sometimes unconscious, is the purpose of this article; to justify or to condemn this polarity is beyond its scope. If words are tyrants, "black" and "white" are rival despots, warring ceaselessly for control of our sympathies and our antipathies.

SUGGESTIONS FOR DISCUSSION AND WRITING

1. Make your own list of ideas, meanings, and associations for the words "black" and "white." Do not repeat any given in this article and pay particular attention to those that come to you most readily. How many positive connotations do you have for "black"? How many negative connotations for "white"? Do your findings bear out the author's thesis?

2. Investigate the use of color in a language other than English to see what the semantic associations and implications are for "black" and "white" or their equivalents. It might be particularly interesting to examine a language that is not the product of a predominantly white culture.

3. The author feels that the attempts of blacks to reverse the color relationships of black and white such as the use of the slogan "Black is beautiful" remain unconvincing. Do you agree or disagree? What is your own reaction to the slogan, and why do you feel as you do?

4. This essay concludes with the statement that "Examples could be multiplied, but the point has been made." Has it? Are you reasonably convinced that the author's thesis is true? Why or why not?

5. The author explicitly states his thesis in the concluding paragraph: "To indicate the existence in our language of a white-black polarity charged with meaning and emotion, sometimes conscious, sometimes unconscious, is the purpose of this article; to justify or condemn this polarity is beyond its scope." Note again the second part of that statement. Shouldn't the author justify or condemn this polarity? Is it enough to merely make it evident? Is he avoiding moral responsibility by not taking a position? Support your answer.

18

Wm. Walter Duncan

HOW "WHITE" IS
YOUR DICTIONARY?

The preceding article indicates just how far the colors black and white may have penetrated our language and our thinking, and created a polarity in the process. In this selection, William Walter Duncan examines the treatment of the terms "black" and "white" in American dictionaries and concludes that a correction and improvement in the treatment of those terms might contribute to overcoming prejudice associated with skin color. Mr. Duncan teaches Speech at Bronx Community College, New York City.

During a recent discussion on semantics in one of my classes, I asked some twenty students to tell me what they think of when the word *white* is mentioned. I got such responses as: "purity," "the color," "snow," "something clean," but not one negative connotation for the word.

I then asked about the word *black* and got: "something very dark," "dirty," "black lies," "death," but not one positive connotation. When I pointed this out to the class, one "white" student immediately exclaimed, "But there are no positive connotations for *black*."

At this point one of the "black" students—all of whom had previously remained silent—responded angrily, and understandably so, point out that in his mind there are many negative connotations for *white* and many positive ones for *black*.

After a few moments of tension among some of the students, I turned the discussion into an examination of the word *black*,

Reprinted from *Etc.*, Vol. 27, No. 1, by permission of the International Society for General Semantics.

using the unabridged edition of *The Random House Dictionary of the English Language*. All of the definitions of the word in this dictionary are either negative or neutral in nature. Not until the phrases, specifically item no. 22, *in the black*, does one find a positive connotation for the word, the sole entry in more than fifty lines of fine print that can be said to be of a positive nature. Even when *black clothing* is mentioned, one finds: "esp. as a sign of mourning: *He wore black at the funeral*."

In contrast with *black*, *white* has a preponderance of positive meanings, but none with negative connotations—not one word about *white* associated with death, as in *white as a ghost*, or with evil, as in *a white mask of deception*.

Now a dictionary is merely a report of the ways words are used. (The precedent set by Samuel Johnson for the expression of personal biases in the definition of some words has long since been rejected by lexicographers.) And the Random House dictionary, in its treatment of the words *white* and *black* is not essentially different from those in other dictionaries. For example, here is the way *Funk & Wagnalls Standard College Dictionary* (Harcourt, Brace & World, 1963) treats the word:

> black adj. 1. Having no brightness or color; Reflecting no light; opposed to *white*. 2. Destitute of light; in total darkness. 3. Gloomy; dismal; forbidding: a *black* future. 4. Having a very dark skin, as a Negro. 5. Soiled; stained. 6. Indicating disgrace or censure: a *black* mark. 7. Angry; threatening: *black* looks. 8. Evil; wicked; malignant: a *black* heart . . .

While all of the dictionaries which I have examined treat the word *black* in a similar manner, the statement that lexicographers merely report the way a word is used, a defense which one editor of a well-known dictionary recently made to me, needs to be examined carefully.

A dictionary is supposedly merely a record of what a language *was* at some point in the past. Even at the moment of publication, a dictionary is dated. No one, therefore, can reasonably expect the dictionaries now in use to have statements about the way the word *black* is currently being used by many people, as in the slogan *black is beautiful,* and only time will tell if *black* is going to become the standard term for *Negro.*

But even if the above arguments are accepted, American dictionaries have not made complete reports of the word *black.* Why, for instance, in listing the phrase *black clothing* were not references to the formal attire which men sometimes wear to look their best, or to the black robes worn by judges or by academicians? Why weren't references made to the *black opal* or *pearl* or to other contexts in which the word carries a positive connotation?

While a dictionary cannot perhaps explain why a *black lie* is a repugnant case of mendacity and a *white* one an excusable falsehood, a dictionary can suggest that a reader compare one phrase with the other. This might lead many to realize the logical inconsistency of the two phrases and possibly the evil we perpetuate when we use them.

While a dictionary cannot be expected to explain why we call some people "white" and others "black" when in reality there are no black or white people—we are all colored—a dictionary can say "a member of the so-called black race," as *Standard College* does, and "a member of the so-called white race," as *Standard College* does not.

While a correction and an improvement of the treatment of the words *black* and *white* in our dictionaries may not eliminate prejudice associated with skin color, it could be a contribution to this cause.

SUGGESTIONS FOR DISCUSSION AND WRITING

1. *Conduct your own informal survey such as the one mentioned in the opening paragraphs of this selection. Ask some friends or family members to tell you what they think of when the*

word "white" is mentioned; then do the same with the word "black." See if your results are consistent with those of the author.

2. Look up the definitions of, and synonyms for, the words "black" and "white" in a dictionary of your choice. Do your findings bear out the author's thesis?

3. The author says that only time will tell if "black" is going to become the standard term for "Negro." What are the advantages and disadvantages of each of these terms? Which do you prefer and why? Do you see any evidence that "black" is replacing "Negro"? Support your answer.

4. Compare and contrast this author's treatment of "black" and "white" with that of the author of the preceding selection.

5. William Zinsser discusses nature of dictionaries in his essay in Part 2. Examine his comments and compare them with those by the author of this article.

19

Haig A. Bosmajian

THE LANGUAGE OF WHITE RACISM

This is the last of three selections dealing with what Haig A. Bosmajian calls "the language of white racism." As that title clearly indicates, Mr. Bosmajian, like the previous author, argues that the burden of responsibility for the racial problem in the United States rests with the white majority and that one step toward overcoming it would be to rid our language of words and phrases that connote racism to blacks. But Mr. Bosmajian goes deeper into the questions which the briefer selections raise and discusses a wider range of language abuses. The author teaches Speech at the University of Washington.

The attempts to eradicate racism in the United States have been focused notably on the blacks of America, not the whites. What is striking is that while we are inundated with TV programs portraying the plight of black Americans, and with panel discussions focusing on black Americans, we very seldom hear or see any extensive public discussion, literature or programs directly related to the source of the racism, the white American. We continually see on our TV sets and in our periodicals pictures and descriptions of undernourished black children, but we seldom see pictures or get analyses of the millions of school-age white suburban children being taught racism in their white classrooms; we see pictures of unemployed blacks aimlessly walking the streets in their black communities, but seldom do we ever see the whites who have been largely responsible, directly or indirectly, for this unemployment and segregation; we continually hear panelists discussing and diagnosing the blacks in America,

From *College English*, December 1969. Copyright © 1969 by the National Council of Teachers of English. Reprinted by permission of the publisher and Haig A. Bosmajian.

but seldom do we hear panelists diagnosing the whites and their subtle and not so subtle racism.

Gunnar Myrdal, in the Introduction to his classic *An American Dilemma*, wrote that as he "proceeded in his studies into the Negro problem [an unfortunate phrase], it became increasingly evident that little, if anything, could be scientifically explained in terms of the peculiarities of the Negroes themselves." It is the white majority group, said Myrdal, "that naturally determines the Negro's 'place.' All our attempts to reach scientific explanations of why the Negroes are what they are and why they live as they do have regularly led to determinants on the white side of the race line." As the July 1966 editorial in *Ebony* put it, "for too long now, we have focused on the symptoms of the disease rather than the disease itself. It is time now for us to face the fact that Negroes are oppressed in America not by 'the pathology of the ghetto,' as some experts contend, but by the pathology of the white community." In calling for a White House Conference on Whites, the *Ebony* editorial made the important point that "we need to know more about the pathology of the white community. We need conferences in which white leaders will talk not about us [Negroes] but about themselves."

White Americans, through the mass media and individually, must begin to focus their attention not on the condition of the victimized, but on the victimizer. Whitey must begin to take the advice of various black spokesmen who suggest that white Americans start solving the racial strife in this country by eradicating white racism in white communities, instead of going into black communities or joining black organizations or working for legislation to "give" the blacks political and social rights. This suggestion has come from Floyd McKissick, Malcolm X, and Stokely Carmichael. McKissick, when asked what the role of the white man was in the black man's struggle, answered: "If there are whites who are not racists, and I believe there are a few, a *very* few, let them go to their own communities and teach; teach white people the truth about the black man." Malcolm X wrote in his autobiography: "The Negroes aren't the racists. Where the really sincere white people have to do their 'proving' of themselves is not among the black *victims*,

but out on the battle lines of where America's racism really *is*—
and that's in their own home communities; America's racism
is among their own fellow whites. That's where the sincere
whites who really mean to accomplish something have to work."
Stokely Carmichael, writing in the September 22, 1966, issue
of *The New York Times Review of Books*, said: "One of the
most disturbing things about almost all white supporters of the
movement has been that they are afraid to go into their own
communities—which is where the racism exists—and work to get
rid of it."

A step in that direction which most whites can take is to clean
up their language to rid it of words and phrases which connote
racism to the blacks. Whereas many blacks have demonstrated
an increased sensitivity to language and an awareness of the
impact of words and phrases upon both black and white
listeners, the whites of this nation have demonstrated little sensitivity to the language of racial strife. Whitey has been for
too long speaking and writing in terminology which, often being
offensive to the blacks, creates hostility and suspicions and
breaks down communication.

The increased awareness and sensitivity of the black American
to the impact of language is being reflected in various ways.
Within the past two years, there have been an increasing number
of references by Negro writers and speakers to the "Through the
Looking Glass" episode where Humpty Dumpty says: "When I
use a word it means just what I choose it to mean—neither more
nor less." "The question is," said Alice, "whether you can make
words mean so many different things." "The question is," said
Humpty Dumpty, "which is to be master—that's all." The
"Through the Looking Glass" episode was used by Lerone Bennett, Jr. in the November 1967 issue of *Ebony* to introduce his
article dealing with whether black Americans should call themselves "Negroes," "Blacks," or "Afro-Americans." In a speech
delivered January 16, 1967 to the students at Morgan State College, Stokely Carmichael prefaced a retelling of the above Lewis
Carroll tale with: "It [definition] is very, very important because I believe that people who can define are masters." Carmichael went on to say: "So I say 'black power' and someone

says 'you mean violence.' And they expect me to say, 'no, no. I don't mean violence, I don't mean that.' Later for you; I am master of my own terms. If black power means violence to you, that is your problem. . . . I know what it means in my mind. I will stand clear and you must understand that because the first need of a free people is to be able to define their own terms and have those terms recognized by their oppressors. . . . Camus says that when a slave says 'no' he begins to exist."

This concern for words and their implications in race relations was voiced also by Martin Luther King who pointed out that "even semantics have conspired to make that which is black seem ugly and degrading." Writing in his last book before his death, *Where Do We Go From Here: Chaos or Community?*, King said: "In Roget's Thesaurus there are some 120 synonyms for 'blackness' and at least 60 of them are offensive—such words as 'blot,' 'soot,' 'grime,' 'devil,' and 'foul.' There are some 134 synonyms for 'whiteness,' and all are favorable, expressed in such words as 'purity,' 'cleanliness,' 'chastity,' and 'innocence.' A white lie is better than a black lie. The most degenerate member of the family is the 'black sheep,' not the 'white sheep.'"

In March 1962, *The Negro History Bulletin* published an article by L. Eldridge Cleaver, then imprisoned in San Quentin, who devoted several pages to a discussion of the black American's acceptance of a white society's standards for beauty and to an analysis of the negative connotations of the term "black" and the positive connotations of the term "white." Cleaver tells black Americans that "what we must do is stop associating the Caucasian with these exalted connotations of the word *white* when we think or speak of him. At the same time, we must cease associating ourselves with the unsavory connotations of the word black." Cleaver makes an interesting point when he brings to our attention the term "non-white." He writes: "The very words that we use indicate that we have set a premium on the Caucasian ideal of beauty. When discussing inter-racial relations, we speak of 'white people' and 'non-white people.' Notice that that particular choice of words gives precedence to 'white people' by making them a center—a standard—to which 'non-white' bears a negative relation. Notice the different connotations when we turn around and say 'colored' and 'non-colored,' or 'black' or 'non-black.' "

Simon Podair, writing in the Fourth Quarter issue, 1956, of *Phylon* examines the connotations of such words as "blackmail," "blacklist," "blackbook," "blacksheep," and "blackball." The assertion made by Podair that it has been white civilization which has attributed to the word "black" things undesirable and evil warrants brief examination. He is correct when he asserts that "language as a potent force in our society goes beyond being merely a communicative device. Language not only expresses ideas and concepts but it may actually shape them. Often the process is completely unconscious with the individual concerned unaware of the influence of the spoken or written expressions upon his thought processes. Language can thus become an instrument of both propaganda and indoctrination for a given idea." Further, Podair is correct in saying that "so powerful is the role of language in its imprint upon the human mind that even the minority group may begin to accept the very expressions that aid in its stereotyping. Thus, even Negroes may develop speech patterns filled with expressions leading to the strengthening of stereotypes." Podair's point is illustrated by the comments made by a Negro state official in Washington upon hearing of the shooting of Robert Kennedy. The Director of the Washington State Board Against Discrimination said: "This is a black day in our country's history." Immediately after uttering this statement with the negative connotation of "black," he declared that Robert Kennedy "is a hero in the eyes of black people—a champion of the oppressed—and we all pray for his complete recovery."

Although King, Cleaver, and Podair, and others who are concerned with the negative connotations of "black" in the white society are partially correct in their analysis, they have omitted in their discussions two points which by their omission effect an incomplete analysis. First, it is not quite accurate to say, as Podair has asserted, that the concepts of black as hostile, foreboding, wicked, and gloomy "cannot be considered accidental and undoubtedly would not exist in a society wherein whites were a minority. Historically, these concepts have evolved as a result of the need of the dominant group to maintain social and economic relationships on the basis of inequality if its hegemony was to survive." This is inaccurate because the terms "blackball," "blacklist," "blackbook," and "blackmail" did not evolve as "a result of the need of the dominant group to maintain social and economic relationships on the basis of inequality if its hegemony was to survive." The origins of these terms are to be found in the sixteenth and seventeenth centuries in England where the origins of these terms were mostly based on the color of the book cover, the color of printing, or the color of the object from which the word got its meaning, as for instance the term "to blackball" coming from "the black ball" which centuries ago was a small black ball used as a vote against a person or thing. A "blackletter day" had its origin in the eighteenth century to designate an inauspicious day, as distinguished from a "red-letter day," the reference being to the old custom of marking the saint's days in the calendar with red letters.

More important, the assertion that the negative connotations of "black" and the positive connotations of "white" would not exist in a society wherein whites were a minority is not accurate. Centuries ago, before black societies ever saw white men, "black" often had negative connotations and "white" positive in those societies. T. O. Beidelman has made quite clear in his article "Swazi Royal Ritual," which appeared in the October 1966 issue of *Africa*, that black societies in southeast Africa, while attributing to black positive qualities, can at the same time attribute to black negative qualities; the same applies to the color white. Beidelman writes that for the Swazi "darkness, as the 'covered' moon, is an ambiguous quality. Black symbolizes 'impenetrability of the future,' but also the 'sins and evils of the past year. . . .' " Black beads may symbolize marriage and wealth in cattle, but at the same time they can symbolize evil, disappointment, and misfortune. "The word *mnyama* means black and dark, but also means deep, profound, unfathomable, and even confused, dizzy, angry." To the Swazi, "that which is dark is unknown and ambiguous and dangerous, but it is also profound, latent with unknown meanings and possibilities." As for "white," *mhlophe* means to the Swazi "white, pale, pure, innocent, perfect, but this may also mean destitute and empty. The whiteness of the full moon, *inyanga isidindile*, relates to fullness; but this term *dinda* can also mean to be useless, simply because it refers to that which is fully exposed and having no further unknown potentialities."

What King, Cleaver, and Podair have failed to do in their discussions of the negative connotations of "black" and the positive connotations of "white" is to point out that in black societies "black" often connotes that which is hostile, foreboding, and gloomy and "white" has symbolized purity and divinity. Furthermore, in white societies, "white" has numerous negative connotations: white livered (cowardly), white flag (surrender), white elephant (useless), white plague (tuberculosis), white wash (conceal), white feather (cowardice), *et cetera*. The ugliness and terror associated with the color white are portrayed by Melville in the chapter "The Whiteness of the Whale" in *Moby Dick*. At the beginning of the chapter, Melville says: "It was the whiteness of the whale that above all things appalled me."

What I am suggesting here is that the Negro writers, while legitimately concerned with the words and phrases which perpetuate racism in the United States have, at least in their analysis of the term "black," presented a partial analysis. This is not to say, however, that most of the analysis is not valid as far as it goes. Podair is entirely correct when he writes: 'In modern American life language has become a fulcrum of prejudice as regards Negro-white relationships. Its effect has been equally potent upon the overt bigot as well as the confused member of the public who is struggling to overcome conscious or unconscious hostility towards minority groups. In the case of the Negro, language concepts have supported misconceptions and disoriented the thinking of many on the question of race and culture." Not only has the Negro become trapped by these "language concepts," but so too have the whites who, unlike the blacks, have demonstrated very little insight into the language of white racism and whose "language concepts" have "supported misconceptions and disoriented the thinking of many on the question of race and culture."

The Negroes' increased understanding and sensitivity to language as it is related to them demands that white Americans follow suit with a similar understanding and sensitivity which they have not yet demonstrated too well. During the 1960's, at a time when black Americans have been attempting more than ever to communicate to whites, through speeches, marches, sit-ins, demonstrations, through violence and non-violence, the barriers of communication between blacks and whites seem to be almost as divisive as they have been in the past one hundred years, no thanks to the whites. One has only to watch the TV panelists, blacks and whites, discussing the black American's protest and his aspirations, to see the facial expressions of the black panelists when a white on the panel speaks of "our colored boys in Vietnam." The black panelists knowingly smile at the racist phrasing and it is not difficult to understand the skepticism and suspicion which the blacks henceforth will maintain toward the white panelist who offends with "our colored boys in Vietnam." "Our colored boys in Vietnam" is a close relation to "our colored people" and "our colored," phrases which communicate more to the black American listener than intended by the white speaker. John Howard Griffin has pointed out something that applies not only to Southern whites, but to white Americans generally: "A great many of us Southern whites have grown up using an expression that Negroes can hardly bear to hear and yet tragically enough we use it because we believe it. It's an expression that we use when we say how much we love, what we patronizingly call 'our Negroes.' " The white American who talkes of "our colored boys in Vietnam" offends the Negro triply; first, by referring to the black American men as "our" which is, as Griffin points out, patronizing; second, by using the nineteenth century term "colored"; third by referring to the black American men as "boys."

Most whites, if not all, know that "nigger" and "boy" are offensive to the Negro; in fact, such language could be classified as "fighting words." But the insensitive and offensive whites continue today to indulge in expressing their overt and covert prejudices by using these obviously derogatory terms. Running a series of articles on racism in athletics, *Sports Illustrated* quoted a Negro football player as saying: 'The word was never given bluntly; usually it took the form of a friendly, oblique talk with

one of the assistant coaches. I remember one time one of the coaches came to me and said, '[Head Coach] Jim Owens loves you boys. We know you get a lot of publicity, but don't let it go to your head.' Hell, when he said 'Jim Owens loves you boys,' I just shut him off. That did it. I knew what he was talking about."
An athletic director at one of the larger Southwestern universities, discussing how much sports have done for the Negro, declared: "In general, the nigger athlete is a little hungrier and we have been blessed with having some real outstanding ones. We think they've done a lot for us, and we think we've done a lot for them" (Sports Illustrated, July 1, 1968). One of the Negro athletes said of the coaching personnel at the same university: "They can pronounce Negro if they want to. They can pronounce it. But I think it seems like such a little thing to them. The trouble with them is they're not thinking of the Negro and how he feels. Wouldn't you suppose that if there was one word these guys that live off Negroes would get rid of, one single word in the whole vocabulary, it would be nigger?" (Sports Illustrated, July 15, 1968). When a newspaperman tried to get the attention of Elvin Hayes, star basketball player at the University of Houston, the reporter shouted, "Hey, boy!" Hayes turned to the reporter and said: "Boy's on Tarzan. Boy plays on Tarzan. I'm no boy. I'm 22 years old. I worked hard to become a man. I don't call you boy." The reporter apologized and said: "I didn't mean anything by it" (Sports Illustrated, July 1, 1968).

Whites who would never think of referring to Negroes as "boy" or "nigger" do, however, reveal themselves through less obviously racist language. A day does not go by without one hearing, from people who should know better, about "the Negro problem," a phrase which carries with it the implication that the Negro is a problem. One is reminded of the Nazis talking about "the Jewish problem." There was no Jewish problem! Yet the phrase carried the implication that the Jews were a problem in Germany and hence being a problem invited a solution and the solution Hitler proposed and carried out was the "final solution." Even the most competent writers fall into the "Negro problem" trap; James Reston of the New York Times wrote on April 7, 1968: "When Gunnar Myrdal, the Swedish social philosopher who has followed the Negro problem in America for forty years, came back recently, he felt that a great deal had changed for the better, but concluded that we have greatly underestimated the scope of the Negro problem." Myrdal himself titled his 1944 classic work *The American Dilemma: The Negro Problem and Modern Democracy*. A book published in 1967, *The Negro in 20th Century America*, by John Hope Franklin and Isidore Starr, starts off in the Table of Contents with "Book One: *The Negro Problem*"; the foreword begins, "The Negro problem was selected because it is one of the great case studies in man's never-ending fight for equal rights." One of the selections in the book, a debate in which James Baldwin participates, has Baldwin's debate opponent saying that "the Negro problem is a very complicated one." There are several indications that from here on out the black American is no longer going to accept the phrase "the Negro problem." As Lerone Bennett Jr. said in the August 1965 issue of *Ebony*, "there is no Negro problem in America. The problem of race in America, insofar as that problem is related to packets of melanin in men's skins, is a white problem." In 1966, the editors of *Ebony* published a book of essays dealing with American black-white relations entitled *The WHITE Problem in America*. It is difficult to imagine Negroes sitting around during the next decade talking about "the Negro problem," just as it is difficult to imagine Jews in 1939 referring to themselves as "the Jewish problem."

The racial brainwashing of whites in the United States leads them to utter such statements as "You don't sound like a Negro" or "Well, he didn't sound like a Negro to me." John Howard Griffin, who changed the color of his skin from white to black to find out what it meant to be black in America, was ashamed to admit that he thought he could not pass for a Negro because he "didn't know how to speak Negro." "There is an illusion in this land," said Griffin, "that unless you sound as though you are reading Uncle Remus you couldn't possibly have an authentic Negro dialect. But I don't know what we've been using for ears because you don't have to be in the Negro community five minutes before the truth strikes and the truth is that there are just as many speech patterns in the Negro community as there are in any other, particularly in areas of rigid segregation where your right shoulder may be touching the shoulder of a Negro PhD and your left shoulder the shoulder of the disadvantaged." A black American, when told that he does not "sound like a Negro," legitimately can ask his white conversationalist, "What does a Negro sound like?" This will probably place the white in a dilemma for he will either have to admit that sounding like a Negro means sounding like Prissy in *Gone With the Wind* ("Who dat say who dat when you say dat?") or that perhaps there is no such thing as "sounding like a Negro." Goodman Ace, writing in the July 27, 1968, issue of the *Saturday Review* points out that years ago radio program planners attempted to write Negroes into the radio scripts, portraying the Negro as something else besides janitors, household maids, and train porters. Someone suggested that in the comedy radio show *Henry Aldrich* Henry might have among his friends a young Negro boy, without belaboring the point that the boy was Negro. As Mr. Ace observes, "just how it would be indicated on radio that the boy is black was not mentioned. Unless he was to be named Rufus or Rastus." Unless, it might be added, he was to be made to "sound like a Negro."

Psychiatrist Frantz Fanon, who begins his *Black Skin, White Masks* with a chapter titled "The Negro and Language," explains the manner of many whites when talking to Negroes and the effects of this manner. Although he is writing about white Europeans, what Fanon says applies equally to white Americans. He points out that most whites "talk down" to the Negro, and this "talking down" is, in effect, telling the Negro, "You'd better keep your place." Fanon writes: "A white man addressing a Negro behaves exactly like an adult with a child and starts smirking, whispering, patronizing, cozening." The effect of the whites' manner of speaking to the Negro "makes him angry, because he himself is a pidgin-nigger-talker." "But I will be told," says Fanon, "there is no wish, no intention to anger him. I grant this; but it is just this absence of wish, this lack of interest, this indifference, this automatic manner of classifying him, imprisoning him, primitivizing him, decivilizing him, that makes him angry." If a doctor greets his Negro patient with "You not feel good, no?" or "G'morning pal. Where's it hurt? Huh? Lemme see—belly ache? Heart pain?" the doctor feels perfectly justified in speaking that way, writes Fanon, when in return the patient answers in the same fashion; the doctor can then say to himself, "You see? I wasn't kidding you. That's just the way they are." To make the Negro talk pidgin, as Fanon observes, "is to fasten him to the effigy of him, to snare him, to imprison him, the eternal victim of an essence, of an *appearance* for which he is not responsible. And naturally, just as a Jew who spends money without thinking about it is suspect, a black man who quotes Montesquieu had better be watched." The whites, in effect, encourage the stereotype of the Negro; they perpetuate the stereotype through the manner in which they speak about and speak to Negroes. And if Fanon is correct, the whites by "talking down" to the Negro are telling that black American citizen to "remember where you come from!"

Another facet of the racism of the whites' language is reflected in their habit of referring to talented and great writers, athletes, entertainers, and clergymen as "a great Negro singer" or "a great black poet" or "a great Negro ball player." What need is there for whites to designate the color or race of the person who has excelled? Paul Robeson and Marion Anderson are great and talented singers. James Baldwin and Leroi Jones are talented writers. Why must the whites qualify the greatness of these individuals with "black" or "colored" or "Negro"? Fanson briefly refers to this predilection of whites to speak with this qualification:

. . . Charles-André Julien introducing Aimé Césaire as "a Negro poet with a university degree," or again, quite simply, the expression, "a great black poet."

These ready-made phrases, which seem in a common-sense way to fill a need—for Aimé Césaire is really black and a poet—have a hidden subtlety, a permanent rub. I know nothing of Jean Paulhan except that he writes very interesting books; I have no idea how old Roger Caillois is, since the only evidence I have of his existence are the books of his that streak across my horizon. And let no one accuse me of affective allergies; what I am trying to say is that there is no reason why André Breton should say of Césaire, "Here is a black man who handles the French language as no white man today can."

The tendency to designate and identify a person as a Negro when the designation is not necessary carries over into newspaper and magazine reporting of crimes. There was no need for *Time* magazine (July 19, 1968) to designate the race of the individual concerned in the following *Time* report: "In New York City, slum dwellers were sent skidding for cover when Bobby Rogers, 31, Negro superintendent of a grubby South Bronx tenement, sprayed the street with bullets from a sawed-off .30 cal. semi-automatic carbine, killing three men and wounding a fourth." *Time*, for whatever reason, designated the race of the person involved in this instance, but the reports on other criminal offences cited by *Time*, on the same page, did not indicate the race of the "suspects." As a label of primary potency, "Negro" stands out over "superintendent." The assumption that whites can understand and sympathize with the Negro's dismay when black "suspects" are identified by race and white "suspects" are not, is apparently an unwarranted assumption, or it may be possible that the whites *do* understand the dismay and precisely for that reason continue to designate the race of the black criminal suspect. To argue that if the race is not designated in the news story then the reader can assume that the suspected criminal is white, is not acceptable for it makes all the difference if the suspect is identified as "a Negro superintendent," "a white superintendent," or "a superintendent." If we were told, day in and day out, that "a *white* bank clerk embezzled" or "a *white* service station operator stole" or "a *white* unemployment laborer attacked," it would make a difference in the same sense that it makes a difference to identify the criminal suspect as "Negro" or "black."

If many Negroes find it hard to understand why whites have to designate a great writer or a great artist or a common criminal as "colored" or "Negro," so too do many Negroes find it difficult to understand why whites must designate a Negro woman as a

"Negress." Offensive as "Negress" is to most blacks, many whites still insist on using the term. In a July 28, 1968 *New York Times Magazine* article, the writer, discussing the 1968 campaigning of Rockefeller and Nixon, wrote: "A fat Negress on the street says, passionately, 'Rocky! Rocky!'" As Gordon Allport has written in *The Nature of Prejudice*, "members of minority groups are often understandably sensitive to names given them. Not only do they object to deliberately insulting epithets, but sometimes see evil intent where none exists." Allport gives two examples to make his point: one example is the spelling of the word "Negro" with a small "n" and the other example is the word "Negress." "Sex differentiations are objectionable." writes Allport, "since they seem doubly to emphasize ethnic differences: why speak of Jewess and not of Protestantess, or of Negress, and not of whiteness?" Just as "Jewess" is offensive to the Jews, so too is "Negress" offensive to the Negroes. "A Negro woman" does not carry the same connotations as "Negress," the latter conveying an emotional emphasis on both the color and sex of the individual. *Webster's New World Dictionary of American Language* says of "Negress": "A Negro woman or girl: often a patronizing or contemptuous term."

When the newspaper reporter tried to get the attention of twenty two year old basketball star Elvin Hayes by shouting, "Hey boy!" and Hayes vigorously objected to being called "boy," the reporter apologized and said: "I didn't mean anything by it." In a few cases, a very few cases, white Americans indeed "didn't mean anything by it." That excuse, however, will no longer do. The whites must make a serious conscious effort to discard the racist clichès of the past, the overt and covert language of racism. "Free, white, and 21" or "That's white of you" are phrases whites can no longer indulge in. Asking white Americans to change their language, to give up some of their clichès, is disturbing enough since the request implies a deficiency in the past use of that language; asking that they discard the language of racism is also disturbing because the people being asked to make the change, in effect, are being told that they have been the perpetrators and perpetuators of racism. Finally, and most important, calling the Negro "nigger" or "boy," or "speaking down" to the Negro, gives Whitey a linguistic power over the victimized black American, a power most whites are unwilling or afraid to give up. A person's language is an extension of himself and to attack his use of language is to attack him. With the language of racism, this is exactly the point for the language of white racism and the racism of the whites are almost one and the same. Difficult and painful as it may be for whites to discard their racist terms, phrases, and clichès, it must be done before blacks and whites can discuss seriously the eradication of white racism.

SUGGESTIONS FOR DISCUSSION AND WRITING

1. Simon Podair is quoted in this essay as saying that "so powerful is the role of language in its imprint upon the human mind that even the minority group may begin to accept the very impressions that aid in its stereotyping. Thus, even Negroes may develop speech patterns filled with expressions leading to the strengthening of stereotypes." What kinds of speech patterns is he referring to? What stereotypes? Are you aware of minority group members using language in this way? If so, give examples.

2. Have you ever been involved in or observed situations in which whites "talked down" to blacks? If so, recount one situation.

3. Do you think that blacks who are disturbed by being referred to as "colored" and "boys" are overly sensitive? Do you think the people using such language are conscious of its implications? Support your answers.

4. Like the two preceding selections, this one is concerned with the connotations and associations of the terms "black" and "white"; but there are some very important differences in this author's discussion of the subject. Point out those differences.

5. Do you agree with the author's conclusion that most whites are unwilling or afraid to give up their linguistic power over blacks? Support your answer.

20

Olivia Mellan

BLACK ENGLISH

Many Americans assume there is only one form of "good English"—that spoken by the educated white majority; and all other forms are considered to be substandard. Accordingly, school children whose speech patterns differ from the standard forms—including large numbers of young blacks—are taught to discard their familiar patterns and adopt those of standard English as a means of gaining social acceptance within the larger community. In recent years, however, many linguists have argued that attitudes and practices such as these are as racist in their ultimate effect as those mentioned in the preceding essays in this section. Here, Olivia Mellan, writing as a graduate student in French at Georgetown University, outlines the differing points of view in the debate over teaching "Black English."

Our melting pot myth is being shattered as black separatism grows in favor and fact. Many blacks do still emulate the values of white society, but many don't, and they resent attempts to assimilate them into a "majority culture." While "black culture" cannot be neatly defined and isolated (nor can "white" or "American" culture), both blacks and whites are becoming increasingly aware of marked differences in styles of dress, behavior patterns, values and attitudes, and these are mirrored in speech as well as "culture." This new awareness is reflected in the charge of "cultural fascism" that is being levied at traditional English classes, where "Standard English" is taught to blacks and their nonstandard "Black English" is frowned upon.

Those who object to our long-standing efforts to eradicate Black English, claim that it harms the black child, brands the

Reprinted by permission of *The New Republic*, © 1970, Harrison-Blaine of New Jersey, Inc.

speech he has used since childhood as defective and by inference slurs the black culture that speech expresses. The child often accepts these judgments, disparaging his own language and culture in the same way whites do. Or, the child turns his back on school, English class in particular, and all that goes with a white-oriented teaching system.

Aside from its psychological effects, "eradicationism" is under attack for another reason: it doesn't seem to be working. At least that's the conclusion of many educators who have been trying to teach black children to read and to speak "white English," and of many linguists. One such is Joan C. Baratz, co-director of the Washington-based Education Study Center, who writes of "the nationwide failure of so many black children to learn to read." The remedy Dr. Baratz and co-director William Stewart prescribe is to teach the black child to read nonstandard Negro English first, "starting where the child is" instead of where he should be. They are convinced that if we ignore the specific language the black child speaks, we block the successful teaching of Standard English, either written or spoken.

Wayne O'Neil, MIT linguistics professor and education lecturer at Harvard, has a similar objection to standard pedagogy. "Traditionally, schools have understood that part of their task is to get students to speak and write properly, where 'properly' is defined by whatever it is that characterizes the language of the middle class," he writes. "They have not been successful in this endeavor. A few individuals assimilate proper speech ways, but most go on speaking, a bit nervously after their school experience, the way they would have had schools never been invented, just as they go on avoiding the plays and books and art that schools concern themselves with—a bit nervous about that, too."

Linguists who have studied the vocabulary and syntax of Black English find it to be a "separate but equally" valid language system, with a highly developed structure of its own. Among the list of syntactic (grammatical), phonological (pronunciation) and lexical (vocabulary) features which distinguish Black English from Standard, there are syntactic features which resemble creole, or African languages. One such is the distinction between "he working" meaning he is working right now) and "he be working," (meaning he is working continuously). This distinction is not present either in white nonstandard dialects or in Standard English. To skeptics who question whether Black English is a separate "language" or merely a substandard "dialect of English," linguists explain that "language" and "dialect" are two points on a continuum, moving from "dialects" (two speech systems which are relatively close in syntax, vocabulary and historical development) to "languages" (where the differences begin to outweigh the similarities). For most linguists, it is irrelevant whether Black English is "language" or "dialect." It functions as a communication system.

The eradicationist school has many defenders, however, with Kenneth B. Clark, the black psychologist and educator, one of the strongest among them. Clark maintains that Standard English is the only language that should be taught in school, and that no attempt should be made to preserve native dialects, except perhaps as "exotic primitives." He accuses those who would preserve Black English of consigning blacks to perpetual inferiority by implying that they cannot be absorbed into the mainstream of American society. And some black parents agree with him. That is what they mean when they say, "Teach my child good English. Don't tell me he can't learn it just like whites do."

Those who see eradicationism as psychologically harmful and educationally inefficient are persuaded there are better alternatives. One of these comes from the Center for Applied Linguistics in Washington, and it's called "bidialectalism" or "biloquialism." It begins by assuming that the black child *should* be taught Standard English, since that is what he needs to function in present-day America. But the biloquialists insist that the child's Black English should be respected, and that it can and should be preserved for appropriate surroundings such as home and playground.

The critics of biloquialism say that it is a disguised racist view, no better than overt eradicationism, and that it would still perpetuate social inequalities, forcing blacks to become "abnormal whites" in order to get ahead. Thomas Kochman, a linguist at Northeastern Illinois State College, attacks the whole concept of social mobility, terming it an improper motivation rather than a sacred value. Even blacks who do learn Standard English, he contends, will not find, that their "improved" speech patterns make it any easier for them to win jobs, better salaries or social acceptance.

Biloquialism has also come under attack from black militants and black parents, and for two contradictory reasons. Some are against it because they believe it less effective than the tried-and-true eradicationist approach in getting a child to speak "good English" all the time. Others attack it because they resent *any* attempt, however modified, to force the language of white society upon blacks. Ironically, critics at both poles have called the biloquial approach racist.

Nevertheless, the professionals who advocate biloquialism are optimistic about its future, because it would work and because most blacks would want it to work. Teaching materials to make it a classroom reality are being developed. One recently completed set of materials and tapes, entitled "English Now," by Irwin Feigenbaum, has just been put out by New Century in New York. Contrasts between Black English and Standard are offered to help the black child master certain Standard English features which "interfere" linguistically with his native dialect. Drills juxtaposing "he work hard" and "he works hard," for instance, are used to reinforce Standard English patterns. The materials are being tested in a North Carolina school system, and will be used in Pontiac, Mich.

In a different vein, a sizable group of white teachers in urban schools has for the past two years been learning black language and exploring black culture in a course called "American Negro Dialect," at Columbia Teachers College. According to William Stewart, the professor since the course's inception, demand for this kind of training is steadily rising.

But biloquialism is not the only alternative to eradicationism. There are linguists who want to bridge the linguistic gap by focusing on the white rather than the black child. Instead of "enriching the lives of urban [black] children by plugging them into a 'second dialect' [Standard English]," Wayne O'Neil asks, "why don't we . . . enrich the suburban kid with an urban dialect?" Ideally, this might "eradicate the language prejudice," the language mythology that people grew into holding and believing."

O'Neil's theory remains untested and is supported by relatively few linguists and sociologists. However, the experts do agree that biloquialism and the O'Neil suggestion could complement one another. Roger Shuy, Sociolinguistics Director of the Center for Applied Linguistics and a special consultant to HEW, thinks that a combined program might not only help blacks learn Standard English, but "might be the best method to successfully reorient attitudes toward language so that eradication of nonstandard dialects will no longer be necessary."

One place to start is in experimental English classes in progressive elementary or secondary schools. Through drills in the two dialects, supplemented by discussions of language contrasts, students would add to their knowledge of both language and cultural differences. A course of this kind is bound to be more interesting, in the beginning at least, than are most English classes today—less apt to turn blacks *and* whites off than "Standard English" pedagogy. Of course there would be problems. White parents would have to be convinced that their children should study Black English and culture. Critics like Kenneth Clark probably would dismiss it as a wasteful expenditure of time and money in pursuit of a dubious goal. But in a time of racial polarization, a dual approach to language would offer one advantage: an opportunity for continuing dialogue between blacks and whites who still want to talk to each other with mutual respect.

SUGGESTIONS FOR DISCUSSION AND WRITING

1. *Just what is "good English" any way? What is "correct English"? Is "Standard English" any better than "Black English"? Is it more "correct?" Support your answers. What is meant by*

the terms "nonstandard" and "substandard"? What are the social implications of these terms?

2. Investigate Black English to determine what some of its dominant characteristics are and how it differs from Standard English.

3. Do you feel that black children should be taught to use Standard English or that they should be taught to use Black English?

4. Define "bidialectism" and "biloquialism." Re-examine the arguments for and against this approach to language learning. What position do you think you would favor on this issue and why?

5. According to this article, some linguists want to bridge the linguistic gap between the black and white cultures by focusing on the white rather than the black child—for example, by educating whites to appreciate urban and black dialects. Do you believe that this might be a sound approach to overcoming language prejudice? Support your answer.

21

Claude Brown

THE LANGUAGE OF SOUL

Subcultures frequently inherit or develop distinctive linguistic features which distinguish their use of language from that of the larger community. So it is with those black people in the United States who find their most natural and expressive words and forms in what Claude Brown identifies here as "the language of soul." In this essay, Mr. Brown, a writer best noted for his autobiographical novel Manchild in The Promised Land, *discusses the language of soul—its roots, its characteristic features, and its future.*

Perhaps the most soulful word in the world is "nigger." Despite its very definite fundamental meaning (the Negro man), and disregarding the deprecatory connotation of the term, "nigger" has a multiplicity of nuances when used by soul people. Dictionaries define the term as being synonymous with Negro, and they generally point out that it is regarded as a vulgar expression. Nevertheless, to those of chitlins-and-neck-bones background the word nigger is neither a synonym for Negro nor an obscene expression.

"Nigger" has virtually as many shades of meaning in Colored English as the demonstrative pronoun "that," prior to application to a noun. To some Americans of African ancestry (I avoid using the term Negro whenever feasible, for fear of offending the Brothers X, a pressure group to be reckoned with), nigger seems preferable to Negro and has a unique kind of sentiment attached to it. This is exemplified in the frequent—and perhaps even excessive—usage of the term to denote either fondness or hostility.

It is probable that numerous transitional niggers and even

established ex-soul brothers can—with pangs of nostalgia—reflect upon a day in the lollipop epoch of lives when an adorable lady named Mama bemoaned her spouse's fastidiousness with the strictly secular utterance: "Lord, how can one nigger be so hard to please?" Others are likely to recall a time when that drastically lovable colored woman, who was forever wiping our noses and darning our clothing, bellowed in a moment of exasperation: "Nigger, you gonna be the death o' me." And some of the brethren who have had the precarious fortune to be raised up, wised up, thrown up or simply left alone to get up as best they could, on one of the nation's South Streets or Lenox Avenues, might remember having affectionately referred to a best friend as "My nigger."

The vast majority of "back-door Americans" are apt to agree with Webster—a nigger is simply a Negro or black man. But the really profound contemporary thinkers of this distinguished ethnic group—Dick Gregory, Redd Foxx, Moms Mabley, Slappy White, etc.—are likely to differ with Mr. Webster and define nigger as "something else"—a soulful "something else." The major difference between the nigger and the Negro, who have many traits in common, is that the nigger is the more soulful.

Certain foods, customs and artistic expressions are associated almost solely with the nigger: collard greens, neck bones, hog maws, black-eyed peas, pigs' feet, etc. A nigger has no desire to conceal or disavow any of these favorite dishes or restrain other behavioral practices such as bobbing his head, patting his feet to funky jazz, and shouting and jumping in church. This is not to be construed that all niggers eat chitlins and shout in church, nor that only niggers eat the aforementioned dishes and exhibit this type of behavior. It is to say, however, that the soulful usage of the term nigger implies all of the foregoing and considerably more.

The Language of Soul—or, as it might also be called, Spoken Soul or Colored English—is simply an honest vocal portrayal of black America. The roots of it are more than three hundred years old.

Before the Civil War there were numerous restrictions placed on the speech of slaves. The newly arrived Africans had the problem of learning to speak a new language, but also there were inhibitions placed on the topics of the slaves' conversation by slave masters and overseers. The slaves made up songs to inform one another of, say, the underground railroads' activity. When they sang *Steal Away* they were planning to steal away to the North, not to heaven. Slaves who dared to speak of rebellion or even freedom usually were severely punished. Consequently, Negro slaves were compelled to create a semi-clandestine vernacular in the way that the criminal underworld has historically created words to confound law-enforcement agents. It is said that numerous Negro spirituals were inspired by the hardships of slavery, and that what later became songs were initially moanings and coded cotton-field lyrics. To hear these songs sung today by a talented soul brother or sister or by a group is to be reminded of an historical spiritual bond that cannot be satisfactorily described by the mere spoken word.

The American Negro, for virtually all of his history, has constituted a vastly disproportionate number of the country's illiterates. Illiteracy has a way of showing itself in all attempts at vocal expression by the uneducated. With the aid of colloquialisms, malapropisms, battered and fractured grammar, and a considerable amount of creativity, Colored English, the sound of soul, evolved.

The progress has been cyclical. Often terms that have been discarded from the soul people's vocabulary for one reason or another are reaccepted years later, but usually with completely different meaning. In the Thirties and Forties "stuff" was used to mean vagina. In the middle Fifties it was revived and used to refer to heroin. Why certain expressions are thus reactivated is practically an indeterminable question. But it is not difficut to see why certain terms are dropped from the soul language. Whenever a soul term becomes popular with whites it is common practice for the soul folks to relinquish it. The reasoning is that "if white people can use it, it isn't hip enough for me." To many soul brothers there is just no such creature as a genuinely hip white person. And there is nothing more detrimental to anything hip than to have it fall into the square hands of the hopelessly unhip.

White Americans wracked the expression "something else." It

was bad enough that they couldn't say "sump'n else," but they weren't even able to get out "somethin' else." They had to go around saying *something else* with perfect or nearly perfect enunciation. The white folks invariably fail to perceive the soul sound in soulful terms. They get hung up in diction and grammar, and when they vocalize the expression it's no longer a soulful thing. In fact, it can be asserted that spoken soul is more of a sound than a language. It generally possesses a pronounced lyrical quality which is frequently incompatible to any music other than that ceaseless and relentlessly driving rhythm that flows from poignantly spent lives. Spoken soul has a way of coming out metered without the intention of the speaker to invoke it. There are specific phonetic traits. To the soulless ear the vast majority of these sounds are dismissed as incorrect usage of the English language and, not infrequently, as speech impediments. To those so blessed as to have had bestowed upon them at birth the lifetime gift of soul, these are the most communicative and meaningful sounds ever to fall upon human ears: the familiar "mah" instead of "my," "gonna" for "going to," "yo" for "your." "Ain't" is pronounced "ain'"; "bread" and "bed," "bray-ud" and "bay-ud"; "baby" is never "bay-bee" but "bay-buh"; Sammy Davis Jr. is not "Sammee" but a kind of "Sam-eh"; the same goes for "Eddeh" Jefferson. No matter how many "man's" you put into your talk, it isn't soulful unless the word has the proper plaintive, nasal "maee-yun."

Spoken soul is distinguished from slang primarily by the fact that the former lends itself easily to conventional English, and the latter is diametrically opposed to adaptations within the realm of conventional English. Police (pronounced pō' lice) is a soul term, whereas "The Man" is merely slang for the same thing. Negroes seldom adopt slang terms from the white world and when they do the terms are usually given a different meaning. Such was the case with the term "bag." White racketeers used it in the Thirties to refer to the graft that was paid to the police. For the past five years soul people have used it when referring to a person's vocation, hobby, fancy, etc. And once the appropriate term is given the treatment (soul vocalization) it becomes soulful.

However, borrowings from spoken soul by white men's slang —particularly teen-age slang—are plentiful. Perhaps because soul is probably the most graphic language of modern times, everybody who is excluded from Soulville wants to usurp it, ignoring the formidable fettering to the soul folks that has brought the language about. Consider "uptight," "strung-out," "cop," "boss," "kill 'em," all now widely used outside Soulville. Soul people never question the origin of a slang term; they either dig it and make it a part of their vocabulary or don't and forget it. The expression "uptight," which meant being in financial straits, appeared on the soul scene in the general vicinity of 1953. Junkies were very fond of the word and used it literally to describe what was a perpetual condition with them. The word was pictorial and pointed; therefore it caught on quickly in Soulville across the country. In the early Sixties when "uptight" was on the move, a younger generation of soul people in the black urban communities along the Eastern Seaboard regenerated it with a new meaning; "everything is cool, under control, going my way." At present the term has the former meaning for the older generation and the latter construction for those under thirty years of age.

It is difficult to ascertain if the term "strung-out" was coined by junkies or just applied to them and accepted without protest. Like the term "uptight" in its initial interpretation, "strung-out" aptly described the constant plight of the junkie. "Strung-out" had a connotation of hopeless finality about it. "Uptight" implied a temporary situation and lacked the overwhelming despair of "strung-out."

The term "cop," (meaning "to get"), is an abbreviation of the word "copulation." "Cop," as originally used by soulful teenagers in the early Fifties, was deciphered to mean sexual coition, nothing more. By 1955 "cop" was being uttered throughout national Soulville as a synonym for the verb "to get," especially in reference to illegal purchases, drugs, pot, hot goods, pistols, etc. ("Man, where can I cop now?") But by 1955 the meaning was all-encompassing. Anything that could be obtained could be "copped."

The word "boss," denoting something extraordinarily good or great, was a redefined term that had been popular in Soulville during the Forties and Fifties as a complimentary remark from one soul brother to another. Later it was replaced by several terms such as "groovy," "tough," "beautiful" and, most recently, "out of sight." This last expression is an outgrowth of the former term "way out," the meaning of which was equivocal. "Way out" had an ad hoc hickish ring to it which made it intolerably unsoulful and consequently it was soon replaced by "out of sight," which is also likely to experience a relatively brief period of popular usage. "Out of sight" is better than "way out," but it has some of the same negative, childish taint of its predecessor.

The expression, "kill 'em," has neither a violent nor a malicious interpretation. It means "good luck," "give 'em hell," or "I'm pulling for you," and originated in Harlem from six to nine years ago.

There are certain classic soul terms which, no matter how often borrowed, remain in the canon and are reactivated every so often, just as standard jazz tunes are continuously experiencing renaissances. Among the classical expressions are: "solid," "cool," "jive" (generally as a noun), "stuff," "thing," "swing" (or "swinging"), "pimp," "dirt," "freak," "heat," "larceny," "busted," "okee doke," "piece," "sheet" (a jail record), "squat," "square," "stash," "lay," "sting," "mire," "gone," "smooth," "joint," "blow," "play," "shot," and there are many more.

Soul language can be heard in practically all communities throughout the country, but for pure, undiluted spoken soul one must go to Soul Street. There are several. Soul is located at Seventh and "T" in Washington, D.C., on One Two Five Street in New York City; on Springfield Avenue in Newark; on South Street in Philadelphia; on Tremont Street in Boston; on Forty-seventh Street in Chicago, on Fillmore in San Francisco, and dozens of similar locations in dozens of other cities.

As increasingly more Negroes desert Soulville for honorary membership in the Establishment clique, they experience a metamorphosis, the repercussions of which have a marked influence on the young and impressionable citizens of Soulville. The expatriates of Soulville are often greatly admired by the youth of Soulville, who emulate the behavior of such expatriates as Nancy Wilson, Ella Fitzgerald, Eartha Kitt, Lena Horne, Diahann Carroll, Billy Daniels, or Leslie Uggams. The result—more often than not—is a trend away from spoken soul among the young soul folks. This abandonment of the soul language is facilitated by the fact that more Negro youngsters than ever are acquiring college educations (which, incidentally, is not the best treatment for the continued good health and growth of soul); integration and television, too, are contributing significantly to the gradual demise of spoken soul.

Perhaps colleges in America should commence to teach a course in spoken soul. It could be entitled the Vocal History of Black America, or simply Spoken Soul. Undoubtedly there would be no difficulty finding teachers. There are literally thousands of these experts throughout the country whose talents lie idle while they await the call to duty.

Meanwhile the picture looks dark for soul. The two extremities in the Negro spectrum—the conservative and the militant—are both trying diligently to relinquish and repudiate whatever vestige they may still possess of soul. The semi-Negro—the soul brother intent on gaining admission to the Establishment even on an honorary basis—is anxiously embracing and assuming conventional English. The other extremity, the Ultra-Blacks, are frantically adopting everything from a Western version of Islam that would shock the Caliph right out of his snugly fitting shintiyan to anything that vaguely hints of that big, beautiful, bountiful black bitch lying in the arms of the Indian and Atlantic Oceans and crowned by the majestic Mediterranean Sea. Whatever the Ultra-Black is after, it's anything but soulful.

SUGGESTIONS FOR DISCUSSION AND WRITING

1. What does the term "nigger" mean to you? What are its connotations for you, and how do you react to the word? Do you approve or disapprove of the use? Why?

2. Investigate the use of soul terms in the white community, particularly in the language of the young. (A good starting point for your study might be the Carnes essay in Part 2.) To what extent has it influenced the larger community? Support your answers.

3. The author says that the language of soul is gradually diminishing. See if you can find evidence to support or refute that claim.

4. What do you think of the author's idea to establish college courses in the language of soul? Would you take such a course? Why or why not?

5. Some readers of this article have charged that it is out of date (it first appeared in print in 1968) and linguistically inaccurate. Do you find any support for these charges in your own reading of the article?

5

THE SILENT LANGUAGES:
VERBAL AND NONVERBAL COMMUNICATION

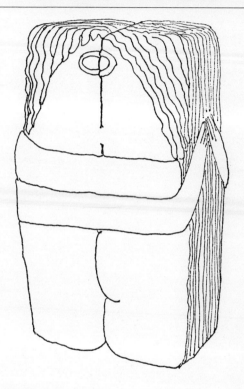

The Kiss, by Constantin Brancusi (1908). Philadelphia Museum of Art: Louise and Walter Arensburg Collection. (Traced from a photograph.) Reprinted from *Etc.*, Vol. 25, No. 2 by permission of the International Society for General Semantics.

22

Julius Fast

CAN YOU INFLUENCE PEOPLE THROUGH "BODY LANGUAGE?"

*Many of us have come to appreciate more fully in recent years
the fact that human beings communicate in far more ways than
through the medium of words alone. In addition to our verbal
language, there are also the "silent languages"—such as our use
of color, time and space, dress and grooming, and eye contact
and gestures. It is with these aspects of communication that the
readings in this part of the book are concerned. This first one, by
Julius Fast, introduces one of these forms that was quick to
arouse popular interest: body language. Mr. Fast is an editor and
free-lance writer, among whose credits is a volume on the subject
of body language.*

The bus was crowded when Peter boarded it and he found himself close to a very pretty girl. Peter enjoyed the bus ride and
admired the girl, in fact, he couldn't keep his eyes off her. Staring at her, he noticed that she had light blue eyes and dark
brown hair, a pleasant combination.

His innocent enjoyment was shattered when the girl turned
to him angrily before she left the bus and said loudly, "You
should be ashamed of yourself!"

"What did I do?" Peter asked the driver in honest bewilder-
ment. "I only looked at her."

"It takes all kinds . . ." the driver shrugged, but did he mean
Peter or the girl? Peter spent a miserable evening wondering

From *Family Circle*, November 1970. "Can You Influence People Through
'Body Language'?" Julius Fast. Reprinted with permission of the publisher
and the author.

just what he had done that was wrong. He would have known what was wrong if he understood some of the rules of body language. Peter violated a very basic law. He looked at the girl beyond the proper looking time.

For every situation there is a proper looking time, a definite period during which you are allowed to meet and hold someone's eyes. In an elevator the time is so brief that it can hardly be considered looking at all. Your eye catches that of a stranger and you look away at once. In a crowded bus, a subway or train, you can look a little longer. But go beyond the proper time—some 10 seconds—and you violate the unwritten but rigid code of body language and take the chance of getting into the same situation that embarrassed Peter.

The girl Peter admired interpreted his stare as insolent or arrogant or insulting in the same way that a cripple interprets the stares of the curious. If we have any consideration, we look only briefly at a cripple or a deformed person, pretending not to look at all.

We look at celebrities in the same way, taking care not to catch their eyes, not to stare at them with too curious a look.

The unwritten laws of body language allow a longer time for staring when we talk to someone, but it is still a limited time. In all conversations we look away frequently and break eye contact. Only a lecturer or a politician addressing an audience can hold eye contact as long as he wishes.

Just what are these unwritten laws of body language? For that matter, just what is body language? Are the rules learned or are they acquired instinctively? Do we all know them, or are they something we must learn? If so, how do we learn them?

These questions have intrigued psychologists ever since they discovered that we communicate with more than the words we speak. Words are only one part of communication. How we use those words is another part. Are our voices loud, angry, overbearing, confident, soft, shy? The quality of a voice can communicate as much as the words. The same words can be tender, mocking, sarcastic or angry, depending on how they are said. We can signal our own authority by talking in a loud, overbearing way. We can use the same words to signal our humility by talking softly and hesitantly. But even beyond voice communication, there are the messages our bodies send out constantly. Sometimes the body message reinforces the words. Sometimes it contradicts them. Sometimes the messages are sent with no accompanying words and we speak in body language alone.

But what gestures make up body language? Most of us are familiar with the common hand gestures. Some people cannot talk without using their hands. They reach out as they explain, almost shaping the words, emphasizing and exaggerating and punctuating with their hands. Other people hardly use their hands at all when they talk. How people use their hands and whether they use them depends on their cultural background. Italians are great hand movers. So are Russians and Latin Americans. Englishmen are stingy about their hand movements; they appear as more controlled and rigid in their behavior.

In the United States, almost any type of hand movement can be found because we have such a mixture of cultures. American etiquette books tell us that waving the hands and gesticulating is ill-mannered and distasteful. It is "unrefined." Refined behavior is always tight and formal. True etiquette can be equated with control and discipline. It can also be equated with an Anglo-Saxon, overcontrolled culture. But our cultural mix in the last century has been too much for books of etiquette.

It is just this cultural mix in America that makes some men more eloquent than others. When body language is used to emphasize the spoken language, to reinforce it, the man who cannot use it is crippled. Too many politicians, awkward with their hands, have learned this to their sorrow. Many have had their images revamped by a reeducation in body language.

A man who uses hand movements when he talks appears freer, more open and more honest to an audience than a controlled nonmover. At certain times, however, a limited amount of hand movement indicates things like solidity, reliability and confidence.

A good poltician knows this instinctively and matches his hand movements to the image he wishes to project. Former President Johnson was apparently taught the proper hand movements because his image was too distant and withdrawn. There was a period, before he learned the gestures, when he appeared awkward and uncomfortable.

It seems obvious that President Nixon has had his body language changed and tailored to match his new image. He does not come across now as the same man who lost the election to John Kennedy in 1960, and the change is largely due to a more controlled, but not nearly so stiff, body movement.

Fiorello H. La Guardia, New York City's mayor in the '30s and early '40s, used to campaign in English, Italian and Yiddish. When he spoke Italian he had one set of hand gestures, another set for Yiddish and still a third for English. Each language demanded its own set of body-language gestures.

But body language is more than hand movements. The eyes play a large part, too. Try holding a fellow pedestrian's eye a bit longer than the proper time. You create an awkward situation and often the only solution is to smile and offer a casual remark, "How are you?" or "Nice day." You may find yourself in conversation with a complete stranger.

The eyes give hidden signals as well as obvious ones. Scientists have found that the pupils dilate unconsciously under pleasant circumstances. Show a man a naked lady, or show a woman a pretty baby, and their pupils dilate. Do the pupils also dilate when a man has a good hand at poker? If so, then perhaps the "natural" poker player is one who unconsciously reads this body-language sign.

What of the rest of the body? Does it also send out unconscious signals?

It does, and the fact that these signals are unconscious means that they are beyond our control. We are not aware that we are sending them out and, therefore, they are more honest than words. It is easy to lie with our voices, but harder to lie with our bodies.

Actors are the exception to this rule. They are trained to lie with their bodies. Recently I talked to Lily Tomlin, who plays a number of characters on "Laugh-In." One of them, a telephone operator, is a masterpiece of body language. The operator torments a customer as she plucks at her breast and twists her face and body. Discussing her movements I told Miss Tomlin that the breast-touching indicated loneliness and introversion; the foot-twisting, self-satisfaction.

"That's what she is," Miss Tomlin agreed. "Lonely and yet self-satisfied with what she is doing. The gestures? They just came naturally once I knew the character."

This is an unconscious adoption of body-language gestures by an actress who first created the character, then lived it and, in living it, naturally used the right body-language gestures.

In addition to the messages we send with our bodies, we also use the space around us to communicate. All of us have our own territories—comfortable distances that we like to keep between us and our friends. We stay closer to people we love, farther away from strangers. When a stranger intrudes on our territory—comes too close to us—we may find it uncomfortable. If the intruder is a wife or husband or lover, we may like the intrusion. It tells us, "I care for you. I love you."

Parents often use space to dominate a child. By looming over him, a parent proves her superiority. The child feels the parent as overpowering and himself as helpless. On the other hand, a parent can draw a child into the circle of her arms and by forcibly invading his space, communicate love and warmth. To do this more easily, the parent may kneel down to the child's level and do away with the looming quality of an adult-child encounter.

Teachers, too, can take a tip from body language in relating to their pupils. The teacher who sits behind a desk is placing an obstacle, the desk, between herself and her pupils. In body language she's saying, "I am your superior. I am here to teach you. You must obey me."

Many educators feel that this is an important and necessary attitude to establish if any "real" teaching is to be done. Other teachers, however, try to do away with the barrier of a desk. They perch on the edge of it and have nothing between them and their students. Still others feel that this is an elevated position, putting the teacher above the student and creating resistance to the teacher. They prefer a position in the center of the room, surrounded by the students, some of whom must turn in their seats to face the teacher.

"This," a teacher once explained to me, "puts me in the center of things. I never sit in a student's seat because I'd be too low. I'd be no better than a student, and a teacher has to be better or why be a teacher? I sit on a student's desk in the center of the room. I'm one of them and yet still a teacher. You'd be amazed at how well they respond."

She is using space to communicate a body-language message. "I'm one of you. I'm on your side even though I'm your teacher."

Which method is most efficient? It's hard to say, except that each teacher must adopt the method that works best for her. If her body language is restricted and tight, sitting on a student's desk may seem simply an affectation—false and unnatural.

The use of the desk as a protective device is familiar to everyone who has watched the Johnny Carson show. Carson uses a desk to separate himself from his guests and to achieve a certain formality. David Frost, when he interviews a guest, does away with a desk and sometimes even does away with chairs, sitting on the stage steps with his guest and using territorial invasion and touch to communicate closeness and warmth. Frost's interviews have a different quality from Carson's because of this different use of space. Perhaps not better, but surely more personal.

The quality of an interview depends not only on the body language of the interviewer, but on his personality as well, and every personality has its own characteristic body-language gestures, even as each culture has its own gestures. We shake our heads up and down for "yes." In India they use the same gesture for "no." To really understand a person's body language we must understand something of their personality, as well as something of their cultural background.

But there are some gestures, such as smiles, that seem to cut across cultural lines. In America there are many common gestures in spite of our cultural mix. Arm-crossing and leg-crossing are two of them. If someone is trying to persuade us and we cross our arms tightly, it is often a sign of resistance. Crossed legs can also be a sign of resistance. When a woman crosses them tightly at the knees and at the ankles, sort of intertwining them, it may indicate resistance to sexuality or a tight, closed personality. (However, it may also be a necessary pose because she's wearing a miniskirt.)

Women in pants tend to give better clues to their emotions by the positioning of their legs. They can sprawl out comfortably. If they sit with open laps they may indicate acceptance, not only sexually, but also intellectually. The well-organized woman may tend to run her legs parallel—as orderly as her life. But I say "tend" because these are still just tendencies. With a skirt, parallel legs are simply a model's pose. Girls are taught in charm schools that this is more graceful. They are also taught the proper arm-crossing.

If all this is true, can we ever really tell anything from a person's body language? Can we use it to control other people or to interpret the true meaning of the messages they send?

We can. We can learn certain tricks of domination to control a situation. We can arrange to be higher than our subordinates, or we can allow our boss to be higher than we are. We can be aware that we dominate our children when we hover over them, that certain facial gestures should be matched to certain body gestures for a smoother appearance—but these are tricks and rather superficial. The real value of body language lies in the insight it can give to our behavior.

Are we tight and rigid about life in general? Our body language can give us a clue to how we are acting and allow us to change our behavior for the better. How a woman sits next to a man on a couch contains a dozen clues to her personality. Does she use her arms as a barrier? Does she cross her legs away from him? Does she turn her body toward him?

How we react to other people's zones of privacy, and how strong our territorial needs are, give other clues. Do we feel uncomfortable when people are close to us? Are we afraid of touching, of being touched? If we are, it might be a sign of our own insecurity, our own fear of revealing ourselves. Understanding this can allow us to take the first step toward dropping the barriers that stand between us and the world.

Only when these barriers begin to fall is it possible to realize not only our own potential as human beings, but the potential of the entire world around us.

SUGGESTIONS FOR DISCUSSION AND WRITING

1. Conduct your own informal experiment with eye contact: In a variety of social situations, determine whether or not a "proper looking time" such as that mentioned in the opening paragraphs of this essay does exist. If so, what is that time period in each of the situations? Try your experiment both with and without conversation.

2. Although this essay concentrates on body language, it also mentions vocal qualities as another form of nonverbal communication. Investigate the role of one or more of the following to see what contribution each makes to the total communication process: vocal tone, pitch, tempo, and volume.

3. Study the body language of a public figure of your choice— either in person or on television. You might use a political figure, an actor or actress, a comedian, or a singer. What techniques of body language do you observe? How much of it appears to be conscious and how much unconscious? Do you detect any disparity between the verbal and nonverbal signals? What does the body language contribute to the total communication? If you prefer, you might observe the body language of a teacher or student.

4. Discuss the use of space as a means of communication in one or more of your classrooms on campus. What does the physical environment tell you? What does the arrangement of people and desks, tables, and so forth tell you?

5. After reading the following essay on nonverbal communication by the Halls, compare and contrast their views on body language with those of this author. Note any differences that you find.

23

Edward and Mildred Hall

THE SOUNDS OF SILENCE

Long before nonverbal communication became a subject of widespread popular interest, anthropologist Edward T. Hall was pursuing his own concern with it, a concern that resulted in two books—the first one on nonverbal communications in their cultural contexts (a book to which this present section of readings owes its title), the second on the use of space as a means of communication. In this essay, written jointly by Mr. Hall and his wife Mildred Reed Hall, the subject of body language, which was introduced in the preceding essay, is more fully developed, along with a number of other dimensions of nonverbal communication.

Bob leaves his apartment at 8:15 A.M. and stops at the corner drugstore for breakfast. Before he can speak, the counterman says, "The usual?" Bob nods yes. While he savors his Danish, a fat man pushes onto the adjoining stool and overflows into his space. Bob scowls and the man pulls himself in as much as he can. Bob has sent two messages without speaking a syllable.

Henry has an appointment to meet Arthur at 11 o'clock; he arrives at 11:30. Their conversation is friendly, but Arthur retains a lingering hostility. Henry has unconsciously communicated that he doesn't think the appointment is very important or that Arthur is a person who needs to be treated with respect.

George is talking to Charley's wife at a party. Their conversation is entirely trivial, yet Charley glares at them suspiciously. Their physical proximity and the movements of their eyes reveal that they are powerfully attracted to each other.

From *Playboy*, June 1971. Reprinted by special permission of *Playboy* magazine and the authors.

José Ybarra and Sir Edmund Jones are at the same party and it is important for them to establish a cordial relationship for business reasons. Each is trying to be warm and friendly, yet they will part with mutual distrust and their business transaction will probably fall through. José, in Latin fashion, moved closer and closer to Sir Edmund as they spoke, and this movement was miscommunicated as pushiness to Sir Edmund, who kept backing away from this intimacy, and this was miscommunicated to José as coldness. The silent languages of Latin and English cultures are more difficult to learn than their spoken languages.

In each of these cases, we see the subtle power of nonverbal communication. The only language used throughout most of the history of humanity (in evolutionary terms, vocal communication is relatively recent), it is the first form of communication you learn. You use this preverbal language, consciously and unconsciously, every day to tell other people how you feel about yourself and them. This language includes your posture, gestures, facial expressions, costume, the way you walk, even your treatment of time and space and material things. All people communicate on several different levels at the same time but are usually aware of only the verbal dialog and don't realize that they respond to nonverbal messages. But when a person says one thing and really believes something else, the discrepancy between the two can usually be sensed. Nonverbal-communication systems are much less subject to the conscious deception that often occurs in verbal systems. When we find ourselves thinking, "I don't know what it is about him, but he doesn't seem sincere," it's usually this lack of congruity between a person's words and his behavior that makes us anxious and uncomfortable.

Few of us realize how much we all depend on body movement in our conversation or are aware of the hidden rules that govern listening behavior. But we know instantly whether or not the person we're talking to is "tuned in" and we're very sensitive to any breach in listening etiquette. In white middle-class American culture, when someone wants to show he is listening to someone else, he looks either at the other person's face or, specifically, at his eyes, shifting his gaze from one eye to the other.

If you observe a person conversing, you'll notice that he indicates he's listening by nodding his head. He also makes little "Hmm" noises. If he agrees with what's being said, he may give a vigorous nod. To show pleasure or affirmation, he smiles; if he has some reservations, he looks skeptical by raising an eyebrow or pulling down the corners of his mouth. If a participant wants to terminate the conversation, he may start shifting his body position, stretching his legs, crossing or un-crossing them, bobbing his foot or diverting his gaze from the speaker. The more he fidgets, the more the speaker becomes aware that he has lost his audience. As a last measure, the lis-tener may look at his watch to indicate the imminent end of the conversation.

Talking and listening are so intricately intertwined that a person cannot do one without the other. Even when one is alone and talking to oneself, there is part of the brain that speaks while another part listens. In all conversations, the listener is positively or negatively reinforcing the speaker all the time. He may even guide the conversation without knowing it, by laughing or frowning or dismissing the argument with a wave of his hand.

The language of the eyes—another age-old way of exchanging feelings—is both subtle and complex. Not only do men and women use their eyes differently but there are class, generation, regional, ethnic and national cultural differences. Americans often complain about the way foreigners stare at people or hold a glance too long. Most Americans look away from someone who is using his eyes in an unfamiliar way because it makes them self-conscious. If a man looks at another man's wife in a certain way, he's asking for trouble, as indicated earlier. But he might not be ill mannered or seeking to challenge the husband. He might be a European in this country who hasn't learned our visual mores. Many American women visiting France or Italy are acutely embarrassed because, for the first time in their lives, men really look at them—their eyes, hair, nose, lips, breasts, hips, legs, thighs, knees, ankles, feet, clothes, hairdo, even their walk. These same women, once they have become used to being looked at, often return to the United States and are overcome with the feeling that "No one ever really looks at me anymore."

Analyzing the mass of data on the eyes, it is possible to sort out at least three ways in which the eyes are used to communicate: dominance *vs.* submission, involvement *vs.* detachment and positive *vs.* negative attitude. In addition, there are three levels of consciousness and control, which can be categorized as follows: (1) conscious use of the eyes to communicate, such as the flirting blink and the intimate nose-wrinkling squint; (2) the very extensive category of unconscious but learned behavior governing where the eyes are directed and when (this unwritten set of rules dictates how and under what circumstances the sexes, as well as people of all status categories, look at each other); and (3) the response of the eye itself, which is completely outside both awareness and control—changes in the cast (the sparkle) of the eye and the pupillary reflex.

The eye is unlike any other organ of the body, for it is an extension of the brain. The unconscious pupillary reflex and the cast of the eye have been known by people of Middle Eastern origin for years—although most are unaware of their knowledge. Depending on the context, Arabs and others look either directly at the eyes or deeply *into* the eyes of their interlocutor. We became aware of this in the Middle East several years ago while looking at jewelry. The merchant suddenly started to push a particular bracelet at a customer and said, "You buy this one." What interested us was that the bracelet was not the one that had been consciously selected by the purchaser. But the merchant, watching the pupils of the eyes, knew what the purchaser really wanted to buy. Whether he specifically knew *how* he knew is debatable.

A psychologist at the University of Chicago, Eckhard Hess, was the first to conduct systematic studies of the pupillary reflex. His wife remarked one evening, while watching him reading in bed, that he must be very interested in the text because his pupils were dilated. Following up on this, Hess slipped some pictures of nudes into a stack of photographs that he gave to his male assistant. Not looking at the photographs but watching his assistant's pupils, Hess was able to tell precisely when the assistant came to the nudes. In further experiments, Hess retouched the eyes in a photograph of a woman. In one print, he made the pupils small, in another, large; nothing else was changed. Subjects who were given the photographs found the woman with the dilated pupils much more attractive. Any man who has had the experience of seeing a woman look at him as her pupils widen with reflex speed knows that she's flashing him a message.

The eye-sparkle phenomenon frequently turns up in our interviews of couples in love. It's apparently one of the first reliable clues in the other person that love is genuine. To date, there is no scientific data to explain eye sparkle; no investigation of the pupil, the cornea or even the white sclera of the eye shows how the sparkle originates. Yet we all know it when we see it.

One common situation for most people involves the use of the eyes in the street and in public. Although eye behavior follows a definite set of rules, the rules vary according to the place, the needs and feelings of the people, and their ethnic background. For urban whites, once they're within definite recognition distance (16–32 feet for people with average eyesight), there is mutual avoidance of eye contact—unless they want something specific: a pickup, a handout or information of some kind. In the West and in small towns generally, however, people are much more likely to look at and greet one another, even if they're strangers.

It's permissible to look at people if they're beyond recognition distance; but once inside this sacred zone, you can only steal a glance at strangers. You *must* greet friends, however; to fail to do so is insulting. Yet, to stare too fixedly even at them is considered rude and hostile. Of course, all of these rules are variable.

A great many blacks, for example, greet each other in public even if they don't know each other. To blacks, most eye behavior of whites has the effect of giving the impression that they aren't there, but this is due to white avoidance of eye contact with *anyone* in the street.

Another very basic difference between people of different

ethnic backgrounds is their sense of territoriality and how they handle space. This is the silent communication, or miscommunication, that caused friction between Mr. Ybarra and Sir Edmund Jones in our earlier example. We know from research that everyone has around himself an invisible bubble of space that contracts and expands depending on several factors: his emotional state, the activity he's performing at the time and his cultural background. This bubble is a kind of mobile territory that he will defend against intrusion. If he is accustomed to close personal distance between himself and others, his bubble will be smaller than that of someone who's accustomed to greater personal distance. People of North European heritage—English, Scandinavian, Swiss and German—tend to avoid contact. Those whose heritage is Italian, French, Spanish, Russian, Latin American or Middle Eastern like close personal contact.

People are very sensitive to any intrusion into their spatial bubble. If someone stands too close to you, your first instinct is to back up. If that's not possible, you lean away and pull yourself in, tensing your muscles. If the intruder doesn't respond to these body signals, you may then try to protect yourself, using a briefcase, umbrella or raincoat. Women—especially when traveling alone—often plant their pocketbook in such a way that no one can get very close to them. As a last resort, you may move to another spot and position yourself behind a desk or a chair that provides screening. Everyone tries to adjust the space around himself in a way that's comfortable for him; most often, he does this unconsciously.

Emotions also have a direct effect on the size of a person's territory. When you're angry or under stress, your bubble expands and you require more space. New York psychiatrist Augustus Kinzel found a difference in what he calls Body-Buffer Zones between violent and nonviolent prison inmates. Dr. Kinzel conducted experiments in which each prisoner was placed in the center of a small room and then Dr. Kinzel slowly walked toward him. Nonviolent prisoners allowed him to come quite close, while prisoners with a history of violent behavior couldn't tolerate his proximity and reacted with some vehemence.

Apparently, people under stress experience other people as

looming larger and closer than they actually are. Studies of schizophrenic patients have indicated that they sometimes have a distorted perception of space, and several psychiatrists have reported patients as filling up an entire room. For these patients, anyone who comes into the room is actually inside their body, and such an intrusion may trigger a violent outburst.

Unfortunately, there is little detailed information about normal people who live in highly congested urban areas. We do know, of course, that the noise, pollution, dirt, crowding and confusion of our cities induce feelings of stress in most of us, and stress leads to a need for greater space. The man who's packed into a subway, jostled in the street, crowded into an elevator and forced to work all day in a bull pen or in a small office without auditory or visual privacy is going to be very stressed at the end of his day. He needs places that provide relief from constant overstimulation of his nervous system. Stress from overcrowding is cumulative and people can tolerate more crowding early in the day than later; note the increased bad temper during the evening rush hour as compared with the morning melee. Certainly one factor in people's desire to commute by car is the need for privacy and relief from crowding (except, often, from other cars); it may be the only time of the day when nobody can intrude.

In crowded public places, we tense our muscles and hold ourselves stiff, and thereby communicate to others our desire not to intrude on their space and, above all, not to touch them. We also avoid eye contact, and the total effect is that of someone who has "tuned out." Walking along the street, our bubble expands slightly as we move in a stream of strangers, taking care not to bump into them. In the office, at meetings, in restaurants, our bubble keeps changing as it adjusts to the activity at hand.

Most white middle-class Americans use four main distances in their business and social relations: intimate, personal, social and public. Each of these distances has a near and a far phase and is accompanied by changes in the volume of the voice. Intimate distance varies from direct physical contact with another person to a distance of six to eighteen inches and is used for our most private activities—caressing another person or making love. At this distance, you are overwhelmed by sensory inputs from the other person—heat from the body, tactile stimulation from the skin, the fragrance of perfume, even the sound of breathing—all of which literally envelop you. Even at the far phase, you're still within easy touching distance. In general, the use of intimate distance in public between adults is frowned on. It's also much too close for strangers, except under conditions of extreme crowding.

In the second zone—personal distance—the close phase is one and a half to two and a half feet; it's at this distance that wives usually stand from their husbands in public. If another woman moves into this zone, the wife will most likely be disturbed. The far phase—two and a half to four feet—is the distance used to "keep someone at arm's length" and is the most common spacing used by people in conversation.

The third zone—social distance—is employed during business transactions or exchanges with a clerk or repairman. People who work together tend to use close social distance—four to seven feet. This is also the distance for conversations at social gatherings. To stand at this distance from someone who is seated has a dominating effect (e.g., teacher to pupil, boss to secretary). The far phase of the third zone—seven to twelve feet—is where people stand when someone says, "Stand back so I can look at you." This distance lends a formal tone to business or social discourse. In an executive office, the desk serves to keep people at this distance.

The fourth zone—public distance—is used by teachers in classrooms or speakers at public gatherings. At its farthest phase—25 feet and beyond—it is used for important public figures. Violations of this distance can lead to serious complications. During his 1970 U. S. visit, the president of France, Georges Pompidou, was harassed by pickets in Chicago, who were permitted to get within touching distance. Since pickets in France are kept behind barricades a block or more away, the president was outraged by this insult to his person, and President Nixon was obliged to communicate his concern as well as offer his personal apologies.

It is interesting to note how American pitchmen and panhandlers exploit the unwritten, unspoken conventions of eye and distance. Both take advantage of the fact that once explicit eye contact is established, it is rude to look away, because to do so means to brusquely dismiss the other person and his needs. Once having caught the eye of his mark, the panhandler then locks on, not letting go until he moves through the public zone, the social zone, the personal zone and, finally, into the intimate sphere, where people are most vulnerable.

Touch also is an important part of the constant stream of communication that takes place between people. A light touch, a firm touch, a blow, a caress are all communications. In an effort to break down barriers among people, there's been a recent upsurge in group-encounter activities, in which strangers are encouraged to touch one another. In special situations such as these, the rules for not touching are broken with group approval and people gradually lose some of their inhibitions.

Although most people don't realize it, space is perceived and distances are set not by vision alone but with all the senses. Auditory space is perceived with the ears, thermal space with the skin, kinesthetic space with the muscles of the body and olfactory space with the nose. And, once again, it's one's culture that determines how his senses are programmed—which sensory information ranks highest and lowest. The important thing to remember is that culture is very persistent. In this country, we've noted the existence of culture patterns that determine distance between people in the third and fourth generations of some families, despite their prolonged contact with people of very different cultural heritages.

Whenever there is great cultural distance between two people, there are bound to be problems arising from differences in behavior and expectations. An example is the American couple who consulted a psychiatrist about their marital problems. The husband was from New England and had been brought up by reserved parents who taught him to control his emotions and to respect the need for privacy. His wife was from an Italian family and had been brought up in close contact with all the members of her large family, who were extremely warm, volatile and demonstrative.

When the husband came home after a hard day at the office,

dragging his feet and longing for peace and quiet, his wife would rush to him and smother him. Clasping his hands, rubbing his brow, crooning over his weary head, she never left him alone. But when the wife was upset or anxious about her day, the husband's response was to withdraw completely and leave her alone. No comforting, no affectionate embrace, no attention—just solitude. The woman became convinced her husband didn't love her and, in desperation, she consulted a psychiatrist. Their problem wasn't basically psychological but cultural.

Why has man developed all these different ways of communicating messages without words? One reason is that people don't like to spell out certain kinds of messages. We prefer to find other ways of showing our feelings. This is especially true in relationships as sensitive as courtship. Men don't like to be rejected and most women don't want to turn a man down bluntly. Instead, we work out subtle ways of encouraging or discouraging each other that save face and avoid confrontations.

How a person handles space in dating others is an obvious and very sensitive indicator of how he or she feels about the other person. On a first date, if a woman sits or stands so close to a man that he is acutely conscious of her physical presence—inside the intimate-distance zone—the man usually construes it to mean that she is encouraging him. However, before the man starts moving in on the woman, he should be sure what message she's really sending; otherwise, he risks bruising his ego. What is close to someone of North European background may be neutral or distant to someone of Italian heritage. Also, women sometimes use space as a way of misleading a man and there are few things that put men off more than women who communicate contradictory messages—such as women who cuddle up and then act insulted when a man takes the next step.

How does a woman communicate interest in a man? In addition to such familiar gambits as smiling at him, she may glance shyly at him, blush and then look away. Or she may give him a real come-on look and move in very close when he approaches. She may touch his arm and ask for a light. As she leans forward to light her cigarette, she may brush him lightly, enveloping him in her perfume. She'll probably continue to smile at him and she may use what ethologists call preening gestures—touching the back of her hair, thrusting her breasts forward, tilting her hips as she stands or crossing her legs if she's seated, perhaps even exposing one thigh or putting a hand on her thigh and stroking it. She may also stroke her wrists as she converses or show the palm of her hand as a way of gaining his attention. Her skin may be unusually flushed or quite pale, her eyes brighter, the pupils larger.

If a man sees a woman whom he wants to attract, he tries to present himself by his posture and stance as someone who is self-assured. He moves briskly and confidently. When he catches the eye of the woman, he may hold her glance a little longer than normal. If he gets an encouraging smile, he'll move in close and engage her in small talk. As they converse, his glance shifts over her face and body. He, too, may make preening gestures—straightening his tie, smoothing his hair or shooting his cuffs.

How do people learn body language? The same way they learn spoken language—by observing and imitating people around them as they're growing up. Little girls imitate their mothers or an older female. Little boys imitate their fathers or a respected uncle or a character on television. In this way, they learn the gender signals appropriate for their sex. Regional, class and ethnic patterns of body behavior are also learned in childhood and persist throughout life.

Such patterns of masculine and feminine body behavior vary widely from one culture to another. In America, for example, women stand with their thighs together. Many walk with their pelvis tipped slightly forward and their upper arms close to their body. When they sit, they cross their legs at the knee or, if they are well past middle age, they may cross their ankles. American men hold their arms away from their body, often swinging them as they walk. They stand with their legs apart (an extreme example is the cowboy, with legs apart and thumbs tucked into his belt). When they sit, they put their feet on the floor with legs apart and, in some parts of the country, they cross their legs by putting one ankle on the other knee.

Leg behavior indicates sex, status and personality. It also indicates whether or not one is at ease or is showing respect or disrespect for the other person. Young Latin-American males avoid crossing their legs. In their world of *machismo*, the preferred position for young males when with one another (if there is no older dominant male present to whom they must show respect) is to sit on the base of their spine with their leg muscles relaxed and their feet wide apart. Their respect position is like our military equivalent: spine straight, heels and ankles together —almost identical to that displayed by properly brought up young women in New England in the early part of this century.

American women who sit with their legs spread apart in the presence of males are *not* normally signaling a come-on—they are simply (and often unconsciously) sitting like men. Middle-class women in the presence of other women to whom they are very close may on occasion throw themselves down on a soft chair or sofa and let themselves go. This is a signal that nothing serious will be taken up. Males, on the other hand, lean back and prop their legs up on the nearest object.

The way we walk, similarly, indicates status, respect, mood and ethnic or cultural affiliation. The many variants of the female walk are too well known to go into here, except to say that a man would have to be blind not to be turned on by the way some women walk—a fact that made Mae West rich before scientists ever studied these matters. To white Americans, some French middle-class males walk in a way that is both humorous and suspect. There is a bounce and looseness to the French walk, as though the parts of the body were somehow unrelated. Jacques Tati, the French movie actor, walks this way; so does the great mime, Marcel Marceau.

Blacks and whites in America—with the exception of middle- and upper-middle-class professionals of both groups—move and walk very differently from each other. To the blacks, whites often seem incredibly stiff, almost mechanical in their movements. Black males, on the other hand, have a looseness and coordination that frequently makes whites a little uneasy; it's too different, too integrated, too alive, too male. Norman Mailer has said that squares walk from the shoulders, like bears, but blacks and hippies walk from the hips, like cats.

All over the world, people walk not only in their own characteristic way but have walks that communicate the nature of their involvement with whatever it is they're doing. The purposeful walk of North Europeans is an important component of proper behavior on the job. Any male who has been in the military knows how essential it is to walk properly (which makes for a continuing source of tension between blacks and whites in the Service). The quick shuffle of servants in the Far East in the old days was a show of respect. On the island of Truk, when we last visited, the inhabitants even had a name for the respectful walk that one used when in the presence of a chief or when walking past a chief's house. The term was *sufan*, which meant to be humble and respectful.

The notion that people communicate volumes by their gestures, facial expressions, posture and walk is not new; actors, dancers, writers and psychiatrists have long been aware of it. Only in recent years, however, have scientists begun to make systematic observations of body motions. Ray L. Birdwhistell of the University of Pennsylvania is one of the pioneers in body-motion research and coined the term kinesics to describe this field. He developed an elaborate notation system to record both facial and body movements, using an approach similar to that of the linguist, who studies the basic elements of speech. Birdwhistell and other kinesicists such as Albert Sheflen, Adam Kendon and William Condon take movies of people interacting. They run the film over and over again, often at reduced speed for frame-by-frame analysis, so that they can observe even the slightest body movements not perceptible at normal interaction speeds. These movements are then recorded in notebooks for later analysis.

To appreciate the importance of non-verbal-communication systems, consider the unskilled inner-city black looking for a job. His handling of time and space alone is sufficiently different from the white middle-class pattern to create great misunderstandings on both sides. The black is told to appear for a job interview at a certain time. He arrives late. The white interviewer concludes from his tardy arrival that the black is irresponsible and not really interested in the job. What the interviewer doesn't know is that the black time system (often referred to by blacks as C. P. T.—colored people's time) isn't the same as that of whites. In the words of a black student who had been told to make an appointment to see his professor: "Man, you *must* be putting me on. I never had an appointment in my life."

The black job applicant, having arrived late for his interview may further antagonize the white interviewer by his posture and his eye behavior. Perhaps he slouches and avoids looking at the interviewer; to him, this is playing it cool. To the interviewer, however, he may well look shifty and sound uninterested. The interviewer has failed to notice the actual signs of interest and eagerness in the black's behavior, such as the subtle shift in the quality of the voice—a gentle and tentative excitement—an almost imperceptible change in the cast of the eyes and a relaxing of the jaw muscles.

Moreover, correct reading of black-white behavior is continually complicated by the fact that both groups are comprised of individuals—some of whom try to accommodate and some of whom make it a point of pride *not* to accommodate. At present, this means that many Americans, when thrown into contact with one another, are in the precarious position of not knowing which pattern applies. Once identified and analyzed, nonverbal-communication systems can be taught, like a foreign language. Without this training, we respond to nonverbal communications in terms of our own culture; we read everyone's behavior as if it were our own, and thus we often misunderstand it.

Several years ago in New York City, there was a program for sending children from predominantly black and Puerto Rican low-income neighborhoods to summer school in a white upper-class neighborhood on the East Side. One morning, a group of young black and Puerto Rican boys raced down the street, shouting and screaming and overturning garbage cans on their way to school. A doorman from an apartment building nearby chased them and cornered one of them inside a building. The boy drew a knife and attacked the doorman. This tragedy would not have occurred if the doorman had been familiar with the behavior of boys from low-income neighborhoods, where such antics are routine and socially acceptable and where pursuit would be expected to invite a violent response.

The language of behavior is extremely complex. Most of us are lucky to have under control one subcultural system—the one that reflects our sex, class, generation and geographic region within the United States. Because of its complexity, efforts to isolate bits of nonverbal communication and generalize from them are in vain; you don't become an instant expert on people's behavior by watching them at cocktail parties. Body language isn't something that's independent of the person, something that can be donned and doffed like a suit of clothes.

Our research and that of our colleagues has shown that, far from being a superficial form of communication that can be consciously manipulated, nonverbal-communication systems are interwoven into the fabric of the personality and, as sociologist Erving Goffman has demonstrated, into society itself. They are the warp and woof of daily interactions with others and they influence how one expresses oneself, how one experiences oneself as a man or a woman.

Nonverbal communications signal to members of your own group what kind of person you are, how you feel about others, how you'll fit into and work in a group, whether you're assured or anxious, the degree to which you feel comfortable with the standards of your own culture, as well as deeply significant feelings about the self, including the state of your own psyche. For most of us, it's difficult to accept the reality of another's behavioral system. And, of course, none of us will ever become fully knowledgeable of the importance of every nonverbal signal. But as long as each of us realizes the power of these signals, this society's diversity can be a source of great strength rather than a further—and subtly powerful—source of division.

SUGGESTIONS FOR DISCUSSION AND WRITING

1. The authors believe that "Nonverbal communication systems are much less subject to the conscious deception that often occurs in verbal systems." Do you agree or disagree? If you agree, can you cite some specific examples to support your position? If you disagree, explain your basis for that position.

2. Set aside one day during which you take particular notice of nonverbal communication as you go about your regular activities. Then prepare a summary of your study for that day, recounting any particularly interesting observations you have made and evaluating the role that nonverbal communications play in our lives.

3. If you are familiar with another culture or subculture, discuss the differences between their nonverbal communications and those of our dominant culture. If you are not familiar with another culture, select one in which you are interested, investigate the differences, and report your findings.

4. Write a paper in which you discuss the effect of space on people living in a highly congested area or in a sparsely populated area. You may wish to contrast the two. If you are familiar with your subject from personal experience, obviously that experience should be the primary source for your paper. If you have never had such experience but are interested in the topic, undertake it as a research project.

5. Review the discussions of the nonverbal communications techniques of minority groups in this essay and consider this subject in relation to the discussions of language and race in the essays in Part 4.

24

Sherri Cavan

TALKING ABOUT SEX BY
NOT TALKING ABOUT SEX

In the strictest sense, this essay by Sherri Cavan is not about nonverbal communications at all, inasmuch as it does discuss the use of language within a given social context. But in a larger sense, the author is dealing not so much with words as the relationship between language and situation. Accordingly, the essay reflects some important aspects of nonverbal communication—the use of setting, situation, and ritual—as well as the communication through which we say one thing and mean quite another. So understood, the essay adds another dimension to the concept of silent language. Ms. Cavan teaches sociology at California State University, San Francisco.

Taboos in our society generally prevent us from talking about sex in a direct or explicit fashion. Any other than an indirect approach to sex talk can categorize the speaker as crude, vulgar, and probably over-preoccupied with the subject.

In our society, sex is a very serious matter. Like income and race, it provides one criterion for imputing moral character. We often evaluate people by their choice of sexual objects. If they appear to show no discrimination, we think them licentious. If they prefer their own sex, we deem them queer. If they have what we think are too many sexual encounters, they are promiscuous; if too few, they are prudes. Those who are compulsive in their sexual behavior we regard as attempting to prove their masculinity. We categorize sexual behavior, if money is exchanged, as prostitution. And the presumed proficiency, style,

Reprinted from *Etc.*, Vol. 25, No. 2, by permission of the International Society for General Semantics.

and attitude of the participants, too, reflect on their general moral character. Like other serious matters, we consider sexual topics more properly approached indirectly rather than directly. Just as it is improper to ask someone how much money he makes yearly, so too it is improper to ask people how often they have sexual intercourse, or whether they want it right now.

Because of taboos, sex talk characteristically takes the form of metaphor and innuendo. An analogous situation arises from the Jewish tradition that regards any direct mention of the name of God as an impropriety. Jews therefore have a variety of institutionalized ways of referring to Him, so that any good Jew will know when God is being talked about even when His name is never explicitly mentioned.

By using metaphor and innuendo, we are able to imply a great deal more than is being said. It is always possible to talk about sex even when it seems as if we were talking about something else. Similarly, the transition from other topics of conversation to the topic of sex can be smoothly made—sometimes the transition not even being noticed by one participant or the other. Discussion of sex can be expressed in such oblique language that the question may always be raised as to whether the participants are, in fact, even talking about sex at any particular moment. Finally, since sex talk is not carried on with the precision of legal contacts, the extent of our commitment to a proposed or nascent sexual relationship can at any given time remain an open question.

THE TIME AND PLACE

How can we be sure that we are talking about sex? How do we manage to say what we want to say, being aware that any direct mention of the subject would immediately classify the speaker as a boor? For adult members of American society, common sense knowledge of the world includes an understanding of situations where sex talk is or is not likely. By and large, we understand sex talk is more likely to occur in a time and place of leisure activities rather than at work. It is understood that we are more inclined to talk about sex at the movies, the beach, in the park, in bars, at vacation resorts, hotels, ski lodges, and at social parties than in offices, on a bus, in a doctor's waiting room, in the supermarket, or at church. This is not to say that casual sex talk never takes place in the latter situations, but only that a particular kind of finesse is necessary in order that what is taking place can be more or less known by both participants.

Similarly, we generally understand that talk about sex is more likely to take place between conversational participants who see each other as compatible sexual partners. This means that participants of the encounter are much more likely to be talking about sex when they are of opposite sexes, more or less the same age, without obvious marital attachments, and of similar social backgrounds. Again, this is not to say that sex cannot be talked about by those of the same sex, those who are clearly married or engaged to someone else, or those who differ considerably in age or social background. But like talking about sex in unpromising settings or on unpromising occasions, it is not as easy to manage. Given the proper conjunction of setting and participants, however, casual sex talk is not only relatively easy to manage, but quite likely to take place.

FLIRTATION

Casual sex talk is broadly any kind of flirtatious sociability. It may be no more than toying with the notion of seduction and being seduced without seriously expecting that seduction will occur, as in a wink or the protracted, cryptic smile. Or it may lead to actually negotiating a physical, sexual encounter—a sociological euphemism for the social euphemism of "making love."

Just as there are socially institutionalized means for knowing when it is likely that one might engage another in casual sex talk, so, too, are there socially institutionalized ways for carrying out such talk. Flirtations may be spontaneously desired by one participant or another, but the way they are carried out tends to make them an almost ritualized formality, much like the *correria* in Latin American countries. There, collective flirtations take place between groups of young men and groups of young women through the ritual means of openly strolling around the plaza. The men proceed in one direction, the women in another, while members of one group are surreptitiously glancing at particular members of the opposite group.

In Rome, "the art of ogling" takes form in many guises. Russell Baker comments:

> There are many techniques for the male. One of the most popular is the Bookkeeper's Stare. A woman approaches. The Roman stares into her eyes, then glances rapidly downward from shoulder to calf like a bookkeeper adding a column of figures . . .
>
> A variation on the Bookkeeper's Stare is the Clockwise Inspection. In this one, the Roman approaches the woman head-on, gazes passionately into her eyes and then rotates his stare in a slow, circular motion around her upper torso, bringing it to rest again upon her eyes.
>
> A third technique in great popularity in Italy is the Broken Barber Pole . . . The Roman approaches the woman head-on, walking very rapidly. He draws alongside her without looking. Then, when he is a half-step past her, he starts to revolve, rapidly casting his eyes backward and downward to survey her from shoulder blades to ankles.
>
> He does not spin all the way around, as a barber pole should, but quickly resumes his forward motion until he is fully balanced for the next woman.[1]

In American society, we find an example of the ritual procedures of casual sex talk by looking at what happens in bars. Bars are commonly understood to be likely places for such activity. In fact, in some bars casual sex talk has a kind of institutional character to it, especially in those places known to be "pick-up" bars. Although professionals such as B-girls and prostitutes engage in rituals for making commercial contacts in bars, by and large casual sex talk rituals tend to be the domain of the nonprofessional; and the rituals of the professionals tend

[1] *San Francisco Chronicle Sunday Punch*, October 9, 1966.

to be attenuated forms of those the nonprofessionals employ.

It should be pointed out that while bars are generally understood to be acceptable settings for casual sex talk, some, more than others, may have a reputation for such activity. Large segments of the population of any city have within their store of common knowledge a partial list, at least, of the bars in the city where "the action is." Even newcomers somehow soon learn where to seek the "action," inasmuch as their knowledge of the social world in general would lead them to the best choice. If no particular bar is known by name, they might seek one in the vicinity of young, unattached (either temporarily or permanently) populations. First choice would be near the places where both men and women work, and second choice near residential areas of studio and one-bedroom apartments. Patrons of various known pick-up bars in San Francisco frequently have heard of such places from friends as far away as New York, who have given them lists of "San Francisco bars that swing." Others have heard of bars "in St. Louis where a guy from Philadelphia said this was a place where you see humanity in action." Even people from such faraway places as New Zealand are able to seek out a San Francisco bar with a reputation for being a fine "body exchange."

WHERE THE ACTION IS

Once the participants have located themselves in the appropriate setting, the ritual of casual sex talk in bars ensues. It is a social game in which it is assumed that all patrons there are open to conversation with strangers. Almost anyone present can be considered a likely participant in a known pick-up bar, more so than in bars generally. The patrons of the latter, however, are similarly disposed unless they elect to sit in the booths or at tables away from the bar, a strategy for proclaiming oneself unavailable for participation.

Given a population of possible female co-participants, the male in the bar can instigate casual sex talk either directly or indirectly. A direct opening move would be one where he starts a conversation with a very general remark, "Do you live around here?" or ". . . work around here?" or "The weather has been particularly nice/ particularly bad/ unusual . . ." Or, "They make the best martinis [Irish coffee, Pim's Cup, etc.] in town here."

An indirect opening requires the assistance of the bartender. This usually takes place when the male is sitting too far from the chosen female to address her directly. The male asks the bartender to "give the lady another of what she's drinking," with the understanding that the bartender will indicate with a nod of his head with whose compliments the drink has arrived. If the woman accepts the drink and conveys her thanks directly to the man with a look and a smile, he may then come over to join her. Once he has joined her in this manner, his opening remarks are almost identical with those which are made when the initial contact is direct, as in "Do you live [work] around here . . .?"

THE STRUCTURE OF THE RITUAL

When a conversation has been initiated between a man and a woman—once the initial overture and acceptance have been completed—the game moves from casual talk-in-general to casual sex talk. The transformation from *just talk* to *sex talk* characteristically takes place by the participants signifying that the latter is acceptable. This signification is made and acknowledged by means of an exchange of ritual information.

The first such bit of ritual information is that concerning the participants' availability for flirtations. Often statements of availability will be made even before names are exchanged; for if it turns out that neither party is available, there may be no reason for self-introductions. Statements which are read as statements of availability are of the following sort: "This is a hard city for a single person to meet people," or "This is the anniversary of my divorce," or even "Are you alone, too?"

Information about availability is strategic information, as it conveys in part at least what the possible nature of the ensuing conversation will be. If the participants do not declare themselves as available, the conversation may continue; but it will be understood then to be simply casual talk.

Casual sex talk can, of course, remain low-keyed at a level of almost imperceptible hints and innuendos. But it can also become more involved and the talk can come to stand as a prologue to subsequent physical involvement. Once such talk has begun, the acknowledgment and management of further involvement is characteristically signified by changes of location, either by a suggestion to move from the place where the conversation began to some other part of the bar, or more probably a booth. Or it may, more definitely, be signified by a suggestion to move to some other setting—another bar, a restaurant, or an apartment. Such requests for changes of location are usually read as statements of interest in something more than the flirtatious sociability of the moment. The response to the request is read as a statement about willingness in whatever else may come of it. Hence, within the context of sex talk in the bar, agreements can be made for sexual activity outside of the bar without either party having to put the proposal into words.

MOVIE HOUSE ACTION

The same structural qualities that appear in other flirtations can be seen in the ritual of the movie house encounter. As with pick-up bars, it is a matter of common knowledge among some segments of the population that certain movie houses have more action than others. Thus, casual sexual encounters can take place in any movie house, although some tend to be much more heavily used for this purpose than others—for example, downtown movie houses and those in the vicinity of high schools.

In movie house encounters, it is again up to the male to make the first overture, which, again, as in bars, is characteristically a change in location. Specifically, he moves to the seat directly adjoining that of the female or the one directly behind her. However, the proclamation of the availability to such encounters must be first signified by the female. She sits in the first nine or ten rows of the theater, with an empty seat on at least one side of her if she is with another female, or a seat vacant on both sides if she is alone. (Uninterested single females can sit on the aisle without being disturbed.) A female's proclamation of her availability can be further heightened by frequent trips up the aisle, ostensibly motivated by the desire for popcorn or candy.

Unlike bars, however, the general patterns of behavior associated with movie houses do not include casual talk of any kind. Hence, any conversational overture in such settings is typically read as a sexual move in and of itself. Under such circumstances, for the female to ignore the overture totally is for her to proclaim her lack of interest. A "polite response," however, virtually stands as a proclamation of interest; where they go from there is now to be treated as a matter open to negotiation.

THE POETRY OF SEX TALK

The enlightened in our society often express concern about the fact that sex and talk about sex are surrounded with metaphor and veiled hints and euphemism. They suggest that lack of candor results in our perceiving sex as mysterious and therefore anxiety-provoking. But when we look at the social rituals involved in a bar or movie pick-up, we might ask if those concerned are not confusing different kinds of anxiety: the pleasurable anxiety of titillation and the anxiety of self-consciousness and torment.

The characteristic feature of middle-class American society is the routinization of life. It would seem that the ritualization of sex talk is a way of eliminating chance and risk from casual encounters, in favor of clear and precise paths, which, if carefully followed, will lead either to success or at least to failure without loss of face.

Perhaps the proliferation of marriage manuals in our time is likewise an attempt to eliminate risk from sexual encounters. If the mystery is removed, if sex is treated openly and candidly, readers of these manuals are led to believe, they can be assured of efficient performance.[2]

Sexual activity is common to all but the very lowest forms of life. But man's sexual activity is different from the rutting of animals. Because human beings are, as Alfred Korzybski said, a

[2] Lionel S. Lewis and Dennis Brissett, "Sex as Work: A Study of Avocational Counseling," *Social Problems*, XV, 8-18.

symbolic class of life, man transforms sexual activity from a routine and mundane biological event into an occasion for ritual and ceremony, in the same way that he has managed to transform the routine activity of the linguistic exchange of information into poetry. We can survive without poetry, of course. But the question is, do we really want to?

Were sexual encounters to be treated and transacted with the same explicit candor as checking out a library book or making a bank deposit, there might be nothing left but simple physical gratification, something which can be achieved by one as well as by two.

Sex talk, as it is practiced in our society, with metaphor and innuendo, veiled hints and accepted formal rituals, remains an eminently social activity.

SUGGESTIONS FOR DISCUSSION AND WRITING

1. *Investigate the taboos in our society that prevent us from talking about sex in a direct or explicit fashion and report your findings. What are some of those taboos? What are their sources? What are their effects? Consider these taboos in relation to the verbal taboos discussed by Bens in Part 2.*

2. *Observe a social situation in which people are "talking about sex by not talking about sex" or recount a situation from your own experience. How accurate do you feel that this author's observations are?*

3. *One reviewer who approved the inclusion of this essay in the present volume nevertheless suggested that students might find the essay "condescending and a little straight in its approach to language and sex." Do you find it either "condescending" or "straight"? If so, in what way(s)?*

4. *What is your reaction to the barroom and movie house "pick-up" rituals described here? Are they reasonably accurate or representative in their descriptions? If not, how are they inac-*

curate or unrepresentative? Are they out of date? If so, can
you offer some up-to-date equivalents?

5. The author concludes that the ritualistic routines discussed
here actually enhance the pleasure of sexual relationships. Do
you agree or disagree with the author? Support your answer.

25

William Hedgepeth

GROWL TO ME SOFTLY
AND I'LL UNDERSTAND

It comes as no surprise to anyone who has read the earlier portions of this book that many young Americans have, for various reasons, become disenchanted with our language as a means of expression. In this essay, William Hedgepeth argues that "there's a whole vast range of not only emotions but of newly grasped sensations that seems doomed to lie locked up, unwordable, in our heads. Our language, in its present form," he continues, "just can't handle it; and people—particularly young people—are slowly becoming aware of this flaw in their tongue." Using the singing style of the late Janis Joplin as a frame of reference, Mr. Hedgepeth says that we need new ways in order to really communicate. Mr. Hedgepeth, a former member of the staff of Look *magazine, is also the author of a book on communal living.*

Bands of light beam from the rear—flare, pale, flutter: blue, green, yellow, red; now it's red. Janis is red, writhing, wrenching words right out her pores. "Puh . . . Puhleeazzze . . ." up straight from her toes, shot through cosmos, amplified 2,000 watts. Stompstompstompstomp. Oh, Momma! Janis Joplin! Room booms: thousands out there, in the dark, feel the vibes. Supercharged. Slow glow grows in eyes: Does she *mean* it? Does she *mean* it? "WAH!" Mike jammed to her teeth, kicking, stomping, keeping time. Crouch down, up slow, louder now—tell us, tell us —"Awww wah hoo heee." Cymbals: crash, crash. Drum thump. Silent. Now it's over. Studden hush. Did she mean it? Did she? Wah? Yes! Yes! The hall explodes. Message gotten. Yes! Yes! And then—*wham*—out of the grayish-hazy auditorium air rolls a

long, blurry clap-whistle-roar like a rattling of the world's
largest sheet of tin. Janis drops the mike, shoulders suddenly
limp, bleats a teeny "thankya" and turns away from the crowd
to grope for a paper cup (Dixie Cup) of Southern Comfort sitting on the organ. Then back to the mike.

No pukey, careful-metered lines sung here. And who here can
possibly disentangle more than a few bare words out of that
jammed-together thunderation of wailed syllables? ("Ahheee-
WOG Pleaghuhh woo," she erupts again.) Not me, anyway. But
everybody gets the point. The point is how she feels, and they
are eager to pick it up, share it, feel it with her. They are
primed for this kind of thing. People don't speak this way to
them anywhere else—even at home. No one lays it on the line;
no one translates deep-felt feelings into language and says it
like they sense it.

Probably because most often they can't. And because they
can't say it, they can't imagine it being said. And because of
that, if, somehow, they were able to, the chances are they
wouldn't—at least not right off. So, as it turns out, there's a
whole vast range not only of emotions but of newly grasped sensations that seems doomed to lie locked up, unwordable, in our
heads. Our language, in its present shape, just can't handle it;
and people—particularly young people—are slowly becoming
aware of this flaw in their tongue.

They're becoming aware that—as a vehicle for conveying new
sensibilities, perceptions of consciousness and the huge input of
new ideas and information—straight English is inadequate. And
because, at present, it's untrained to operate in this dimension,
people are feeling around elsewhere for ways to express the
new reality in words (or in wails, grunts, growls, shrieks or
sounds no one's yet labeled). In parts of California, for example,
young people are evolving a speech form some call "Sunbear."
"It's based on how things sound and feel. It's street talk, family
talk," says a turned-on girl in Palo Alto. "But our parents would
never understand a word we're saying. Like, when we start rapping, we stop all the usual connections between thoughts."

"LAAww, ahh wahh . . ." (and louder) "OOOHHHh hooo-
wooo Unngggghh" (like a stomp in the chest). Janis is looking

out into the rotating, multicolored spots and undulating against them and against the sexual pulse-bump-mega-beat of the band. She humps and bumps, howling, and, for a moment, becomes an upright elastic gyration in the stuttering quick-flicker of the strobes. "Uhh uhhhh huh, awoooooo"—low, and with much anguish. Some near the front nod in sympathy. She is speaking now to them beyond words. Ahhhh.

Words develop from a mental tagging of experience. Today, though, the sudden gush of new sorts of experiences—in both inner and outer space—has not only outpaced the development of our language but also shown up the limitations of its structure. It's not that conventional language has become inadequate for communicating fresh concepts merely because of a lack of new words; it's because of the whole way of thinking that it forces us into.

Psychologists say all higher levels of thinking depend on language. But at the same time, the structure of whatever language we use affects the way we see the world—influences, in fact, our attitudes and thought processes themselves. The difficulty today is that our brains have out-evolved our tongue. Every major language, says Dr. Mario Pei, started as a rough-hewn tool "fit only for material communication, and then proceeded to polish and refine itself to the point of becoming a vehicle for abstract, cultural thought."

Obviously, our language has done well in keeping its technological terminology polished up. But just where we need it most today, it lets us down. It's clear that there are important new realms of the mind, of interpersonal involvements and levels of perception that defy its ability to convey or communicate—or even to conceive. The whole business nowadays of people talking about ineffable vibrations they receive from this or that suggests the existence of dimensions of reality beyond the outer limits of our language's vocal range. Our language, after all, is a thought trap: when certain sorts of notions don't fit into its framework they remain unrecognized. It's a monstrous handicap. We are so crippled we haven't even the words to think about all those thoughts that might-have-been.

Then, too, there are concepts expressible in other tongues that simply don't translate into ours—except, perhaps, as vague approximations. The Hopi Indians, for example, can put forth ideas and feelings we can't even think about. The Hopi have a whole conception of time and space that's so far removed from *our* frame of reference it seems the work of Martians. What this means, in other words, is that there are other ways of regarding reality. "A change in language," wrote Benjamin Whorf, "can transform our appreciation of the Cosmos."

But today, our awareness of the Cosmos, our exploratory experiences (whether psychedelic or otherwise) into human consciousness, the whole content of our collective minds, in fact, have grown beyond the present capability of *any* conventional language to express. At the same time, the growing global nature of the human community is about to place enormous demands upon our capacity for interpersonal communication. "Our new environment compels commitment and participation. We have become irrevocably involved with, and responsible for, each other," says McLuhan. Our future, then, requires more than everyone becoming merely multilingual. What we need is a new basis for communication—a new language and, along with it, a newly understood function for language itself.

As it stands, we are harnessed to a tongue that's actually doing bad things to us. Much of our tradition-bound speech is structured in a way that creates a polarity between us and everyone (and everything) else. Our language forces us to conceive so much of life as an endless, goal-focused struggle, a war. And success, in even the most mild endeavors, is depicted in outright battlefield terminology: Wet grapple with, strive, clash, cross swords, lock horns, tussle, contend, engage, fight for or take the offensive to achieve (with flying colors) a triumph, victory, conquest, a win, a mastery, a put-down, a killing, etc. Roget's Thesaurus devotes 28 lines to "Peace" and 162 lines to "Warfare." Thus, at a time when we need to be dismantling barriers to human unity, we continue to generate tension as we talk —and our talk, in turn, influences our behavior. We tend, too, in this way, to use language not as a means of touching souls with others but as a defense, a barrier, with words deployed as little bricks to wall us in and hold other people off. Language tries to deal with reality by manipulating symbols of reality. It hinges on the mind's ability to link sounds with meanings and thereby transfer those meanings. Until we all become telepathic, we can't hope to grasp more than a hazy fraction of what's in another head; but meanwhile, we have to clear our existing channels of communication of all the subterfuge and conflict-laden verbosity that stand between us and what we could be.

Among young people, at least, a real frustration factor enters in here. For too long now, abstract feelings have largely been left in nonlinguistic limbo while our language has developed itself along more "practical" lines. To make things worse, so much irrational emotional baggage has been heaped on so many words that our ability to voice a gut-felt notion is stifled—unless we fall back on euphemisms that remove us even further from reality. If words are sounds that symbolize meanings, it's obviously the meanings not the sounds that are the things we try to get across. OK? Then why do you persist in the idea that "intercourse" or "lovemaking" is acceptable while — — — — is an unprintable moral affront? It's a perfect example of thinking backward, reacting to the symbol rather than the subject—a response so senseless that no one even knows why he does it. Somewhere along the line, things just got so turned around that now people are scared of their own words. We make ourselves feel guilty about our speech and sull up like treed possums when "unmoral" words are uttered—or perhaps it's just those word-sounds that touch a nerve or feeling or say a thing directly.

So, while the framework of our language hamstrings the brain's ability to think, we cramp our speech even further, just out of sheer perverseness. As a result, we go about transmitting at almost inaudibly low intensities with equipment that's inadequate to begin with.

If there is transfer of meaning, there is language. But this transfer doesn't have to be in sequential order nor in sentences nor even in words. Numbers or tones or computer beeps will do it. There are some American Indian tongues in which the verb can include the subject, object and all modifiers so that the entire sentence is a single word. The key element in this is a community of understanding, a willingness to comprehend each other's feelings, a group-consciousness—a quality of "us-ness." And it is precisely this aspect of speech—already a feature with many young people—that can spread worldwide.

Present national languages are a product of fragmentation. Today, though, due to global electronic communication, growing literacy, population density and travel, the drift is toward putting things back together. We're moving toward a world culture and ultimately universal consciousness. Eventually, an international language will supersede national languages—but hopefully sooner, for the lethal potential of this planet is already too great to tolerate continued mass misunderstanding, concealment of feelings and anything less than undistorted universal rapport.

Whatever it may be, our new language must serve this new function: as a common ground for interpersonal honesty; and, by way of that honesty, a greater breadth of nonverbal understanding—i.e., "us-ness." New language, too, can mean a new freedom of thought. We will, at last, use words at peak capacity, and without guile, to make clear who we are and how we feel, to feel our own words and to level with each other by committing ourselves to what we say.

On a personal level, there'll be no need to cling to formal grammar to convey meaning. Speech doesn't have to be linear; it can come out as a compressed overlay of facts and sensations and moods and ideas and images. Words can serve as signals, and others will understand. The way a man feels can be unashamedly expressed in sheer sound, such as a low, glottal hum, like the purring of a cat, to indicate contentment. People need only enough openness about themselves not to feel silly about an honest sound. If it says it, say it. Feelings have meaning. Sounds have meaning. Open language can be a joy—a language we can grow with, growl with. Words can cramp your style.

Janis glares out across the darkened auditorium with a pained grimace and an "Ohhh ahh hoo hiweee" that tears at the very root of the heart. She leans back now and moos some sorrowful something into the mike—low, now high, shrill, other worldly, like a haunt, a siren, wraith, denizen of the darks, dawn goddess, knobby nymph, mooncalf, Ophelia: "UUnnh hoo youpleuzz Yeahhh." Lord, she can't live through this—being eaten inside out with pain. Run to her. Clasp her shoulders, cradle her tortured head. "PUHleazzee. . . ." (Crowd: yeh, yeh, do it, do it.) "Yawhoo oo. . . ." Up now, quick, before she dies, seize her. Cool her. Blow in her face. Marry her. Kiss her cheeks. Ply her limp lips with Southern Comfort. Anything, anything. Oh God . . . Janis, Janis, you've not said a word but I understand. We're in love. We don't need words, just meanings, just sounds of feeling, noises that say things. Oh, roar, hiss, bleat, bark, purr to me, snarl sweetly to me. Ahhhh . . . snaarrrll . . . ahhhhh, yes, I know, I know. . . .

SUGGESTIONS FOR DISCUSSION AND WRITING

1. Can you think of another singer who, like Janis Joplin, communicates extensively by nonverbal means? Study the work of such a performer and analyze his or her use of nonverbal techniques.

2. The author discusses at length the limitations of our language and the need for new forms of communication. Consider this idea in light of what some of the earlier essays say about it. See especially the essays by Carnes, Hayden, and Corbett.

3. If you are familiar with the work of Marshall McLuhan, you are undoubtedly aware of a relationship between his ideas and the language of the young as discussed here and elsewhere in this volume. Write a paper in which you explore that relationship. Again, a good starting point might be the Carnes essay.

4. Compare the author's comments on obscenity with those by the authors who treated this topic in earlier essays, particularly Bens, Rothwell, and Hayden.

5. If you are familiar with any of the new forms of speech such as the one mentioned here—"Sunbear," explain how it works and, if possible, comment on its origin and purpose. If you have no experience with such forms, you might like to investigate the subject and report your findings.

26

Alan Watts

GETTING IN TOUCH WITH REALITY: NON-VERBAL INTELLIGENCE

The first three essays in this section called our attention to some of the nonverbal means by which we communicate; the immediately preceding selection called for the development of ways to transcend our language as we presently know it in order to communicate fully. Here, Alan Watts also returns to the philosophic basis of language from which this volume began—reminding us of the limits of language, then differentiating between verbal and nonverbal intelligence, and urging that we go beyond words and concepts to get in touch with reality. Mr. Watts is a writer and lecturer with particular interests in Eastern religions and psychology.

In a recent issue of THE CENTER MAGAZINE there was a very cogent discussion of the whole biological crisis. That shows that the Center[1] is intellectually aware that there is such a crisis. But the problem is this: We do not always act upon those things which we understand intellectually. Intellectual understanding is not always of sufficient conviction to move us to practical action. Something more than the verbal translation of a situation is necessary to get us to act. Also, we do not realize that we are not simply egos inside skin capsules, we are organism environments. The external world of nature is as much you as your own heart is. It is an extension of your own body. We know that and can state

Reprinted, with permission, from the July/August issue of *The Center Magazine*, a publication of the Center for the Study of Democratic Institutions in Santa Barbara, California.

[1] The Center for the Study of Democratic Institutions, Santa Barbara, California.

it verbally, but we may now feel it in the same sense that we feel that we are in love, or that we feel cold or hot, or hungry. We must get to where we can feel the outside world the same way we are conscious of ourselves. There can't be an inside without an outside; one implies the other. Though the inside of you and the outside of you are explicitly different, they are implicitly one.

Therefore in centers such as this we have to add to the intellectual discipline other kinds of disciplines that enable us actually to experience our relationship to nature, to the universe, or whatever you wish to call it. That is what is lacking in the academic world of the West. The final words in Wittgenstein's *Tractatus* were: "Of that which one cannot speak, thereof one should remain silent." He showed that the intellectual quests of Western philosophy were barren. At that moment all departments of philosophy should have become departments of meditation, departments for the practice of silence. But you can't do that in the university. In the university, it is publish or perish. And in a university if people sit and are silent one doesn't know whether they are working or goofing off. But after Wittgenstein that was the moment for departments of philosophy to become departments of Yoga, or contemplation in the Western tradition, or Zen in the Japanese tradition. One must get the actual experiential, gutsy feeling instead of only concepts and ideas. The concept is useful if you know what you are doing, if you understand it is merely a sort of caricature of what is going on in the world. What is going on in the world is not the concept. Korzybski says the map is not the territory. It is because we do not fully realize this difference between the symbol and the reality, the sign and what it represents, that we are in the mess we're in.

I would suggest to the Center that it should invite people here who are experts in non-verbal intelligence. This is not to say that verbal intelligence is bad, or wrong. It is very good, if it's put in its place. The expert in non-verbal intelligence gets you to practice at it. He might get you to practice breathing, the art of archery, surfboard riding, dancing. Through these things you get in touch with a reality that is not concepts. It is a multidimensional reality. When I look at a plant, I see a form of intelligence, because of the order of its wonderful arrangement. I say it

is intelligent. There are two kinds of intelligence, the linear and
the non-linear. If this room were in total darkness, and if for
understanding its contours and shape I had only a very thin-
beamed spotlight, I would have to scan the room, back and forth,
back and forth, and remember everything that I had scanned, and
then piece together an image of the room. That would be a linear
approach. But if I turn on a floodlight I see the whole thing
simultaneously. That would be a non-linear, field approach to
the same reality. When we spell things out in words or numbers,
we can think of only one thing at a time. Trying to translate a
multidimensional world into a linear system of symbols is like
trying to drink a gallon of water with a fork.

All the mental functions, whether they are emotive, intuitive,
intellective, are important and equal, but different in the same
way that the colors in a spectrum are different. A life based only
on logical propositions and only on concepts would be as barren
and futile as eating the menu instead of the dinner.

SUGGESTIONS FOR DISCUSSION AND WRITING

1. *The author quotes Ludwig Wittgenstein as saying "Of that
   which one cannot speak, thereof one should remain silent."
   Explain as specifically as you can what this statement means.
   What is its relevance to this essay?*

2. *Have you ever known someone who had quite limited verbal
   intelligence but extensive nonverbal intelligence? Or have you
   known someone in the opposite situation—one with marked
   verbal intelligence who appeared to have little nonverbal
   intelligence? In either case, share your knowledge and experience of that person with your classmates.*

3. *Alfred Korzybski was a pioneer and influential thinker in the
   field of semantics. The author cites Korzybski's idea that "the
   map is not the territory"—another way of saying that the word
   is not the thing it represents. Just what does Korzybski mean,*

and what are its implications for students of language? See if you can answer these questions in light of your previous reading in this volume.

4. If you are already familiar with the ideas of Alan Watts, show how his philosophy would inevitably lead him to the position he takes on language in this essay. Students who are not familiar with Watts' work might like to read some of his other essays or books in order to examine the philosophic basis for that position.

5. Using this essay as your basis, discuss the concept of non-verbal intelligence as it relates to the discussion of nonverbal communication elsewhere in this volume—for example, in the essays by Cogley, Maddocks, Carnes, the Halls, and Hedgepeth.

6

THE LAST WORD:
LANGUAGE AND CULTURE

"All right, all right, class — now that we've had our little laugh ..."

27

James Peacock

THE SILENT LANGUAGE

The essays in this final section bring together several aspects of language that were treated earlier in this volume and examine them in light of their cultural implications. Thus, the section involves at one and the same time a return to the study of the relationship between language and reality, which we explored in the first few essays of the book, and a further extension of the subject in terms of the possibilities for enhancing human communications. In this first selection, James Peacock, who teaches Anthropology at the University of North Carolina, takes up another dimension of the "silent languages" discussed in the preceding section and sheds light on the cultural contexts of ritual behavior.

According to a Russian story, a worker in a certain factory pushed a wheelbarrow through the exit gate every afternoon at quitting time. Every time he pushed the wheelbarrow through the gate, the guards inspected the wheelbarrow. The wheelbarrow was always empty so the worker always got through. Then after many months it was discovered that the worker had been stealing wheelbarrows.

The story illustrates the danger of too narrow a field of vision —perceiving the contents but not the container, the part but not the whole, the element but not the system.

The first requirement for "reading other cultures" is simply to avoid the narrow view, to deliberately widen the field of vision beyond the conventional boundaries, to try to see the total system.

Upon broadening his view, the observer invariably becomes

From *College Composition and Communication*, May 1971. Copyright © 1971 by the National Council of Teachers of English. Reprinted by permission of the publisher and James Peacock.

intensely aware of a massive fact about human behavior—that it is ritual as well as rational.

On a Sunday morning a few weeks ago as I was writing this paper I enjoyed the additional task of babysitting while my wife sang at a church. At noon, our middle daughter, Claire, age 3, whined in chewing on an empty ice cream cone she had found, and I realized that she and our oldest daughter, Louly, age 6, were hungry. So I fixed a snack of bologna and V-8 juice to sustain Claire and Louly until my wife got home and fried the chicken. Claire and Louly both complained that they would prefer the fried chicken to the bologna and V-8 juice and asked why I didn't go ahead and fry the chicken. I replied that I didn't know how. Claire then said the following which I quote verbatim: "Yes, you do know how, but daddies don't cook."

Claire's conclusion—which was only partially correct—was that her father was a ritual man as well as a rational man. The father's decision was made not merely for technical reasons such as lack of knowledge but because of convention and tradition: daddies don't cook.

In the metaphor of Edward Hall, from whose work the title of this essay is taken, traditions form a silent language. Traditions and conventions are silent in the sense that they are often unconscious. People who claim to act rationally—motivated only by such considerations as efficiency—unconsciously are guided by rigid and pervasive traditions. To lay bare these traditions has long been a central task of the anthropologist, not to mention the satirist, and Hall merely continues this old task, as, for example, in his analysis of traditions concerning time.

Hall claims to have uncovered a set of rules that businessmen in the USA follow with remarkable consistency. If an American businessman is only 3 minutes late for an appointment, he makes no apology. If he is 4 minutes late, he makes an unintelligible apology. Not until he is 5 minutes late does he make an intelligible apology. Hall assures us that he bases his formulation on extensive observation of businessman behavior.

Hall claims further that a country exists whose name he does not supply where 40 minutes late equals our 3 minutes, 50 minutes late equals our 4 minutes, and one hour late equals our 5 minutes late in terms of the etiquette of making apologies. According to Hall, an American ambassador arrived in this country and was paid a visit by a local diplomat. The diplomat arrived for his appointment not so early as to be obsequious nor so late as to be disrespectful; he arrived 50 minutes late. The American ambassador was later heard to remark, "How can you depend on these people when they arrive an hour late for an appointment, then just mutter something?" Hall claims the ambassador felt this way because he was governed by American traditions of punctuality. Not warned of the native system, he became irritated when, after a fifty-minute wait, he received only the muttered equivalent of the American apology for a four-minute tardiness.

Hall has much to say about the uniquely Western tradition of envisioning time as a line. For centuries the West has conceived of a time-line stretching between the past and the future, divided into centuries, years, months, weeks, days, minutes, and seconds. Any and every event we unhesitatingly classify along that line: the Age of Dinosaurs is many intervals back, the Civil War is much nearer our present position, gestation may stretch 9 months along the line, the act of birth is only a point. The future is similarly envisioned as a movement along the straight and narrow path to progress. Man should make a determined movement down the line, and we are impatient with interruption. For those who have grown up thinking that time is linear, it is completely natural to assume that this is the way time *is*.

Trobriand islanders of the Western Pacific hold different assumptions. The Trobrianders, it is said, do not particularly mind interruptions, or even conceive of the concept "interruption"; to them, time is not a line along which one moves but a puddle in which one wallows.

One need not go to a nonliterate tribe to find time-thought that differs from the Western. After spending a year in Southeast Asia during 1969–70 I am still struck by the Indonesian concept of "mengisi Waktu." If I were being introduced to speak at an Indonesian meeting of this type, the chairman might say, "Now Mr. James will mengisi waktu—fill up time." The concern is not with saying anything but with filling up time. The pattern is visible in many spheres of Indonesian life. They often are more concerned with filling a slot in an elaborate schedule or calendar than with getting something done. This pattern reflects long-standing Hindu-Buddhist traditions, as well as problems of bureaucracy in modern Indonesia.

According to Marshall McLuhan, even the Americans are coming to perceive time non-linearly. To make a McLuhanesque pun, Americans are reaching the end of the line, partly due to TV. TV, unlike the classical novel, teaches absorption in the immediate and now. What TV viewers want is to crawl inside the set and experience what is in there rather than to follow a plot. McLuhan claims that the TV child simply doesn't think in terms of lines and futures, careers and plans, schedules and assignments, and so he has trouble functioning in a school system organized in these terms.

McLuhan's view is of course extreme and often half-baked, but it does highlight the presence of time traditions that differ from the traditional White Anglo-Saxon Protestant or WASP pattern of the straight and narrow line. Black Time is probably quite different from White Time, and even White Time varies from subculture to subculture. Here in the South, the fundamentalist's notion of salvation as a sudden and dramatic instant of conversion experience doubtless encourages an emphasis on the sudden and the now; the classical Protestant conception as achieved by methodically and piously scheduling an entire life as a career to fulfill God's plan has long encouraged a Northern WASP emphasis on the linear and the future.

Up to now I have dealt with ritual behavior in the broadest sense, considering as ritual behavior any aspect of behavior that can be shown to express traditions, such as traditions concerning time. Ritual behavior can also be defined in a narrower sense. It is behavior which expresses traditions so sacred and powerful that to express these traditions by action automatically causes the most wonderful and amazing effects: the rains come, harvests increase, diseases are cured, and the cosmos is ordered.

This type of ritual is the subject of the *Time* magazine essay of several weeks ago entitled "Ritual—The Revolt Against The Fixed Smile."[1] In some ways the *Time* essay is off base, for

---

[1] *Time*, Oct. 12, 1970, p. 42.

example, in its theme that once upon a time ritual was an orgy or at least a spontaneous expression of self, whereas now it is only a fixed smile found on the face of

> the lady with a champagne bottle weighed down by her furs and obligatory Fixed Smile, [who] whacks like an inept murderer at the prow of a receding ship" OR "the politician, equipped with a trowel and the Fixed Smile, [who] gobs mortar on a cornerstone, or noshes his way along the campaign trail."

Time asks, in its inimitable way, "Is this the best the American can do for a bill of rites?"

This is a naive view, for the key to all ritual, modern or ancient, is the Fixed Smile. Only by the most meticulous and rigid conformity to the rules of ritual traditions—kneel here, stand there, hold this with the left hand, that with the right, weep in this manner, smile in that—may the magical powers of the rite be unleashed. It's not the fixity of the smiles that troubles modern ritual but the lack of fixity of the traditions they express.

The virtue of the *Time* essay, however, is to bring out the craving for better ritual felt by modern youth, especially students, and since this is an audience of teachers, I would like to offer a couple of thoughts on this point.

Where I live, in Chapel Hill, North Carolina, people used to go to school in the church, but now they go to church in the school. For example, the Unitarians meet at the Friends School and the Church of the Reconciliation meets at Guy B. Phillips Junior High. One of the reasons is problems of space, but possibly a deeper trend is reflected too. Society is shifting from locating the sacred in church (or in the synagogue and mosque) to locating it in the school. Increasingly perceiving sacred qualities in the school, society is increasingly upset by the current revolution in school ritual. Bombings, strikes, and protest marches replace the old rituals of fraternity parties and football games, and the old ritualists, the football players, the jocks, spearhead the attack on the new, the radicals; this conflict between jocks and radicals has occurred on campuses from Cornell to New Mexico. Under any circumstances the public will react to such upheavals, but especially if they occur in the institutions that are increasingly a focus of ritual sentiments, the schools.

What I'm trying to do here is not present any grandiose theory, but just to illustrate a characteristically anthropological way of thinking centered upon the notion that man is a ritual animal. This type of thinking furnishes one of many paths toward reading other cultures, even when the other culture is simply that of the students.

SUGGESTIONS FOR DISCUSSION AND WRITING

1. *Most of us have at one time or another encountered traditions or conventions that were unfamiliar to us and that, in many instances, led to some breakdown in or impediment to communication. Recount a personal experience along these lines, paying particular attention to the elements of language and communication involved.*

2. *If you are familiar with the traditions and conventions of another culture or subculture, discuss one or more of them in relation to a more familiar culture, explaining the purpose of each and the manner in which it functions. Here, as with some of the earlier assignments, you may wish to regard the culture of the young as different from the established culture.*

3. *Locate a copy of the October 12, 1970 issue of* Time *magazine and read the essay entitled "Ritual—The Revolt Against the Fixed Smile." See if you agree or disagree with this author's evaluation of the* Time *essay.*

4. *Are you aware of "the craving for better ritual felt by modern youth, especially students" that this author mentions? Discuss the matter.*

5. *Examine some of the ritual behavior associated with colleges and universities, for example—commencement exercises, fraternity initiations, or sporting events, and write a paper about the social and cultural functions of such rituals.*

28

Norman Cousins

THE ENVIRONMENT OF LANGUAGE

As we have seen from our earlier reading, the reciprocal relationship between thought and language is, in the judgment of many linguists and other scholars, well established. Here, Norman Cousins returns to an aspect of language discussed at considerable length in Part 4—"the dangerous misconceptions and prejudices that take root in language and that undermine human values." Like the authors of those earlier essays, Mr. Cousins points out the emotional values associated with the words "black" and "white," but he deals with a wider spectrum of colors on a broader cultural plane in developing his metaphor, "the environment of language." After a long career as editor of Saturday Review, *Mr. Cousins has undertaken a new publishing venture—* World Magazine.

1) The words men use, Julian Huxley once said, not only express but shape their ideas. Language is an instrument; it is even more an environment. It has as much to do with the philosophical and political conditioning of a society as geography or climate. The role of language in contributing to men's problems and their prospects is the subject of an imaginative and valuable study now getting under way at Pro Deo University in Rome, which is winning recognition in world university circles for putting advanced scholarship to work for the concept of a world community.

2) One aspect of the Pro Deo study, as might be expected, has to do with the art of conveying precise meaning from one language to another. Stuart Chase, one of America's leading seman-

Norman Cousins, "The Environment of Language," published in *Saturday Review*, April 8, 1967, Copyright © 1967 by Saturday Review, Inc. and reprinted with permission of the publisher and author.

ticists, has pointed out that when an English speaker at the United Nations uses the expression "I assume," the French interpreter may say "I deduce" and the Russian interpreter may say "I consider." When Pope Paul VI sent a cable to Prime Minister Alexei Kosygin and Party Chairman Leonid Brezhnev on their accession to office, he expressed the hope that the historic aspirations of the Russian people for a fuller life would be advanced under the new leadership. As translated into Russian by the Vatican's own interpreter, the Pope's expression of hope came out in a way that made it appear that the Pope was making known his endorsement of the new regime. The eventual clarification was inevitably awkward for all concerned.

3) The Pro Deo study, however, will not be confined to problems of precise translation. The major emphasis has to do with something even more fundamental: the dangerous misconceptions and prejudices that take root in language and that undermine human values. The color of a man's skin, for example, is tied to plus-or-minus words that inevitably condition human attitudes. The words "black" and "white," as defined in Western culture, are heavily loaded. "Black" has all sorts of unfavorable connotations; "white" is almost all favorable. One of the more interesting papers being studied by the Pro Deo scholars is by Ossie Davis, the author and actor. Mr. Davis, a Negro, concluded on the basis of a detailed study of dictionaries and *Roget's Thesaurus* that the English language was his enemy. In *Roget's*, he counted 120 synonyms for "blackness," most of them with unpleasant connotations: blot, blotch, blight, smut, smudge, sully, begrime, soot, becloud, obscure, dingy, murky, threatening, frowning, foreboding, forbidden, sinister, baneful, dismal, evil, wicked, malignant, deadly, secretive, unclean, unwashed, foul, blacklist, black book, black-hearted, etc. Incorporated in the same listing were words such as Negro, nigger, and darky.

4) In the same *Roget's*, Mr. Davis found 134 synonyms for the word "white," almost all of them with favorable connotations: purity, cleanness, bright, shining, fair, blonde, stainless, chaste, unblemished, unsullied, innocent, honorable, upright, just, straightforward, genuine, trustworthy, honesty, etc. "White" as a racial designation was, of course, included in this tally of desirable terms.

5) No less invidious than black are some of the words associated with the color yellow: coward, conniver, baseness, fear, effeminacy, funk, soft, spiritless, poltroonery, pusillanimity, timidity, milksop, recreant, sneak, lilylivered, etc. Oriental peoples are included in the listing.

6) As a matter of factual accuracy, white, black, and yellow as colors are not descriptive of races. The coloration range of so-called white people may run from pale olive to mottled pink. So-called colored people run from light beige to mahogany. Absolute color designations—white, black, red, yellow—are not merely inaccurate; they have become symbolic rather than descriptive. It will be argued, of course, that definitions of color and the connotations that go with them are independent of sociological implications. There is no getting around the fact, it will be said, that whiteness means cleanliness and blackness means dirtiness. Are we to doctor the dictionary in order to achieve a social good? What this line of argument misses is that people in Western cultures do not realize the extent to which their racial attitudes have been conditioned since early childhood by the power of words to ennoble or condemn, augment or detract, glorify or demean. Negative language infects the subconscious of most Western people from the time they first learn to speak. Prejudice is not merely imparted or superimposed. It is metabolized in the bloodstream of society. What is needed is not so much a change in language as an awareness of the power of words to condition attitudes. If we can at least recognize the underpinnings of prejudice, we may be in a position to deal with the effects.

7) To be sure, Western languages have no monopoly on words with connotations that affect judgment. In Chinese, whiteness means cleanliness, but it can also mean bloodlessness, coldness, frigidity, absence of feeling, weakness, insensitivity. Also in Chinese, yellowness is associated with sunshine, openness, beauty, flowering, etc. Similarly, the word black in many African tongues has connotations of strength, certainty, recognizability, integrity, while white is associated with paleness, anemia, unnaturalness, deviousness, untrustworthiness.

8) The purpose of Pro Deo University in undertaking this study is not just to demonstrate that most cultures tend to be

self-serving in their language. The purpose is to give educational substance to the belief that it will take all the adroitness
and sensitivity of which the human species is capable if it is to
be sustained. Earth-dwellers now have the choice of making
their world into a neighborhood or a crematorium. Language is
one of the factors in that option. The right words may not
automatically produce the right actions but they are an essential
part of the process.

SUGGESTIONS FOR DISCUSSION AND WRITING

1. *Consider the title of this essay—"The Environment of Language." What is the metaphorical basis for the title? In what
   way is language like an environment? What is the relationship
   between man and his environment? What are the effects of
   the environment on man? Of man on the environment? Do
   you consider this to be an effective metaphor? Support your
   answer.*

2. *What does the author mean when he says that "most cultures
   tend to be self-serving in their language"? Using the relevant
   selections in this book as a starting point, evaluate that
   statement.*

3. *If it is a biological fact that all people are "colored," what is
   the basis for calling blacks "colored"? Who, then, are
   "whites"? Investigate the origins of these terms and see if you
   can determine how and why they have been used over the
   years.*

4. *Do you approve of the emphasis of the Pro Deo study on "the
   dangerous misconceptions and prejudices that take root in
   language and that undermine human values"? Or do you
   think that it would be more valuable to emphasize the problems of precise translation? Perhaps you feel that there is
   another even more important linguistic study to be undertaken. In any case, support your response.*

5. *Investigate the Pro Deo study on which this essay is based
   and see if you can find out what has become of the project.
   Write a report on your findings.*

29

Mario Pei

PROSPECTS FOR A
GLOBAL LANGUAGE

*Much has been said about many aspects of language in this book,
and most of it has been aimed at improving communication—
not only between people but between cultures. Yet little has been
said up to this point about breaking the verbal barriers between
people who speak different tongues. Perhaps this very fact vali-
dates the question with which linguist Mario Pei opens this
essay: "Is the average American both ignorant and indifferent
in the matter of one language for world use?" Mr. Pei, long a
proponent of a single language for international use, wonders if,
given our 3000 different languages and a globe shrunk by electronic media and air travel, we will take action to avoid a contemporary equivalent to the Tower of Babel.*

Is the average American both ignorant and indifferent in the
matter of one language for world use? The issue is far more alive
in Europe, where a person cannot travel for twenty-four hours
in any single direction without having to cross both political and
linguistic boundaries. There are, however, in the world a few
large countries, such as the U.S.S.R., Canada, Brazil, China, and,
of course, the U.S.A., where the traveler can go in a straight line
by train, bus, or car for days and nights and still find himself
facing the same language. But even in these land giants the
linguistic uniformity may be qualified. The U.S.S.R. has its Ta-
djik, Armenian, Georgian, Ukrainian, and other tongues; Canada
its French-speaking province; Brazil its jungle areas where Por-

Mario Pei, "Prospects for a Global Language," published in *Saturday
Review*, May 2, 1970. Copyright © 1970 by Saturday Review, Inc., and
reprinted with permission of the publisher and author.

tuguese is unknown; China its extensive Cantonese, Wu, and Fukienese regions, where the local, so-called dialect differs from the national language as much as English does from German; and even the standardized U.S. has its occasional Indian reservations, or Spanish-speaking Mexican and Puerto Rican sections. The traveler can always take comfort, however, from the fact that he is speaking what the Soviets call the country's "binding language": Russian, Portuguese, North Mandarin, or English, as the case may be.

In the case of the U.S., this extensive linguistic uniformity tended to make most Americans both ignorant of and indifferent to the problem of international communications, that is, until the Second World War. Prior to that time, few Americans had had occasion to travel abroad, and then largely as privileged tourists, for whom everything, including linguistic interchange, was made easy. The foreigners who had come to these shores as immigrants made it their business to learn the language quickly, because it was to their advantage to do so. But the Second World War caused some twelve million Americans to travel to the most far-flung countries in the world, where they did not enjoy the status of pleasure tourists, where the bulk of the populations with which they came in contact had never acquired any English, and where their American speech was not understood, no matter how loudly or slowly they spoke it. At this point, a consciousness of the diversity of the world's tongues, and the troubles and dangers inherent in the lack of linguistic communications, began to impinge itself upon the average American, never again to be lost. This awareness became all the stronger after the war, when Americans did not draw back into their shell—as they had in the 1920s—but instead insisted on taking a predominant role in world affairs.

It is, therefore, no wonder that a Gallup Poll conducted in 1950 on the desirability of a world tongue for international use—to be imparted to the children of all nations on a basis of parity with their national tongues—drew in the United States a 76 per cent "yes" vote, substantially equal to what it drew in such language-conscious countries as Canada, Norway, Finland, and the Netherlands. The poll, repeated in 1961 in the United States alone, showed the "yes" vote having risen to 84 per cent, paralleling the response obtained in Japan in a similar poll conducted by a Japanese organization.

The need for international language for world communications goes back to the episode of the Tower of Babel in the Book of Genesis. As the various groups parted company, each speaking its own tongue, they gave rise to different ethnic units. That the need for communication among those freshly formed units existed even in early days is witnessed by the hieroglyphic carvings that show ambassadors from foreign lands arriving at the court of the Pharaohs accompanied by interpreters.

But the need, while real enough, was relatively small. Few people traveled afar in those days. Yet, it is significant that during the one historical period whose relative universality and extent of trade and travel approached today's, the need was met. When the Roman Empire was at its peak, two languages, Greek and Latin, reigned in a sort of symbiosis throughout the vast area of the Mediterranean basin and beyond. The western part of the Greco-Roman world had Rome's Latin as its popular spoken tongue, the eastern part had Greek. In addition, Latin was the language of administration, government, the military establishment, and the law throughout the Empire, while Greek was the language of culture, poetry, philosophy, and refinement. The other languages of the ancient world—Gaulish, Iberian, Etruscan, Oscan, Punic, Numidian, and the numerous tongues of Asia Minor—became more and more localized as time went on. Most of them eventually shriveled up and disappeared. A measure of linguistic universality had been reached.

With the Renaissance and the great voyages of exploration and discovery, there came to the fore what is often described as linguistic nationalism. This meant that as the spoken vernaculars became more and more literary, they also became official in each country, so that the rôle of scholarly Latin grew more restricted. The term "linguistic nationalism" is perhaps inexact. It was rather a matter of greater participation in intellectual life on the part of an ever expanding middle class composed of merchants and artisans, who did not care to learn Latin and insisted on carrying on their activities in the national vernacular they had acquired from birth. The net result of this gradual change, which went on for centuries, was that by the fifteenth century each great Western nation was using its own national tongue in its official and literary writings, with Latin becoming more and more the prerogative of a shrinking scholarly and ecclesiastical class.

It was precisely at this period that people began to become aware of their linguistic deficiencies and their new linguistic needs. Travel and trade were becoming more international as well as more extensive, but a common language for international travelers and traders no longer existed. Those who traveled and traded (and they were still a minute fraction of each country's total population) began to miss the advantage their remote ancestors had enjoyed in the common Latin of scholarship.

In the seventeenth century the French philosopher Descartes came out with a new, revolutionary idea, that of *creating*, artificially, a language that could be used internationally by all sorts of people. His idea was quickly taken up, and several of his contemporaries offered constructed languages based on the logical progression of ideas and having no link whatsoever with existing languages.

Side by side with these attempts at constructed languages, there was also a startingly modern proposal, advanced by the Bohemian scholar Comenius, to use existing languages not on a universal, but on a zonal basis (English and French for western Europe, Russian for eastern Europe).

Since the seventeenth century, about 1,000 proposals of various kinds have been advanced. These include the world-wide use of an existing national language, such as English or French; the use of two or more existing languages, either on a zonal basis or in complementary distribution; modifications of existing languages, such as Basic English; fully constructed languages not based on any existing language, like the older American Ro and the more recent Suma, proposed by Dr. B. Russell; and constructed languages, such as Volapük, Esperanto, and Interlingua, in which existing languages are utilized to supply or suggest elements of vocabulary or grammatical structure, with a view to the greatest possible ease for the greatest number of learners. Most of them have fallen by the wayside, though many still persist, notably the extension of an existing, widespread language, such as English, French, or Russian, into a world tongue; the idea of using widespread languages zonally (as suggested by Stalin shortly before his death) or to complement each other (like the *Monde Bilingue* movement of France for the use of French and English in a fashion similar to the use of Greek and Latin in the ancient world); national languages modified to insure greater ease of learning, like Basic English; and such fully constructed languages as Esperanto, Ido, or Interlingua.

All these movements point to the fact that an awareness of the problem exists. Why has none taken the upper hand? In part, because of national rivalries and the belief that a national language is the conveyer of the culture and ideology of the nation that speaks it. In part, because of the difficulty of choosing among so many contenders, each of which claims to be the sole solution. In part, because of the tendency of government bureaucracies to get along with the status quo, however unsatisfactory.

English speakers point triumphantly to the fact that more and more people are learning English, and think their language is going to achieve a world status unofficially and, so to speak, by default. What they overlook is that in far too many quarters the English language is viewed as the mouthpiece of a real or fancied Anglo-American cultural, political, and economic imperialism, and that resistance to English penetration is stiffening in many parts of the world. They also overlook the fact that even the rosiest estimates of the spreading of English account for only one out of ten of the world's total population who can be reached through that language. Worst of all, they forget that acceptance of a fully foreign language for purposes of study and self-improvement is quite different from acceptance of that same language on an official basis. The Russian or French or Japanese student who laboriously follows a course in English for strategic or commercial or scientific purposes, the Arab or Indonesian who picks up enough English words to permit him to work for an American oil company, will rebel at the idea that the language he accepts and uses for immediate practical ends is destined to become the world's official tongue in preference to his own.

Esperanto, most popular and widely known of the constructed languages, has been in existence since the 1880s, when its creator, Dr. Lazarus Zamenhof, offered it to the world in the hope that it might reduce national antagonisms and promote human brotherhood. It arouses no national antipathies, and presents such notable features as ease of learning combined with a possibility of expressing nuances of meaning that make it second to none. That is why it has spread to the point where perhaps fifteen million people throughout the world are able to use it, in one fashion or another. But Esperanto runs into the charge of being artificial (this is a little like accusing an automobile of being artificial in comparison with a horse), as well as into the great stumbling block of bureaucratic governmental inertia. Were a few important governments to adopt it as a full-fledged national second language, it would probably spread far faster than it has so far.

The need for an international language is now growing at a much faster rate than ever before. It has been growing since the beginning of the nineteenth century, when new and rapid means of transportation—the steamship and the railroad—began to make travel easier, cheaper, and more comfortable.

It must be emphasized that the vast expansion of international travel and intermingling of people with different language backgrounds only in small part is of the pleasure tourist variety. The international travelers of the present and the foreseeable future include millions of migrant agricultural and industrial workers who seek employment outside their own countries, such as the Mexicans and Puerto Ricans in our Midwest, or the Italians, Spaniards, Greeks, and Portuguese who travel seasonally to work in industrial plants located in France, Germany, Belgium, and Switzerland. They include throngs of commercial and business representatives, scientists, engineers, technicians, members of the armed forces (not merely those of the U.S., of whom nearly three million are scattered throughout the world, but of all nations; consider also European NATO and Warsaw Pact forces); members of the various foreign services, government employees, students, professors and research workers, missionaries and other ministers of the various faiths.

Faced with the world's three thousand languages or even with the hundred that may be described as important, these people urgently feel the need. Left to themselves, they are tongue-tied and helpless, relying on sign language and on the possibility that someone in the group they want to communicate with may know one of the languages with which they are acquainted.

The need is acute enough now, as witnessed by the response to popular polls, and the fact that fewer people said they didn't know or didn't care than is normally the case with major issues of national policy. In the years to come, that need will become more acute, as international travel and international communications and relations of all kinds take on ever broader scope. Eventually, the need will force itself upon the consciousness of even the most unresponsive of government bureaucrats.

Perhaps, as we approach that point, popular awareness will be translated into action, as was and is the case with other long-felt needs. The mere fact that it hasn't happened yet does not mean it cannot happen soon. It would not be unwise for official bodies to devote some serious attention to the need now, while it is in its final academic stages, and before it reaches the point of popular action and the customary crash solution.

SUGGESTIONS FOR DISCUSSION AND WRITING

1. How would you answer the question with which the author opens his article: "Is the average American both ignorant and indifferent in the matter of one language for world use?" What about the "average American"? And what about you? Are you ignorant of the matter? Indifferent? Explain your answers.

2. If you have traveled in areas or countries where you were unfamiliar with the language, what kind of problems did you encounter and how did you overcome them? What suggestions do you have for minimizing such problems for other people in similar situations?

3. Investigate one of the "artificial" languages such as Esperanto or Interlingua, which has been created to serve as an international language, and prepare a report on your findings.

4. The author gives three reasons why there has been so little progress toward creating a global language (paragraph 11). Evaluate each of those reasons in light of your own knowledge and beliefs about language.

5. Some linguists feel that the very concept of an international or global language is based on a naive and unrealistic view of language. Investigate some of the research that has been done on this matter and report your findings.

30

Edmund S. Glenn

ON COMMUNICATING ACROSS CULTURAL LINES

Before reading this last essay, you might like to look again at the cartoon that introduces this section and the first cartoon in the book. They reflect in visual form some of the same themes that Edmund S. Glenn develops here—among them the difficulty that people have in understanding one another if they do not share the same experiences, and the common assumption that "our values are right values simply because, for us they are obvious values." Despite any verbal skills and knowledge of language that we may possess, these remain two of the primary obstacles to communicating with, and understanding, other people. Mr. Glenn works with National Council for Community Services to International Visitors, Washington, D.C.

There is a folk tale that comes to us from the foothills of the Himalayas. A man was trying to explain to a blind friend what colors are. He began with the color white.

"Well," he said, "it is like snow on the hills."

"Oh," the blind man said, "then it must be a wet and dampish sort of color, isn't it?"

"No, no," the man said. "It is also the same color as cotton or wool."

"Oh yes, I understand. It must be a fluffy color."

"No, it is also like paper."

"Then it must be a crackling or fragile color," said the blind man.

Reprinted from *Etc.*, Vol. 26, No. 4, by permission of the International Society for General Semantics.

"No, not at all. It is also like china."

"Oh, then it must be a hard, smooth color."

It is very difficult for people to understand one another if they do not share the same experiences. Of course, we all share the experience of being human, but there are many experiences which we do share and which are different for all of us. It is these different experiences which make up what is called "culture" in the social sciences—the habits of everyday life, the cues to which people respond, the automatic reactions they have to whatever they see and hear. These often differ, and the differences may introduce misunderstandings where we seek understanding.

At the very beginning of the cultural exchange program, a French visitor came to the United States under the technical assistance program of the agency for International Development.

He said to an American friend, "Why aren't you people more frank with us?"

The American said, "Why? What do you mean?"

The Frenchman said, "You tell us that you are for free enterprise, but I have been traveling throughout the United States and I have seen that practically all the production—all the plants and factories—are nationalized."

The Frenchman's assumption arose from the fact that in France only buildings belonging to the French government fly the French flag, but in the United States it is customary for factories, schools, and many other buildings to fly the American flag. What the Frenchman analyzed was not the immediate perception. He analyzed the economic system, and what he saw he evaluated in his own way.

Another instance of a misunderstanding of this sort occurred when a group of Soviet technicians visited this country. They were quite friendly and open minded, and they wanted to see and to learn.

One of my colleagues who was traveling with them overheard one of them saying to another, "What? Another police regiment? Still another police regiment? I can't count them any more!"

My colleague suddenly realized that the Russian was referring to a uniformed guard in the bank where he and his friends had gone to cash some checks. They saw that the uniform of this guard was different from that of the guard in another bank or of the one at the airport or at various factories and businesses they had visited, so they assumed that each belonged to a different regiment of federal police.

Now, what do you do to dispel such a misunderstanding? If the Russians had been told that these men were not federal police, but just people hired by the bank or plant to guard its property, they might have concluded that American capitalists are so powerful as to have private armies of their own. To clarify the misconcept, the escort took the Soviet guests to a part of Washington where there are quite a few pawn shops, sports shops, and gun shops. He showed them that anyone could buy a gun if he had the price. The Russians were terribly surprised. They asked, "Doesn't this encourage crime?"

The escort admitted that it might, and he added, "Some Americans dislike the situation and wish Congress could enact a law to change it, but that is not possible because our Constitution doesn't permit Congress to pass any laws that would deny people the right to bear arms. We are a country which issued from a revolution, and we want to be quite sure that the people have the means to revolt again should they come to dislike the government." So the misunderstanding was corrected.

Misinterpretations of this type can take place at a variety of levels. They can take place at the level of understanding, at the level of ideas or values, and sometimes at the level of feelings. The most serious, in my opinion, are those that take place at the level of feelings. Very often misunderstandings at this level come, not from ill will, but from good will. Sometimes we hurt another's feelings without wanting to do it and without knowing that we are doing it. Those misunderstandings which come from ill will can be left to the Council of Churches. I am here concerned only with those that are unintentional.

Here is an example. A young Japanese student came to the United States, and he was overwhelmed by the cordial reception he was given. He said, "The American people are wonderful. They are so warm, so friendly—much beyond my expectations."

Some time later I was told that while traveling in the West, this same young man had had dinner with an American family and had remarked that he greatly admired the country's efficiency, organization, and accomplishment. But, he said, there was one thing he would never quite understand, and that was why Americans were so cold, so distant.

His host was deeply hurt and asked him, "How can you consider us cold and unfriendly when so much foreign aid was voted by American citizens and paid for by American taxpayers?"

"Yes," said the young man, "this is precisely what I cannot understand—how people who are so generous can be so cold at the same time."

The visit ended on a bit of a sour note.

The point here is that both the first and last statements by the young man are typical. Very often, upon arrival in this country our foreign visitors are astonished by the warmth and friendliness of the American people. But often after a few months they begin to feel homesick and lonely, and they blame the Americans for causing these feelings by being cold. Now, why is this? I believe it is simply a question of different rhythms.

Americans have one rhythm in their personal and family relations, in their friendliness and their charities. People from other cultures have different rhythms. The American rhythm is fast. It is characterized by a rapid acceptance of others. However, it is seldom that Americans engage themselves entirely in a friendship. Our friendships are warm, but they are casual—and they are specialized. By specialized I mean, for example, you have a neighbor who drops by in the morning for coffee. You see her frequently, but you never invite her for dinner—not because you don't think she could handle a fork and a knife, but because you have seen her that morning. Therefore, you reserve your more formal invitation to dinner for someone who lives in a more distant part of the city and whom you would not see unless you extended an invitation for a special occasion. Now, if the first friend moves away and the second one moves nearby, you are likely to reverse this—see the second friend in the mornings for informal coffee meetings, and the first one you will invite more formally to dinner.

We are, in other words, guided very often by our own convenience. We make friends easily, and we don't feel it necessary to go to a great amount of trouble to see friends often when it becomes inconvenient to do so. There is a family whom my family and I like very much, but we haven't seen them for years. It has become inconvenient. Most of us have had that experience, and usually no one is hurt by it. But in similar circumstances people from many other cultures would be hurt very deeply.

A friend of mine—a famous psychologist, an American of Greek descent—has some friends who came from Greece a while back, and after visiting him on the West Coast they finally settled in Cleveland. Recently the psychologist had to make a trip to Washington, and when his friend learned that he was coming across the country, he said, "Of course you are going to stop over in Cleveland to see me." My friend did so because he realized that this was part of the rhythm of Greek friendships. He could not cross the country, flying over Cleveland, without making a special point to stop and spend a few days with his friend.

It is only when we assume that other people do as we do and they assume that we do as they do that feelings are hurt. Often, for example, foreign visitors feel that our family system shows us to be cold hearted and that we treat our parents badly. They don't live with us. There are not three or four generations in the household; no cousins, no aunts share our homes. The fact is, of course, that we aren't cold; we do things differently. We prize independence. My father, when he lived, didn't want to live with me. I would have been a pain in his neck.

Here is another example of what I mean by a specialized relationship. In Washington an Urban Volunteer Corps was organized. This corps was made up of people who gave one or two days of their time to tutoring children who were retarded in their reading, thereby enabling them to stay in school. This was done in an organized way, with tutors assigned to specific schools. When did they see the children they taught? During the lesson. For the most part there was no further contact and no further obligation.

This question also leads to a point of values. We often assume that our values are the right values simply because, for us they are the obvious values. An African friend of mine, an ambassador in Washington, recently said, "One of the things which has caused misunderstandings between your people and mine is that you Americans always speak of individualism as being good. We do not consider individualism good. You always oppose government to individualism. What we oppose to individualism is not the government, but the family, the clan, the small community of natural primary relations. We feel that an individualist is a lonely man."

If you talk to a Frenchman, on the other hand, he will say, "You Americans are not individualistic at all. You have no sense of individualism." To us an individualist is someone who takes care of his own life, who sets a goal for himself and goes to it. If two young men decide that their goal in life is to make good in the hardware business, and if each of them does it independently, we would say that these are two individualists. The French call individualism something entirely different. They say an individualist is someone who is different from others. If there are two people in the hardware business there can be no individualism. There is one too many. Different understandings, different senses of value, but nevertheless both views are perfectly legitimate as long as we understand each other.

Another situation which often creates misunderstandings is that in our culture, silence is a negation. If you express an opinion and there is a little silence and then the subject is changed, you know you have said something with which the person you are talking to does not agree. In many other cultures, in contrast, silence is a sign of agreement. When the Russians, French, Portuguese, Spanish, or Italians express an opinion and you do not reject it explicitly, they assume you have accepted it. Later, when they find you haven't they feel you are hypocritical.

Cultures also differ in their attitudes about the value of oral argument and of reasoning things out. In many cultures an articulate statement of principles and the defense of principles are the marks of a good man or woman. There is a great belief that by arguing, truth will emerge. Americans don't usually believe this. We believe that arguments can lead only to friction; and, rather than arguing and becoming unfriendly, we would rather not mention the subject. We believe in seeing and touching and doing. That is what shows us reality. By way of contrast, in many other cultures what we sense as reality is something we merely see, but do not necessarily understand in principle. It is something without value. This again is a different orientation in the search for truth.

Some time ago I took the minutes of the Security Council of the United Nations, a document in three languages the meaning of which was agreed upon. Such differences as there were to be found were differences in form, and I wished to find out whether these differences could reveal some of the subconscious patterns of thought of the people who spoke the various languages. There was between Russian and English a constant introversion of subject and predicate. Where in English it was said that A is B, in Russian it appeared as B is A. In English we may say: "The first point on the agenda was the political question." This would appear in Russian as "The political question was the first point on the agenda." This difference may seen insignificant. In either case, people knew they had to appear in a certain room at 10:30 in the morning on the East River Drive in New York even if they disagreed from then on.

Yet it was quite revealing that all the subjects of Russian sentences were more abstract and more general than the predicates. All the subjects of the English sentences were more concrete, more particular, than the predicates. The point of the agenda is something you can see—it is something that is limited in time and space and location. The political question is broader, more difficult to define. And yet the subject, the obvious part of the sentence, appeared to the Russians to call for the abstract. This was confirmed by another pattern—that of sentences constructed with a subordinate clause which could be eliminated. Again, the subordinate clauses which could be eliminated in a

Russian sentence always dealt with questions which were concrete, practical, and immediate. In English what could be eliminated was the abstract, the general, and the distant.

This can be compared to the economies of the two countries. In the Soviet Union there is a general plan, and all the actions of individuals are guided by it, determined deductively from the plan. In America we have many choices by dollar spenders, the aggregate of which makes up statistically our national economy.

Most visitors are well informed about the United States, but the information—as is most information acquired when one is far away from the subject—is usually the sort that is found in books and not the sort one finds in life.

So there are many ways in which misunderstandings between people from different cultures can occur. I believe that the best way to avoid these misunderstandings is to encourage foreign visitors to talk about their countries and to describe their people's way of doing things—their customs. One can then contrast this with a description of our way of doing things. Cultural change often occurs in such a meeting. In short, I believe that the greatest hope for all humanity is to learn from one another.

SUGGESTIONS FOR DISCUSSION AND WRITING

1. *The author uses the opening illustration of the Himalayan folk tale to make the point that "It is very difficult for people to understand one another if they do not share the same experiences." Consider the matter in light of your own experience, and then see if you can offer a similar illustration that makes the same point.*

2. *If you have had or observed experiences such as those of the French visitor and the group of Soviet technicians involving false assumptions based on cultural differences, recount one of them. How might the misunderstanding have been avoided?*

3. *Read again the anecdote about the Russian visitors' reaction to the sale of guns in the United States. What do you think of the explanation the American escort gave them? Does it really correct the misunderstanding or does it, perhaps, create a new one?*

4. *Discuss the author's statement "We often assume that our values are the right values simply because, for us they are the obvious values." Consider your previous reading in this volume, and do not overlook the introductory cartoon or the one that precedes the essays in this section.*

5. *The author tells us that "Cultures differ in their attitudes about the value of oral argument and of reasoning things out." Discuss this statement in light of your own experience and your previous reading in this book.*

The limits of my language are the limits of my world.
Ludwig Wittgenstein

BIBLIOGRAPHY

This bibliography is divided into two parts. The first consists of those items that are referred to in one or more of the selections in this text and that are especially relevant to its subject matter. Materials listed in the second part were chosen either because they were helpful in the preparation of this book or found to be of particular interest to students. Many of them, of course, meet both criteria.

A. Items Referred to in the Reading Selections

Andrews, James R. "Confrontation at Columbia: A Case Study in Coercive Rhetoric," *Quarterly Journal of Speech*, 55 (February 1969).

Avorn, Jerry L., and members of the staff of the *Columbia Daily Spectator. Up Against The Ivy Wall*. New York: Atheneum, 1968.

Birdwhistell, Raymond. *Kinesics and Context: Essays on Body Motion and Communication*. Philadelphia: University of Pennsylvania, 1970.

Booth, Wayne. " 'Now Don't Try to Reason with Me': Rhetoric Today, Left, Right, and Center," *The University of Chicago Magazine*, 60 (November 1967).

Bowers, John Waite, and Donovan J. Ochs. *The Rhetoric of Agitation Control*. Reading, Mass.: Addison-Wesley, 1970.

Davis, Flora. "The Way We Speak 'Body Language,' " *The New York Times Magazine*, May 31, 1970.

Fast, Julius. *Body Language*. Philadelphia: M. Evans, 1970.

Griffin, Leland M. "The Rhetorical Structure of the 'New Left' Movement: Part I," *Quarterly Journal of Speech*, 50 (April 1964).

Haiman, Franklyn S. "The Rhetoric of 1968: A Farewell to

Rational Discourse," *The Ethics of Controversy: Politics and Protest.* Lawrence, Kansas: University Press of Kansas, 1968.

Hall, Edward T. *The Hidden Dimension.* New York: Doubleday, 1966.

————. *The Silent Language.* New York: Doubleday, 1959.

Hayden, Tom. *Trial.* New York: Holt, Rinehart and Winston, 1970.

Katope, Christopher, and Paul Zolbrod, eds. *The Rhetoric of Revolution.* New York: Macmillan, 1970.

Korzybski, Alfred. *Science and Sanity: An Introduction to Non-Aristotelian Systems and General Semantics.* 4th ed. Lakeville, Conn.: Institute of General Semantics, 1962.

McEdwards, Mary G. "Agitative Rhetoric: Its Nature and Effect," in *The Rhetoric of Our Times,* ed. J. Jeffrey Auer. New York: Appleton-Century-Crofts, 1969.

McLuhan, Marshall. *Understanding Media: The Extensions of Man.* New York: McGraw-Hill, 1964.

Ogilvy, David. *Confessions of An Advertising Man.* New York: Atheneum, 1963.

O'Neil, Wayne. "The Politics of Bidialectism," *College English, 33,* No. 4 (January 1972).

Pei, Mario. *Words in Sheep's Clothing.* New York: Hawthorn, 1969.

Sagarin, Edward. *The Anatomy of Dirty Words.* New York: Paperback Library, 1962.

Sapir, Edward. *Language: An Introduction to The Study of Speech.* New York: Harcourt Brace Jovanovich, 1921.

Scott, Robert L., and Donald K. Smith. "The Rhetoric of Confrontation," *Quarterly Journal of Speech, 55* (February 1969).

Steiner, George. *Language and Silence.* New York: Atheneum, 1970.

Time, Editors of. "Ritual—The Revolt Against The Fixed Smile," *Time,* October 12, 1970.

Whorf, Benjamin Lee. *Language, Thought, And Reality: Selected Readings of B. L. Whorf,* ed. by John B. Carroll. New York: Wiley, 1956.

B. Items Found Helpful in Preparing This Book or Of Particular
Interest to Students

Allen, Harold B., ed. *Readings In Applied English Linguistics.*
2nd ed. New York: Appleton-Century-Crofts, 1964.

Anderson, Wallace L., and Norman Stageberg, eds. *Introductory
Readings on Language.* 3rd ed. New York: Holt, Rinehart and
Winston, 1970.

Bailey, Dudley, ed. *Introductory Essays on Language.* New York:
W. W. Norton, 1965.

Braddock, Richard, ed. *Introductory Readings on The English
Language.* Englewood Cliffs, N.J.: Prentice-Hall, 1962.

Brown, Roger. *Words and Things.* New York: Macmillan,
1958.

Bosmajian, Haig A., ed. *The Rhetoric of Nonverbal Communication.* Glenview: Scott, Foresman, 1971.

Chase, Stuart. *The Power of Words.* New York: Harcourt Brace
Jovanovich, 1954.

Clark, Virginia P., Paul A. Escholz, and Alfred F. Rosa, eds.
Language: Introductory Readings. New York: St. Martin's,
1972.

Condon, John C., Jr. *Semantics and Communication.* New York:
Macmillan, 1966.

Dean, Leonard F., Walker Gibson, and Kenneth G. Wilson, eds.
The Play of Language. 3rd ed. New York: Oxford University
Press, 1971.

Etc.: A Review of General Semantics. Published quarterly by the
International Society for General Semantics, San Francisco.

Ford, Nick Aaron, ed. *Language in Uniform: A Reader on Propaganda.* New York: Odyssey Press, 1967.

Gibson, Walker, ed. *The Limits of Language.* New York: Hill
and Wang, 1962.

Guth, Hans P. "The Politics of Rhetoric," *College Composition
and Communication,* 23 (February 1972).

Hall, Robert A., Jr. *Linguistics and Your Language.* New York:
Doubleday, 1960.

Hayakawa, S. I. *Language in Thought and Action*. 3rd ed. New York: Harcourt Brace Jovanovich, 1972.

―――――, ed. *The Use and Misuse of Language*. New York: Fawcett, 1962.

Johnson, Wendell. *People in Quandaries: The Semantics of Personal Adjustment*. New York: Harper and Row, 1946.

Kerr, Elizabeth M., and Ralph M. Aderman, eds. *Aspects of American English*. 2nd ed. New York: Harcourt Brace Jovanovich, 1971.

Kottler, Barnet, and Martin Light, eds. *The World of Words: A Language Reader*. Boston: Houghton Mifflin, 1967.

Laird, Charlton, and Robert M. Gorrell, eds. *English as Language: Background, Development, Usage*. New York: Harcourt Brace Jovanovich, 1961.

―――――, eds. *Reading About Language*. New York: Harcourt Brace Jovanovich, 1971.

Lee, Irving J. *Customs and Crisis in Communication*. New York: Harper and Row, 1954.

Littell, Joseph Fletcher, ed. *The Language of Man*. Evanston: McDougal, Littell, 1971.

Malarkey, Stoddard, ed. *Style: Diagnosis and Prescriptions*. New York: Harcourt Brace Jovanovich, 1972.

Malmstrom, Jean. *Language in Society*. New York: Hayden, 1965.

Matson, Floyd W., and Ashley Montagu, eds. *The Human Dialogue: Perspectives on Communication*. New York: Free Press, 1967.

Ogden, C. K., and I. A. Richards. *The Meaning of Meaning*. 3rd. ed. New York: Harcourt Brace Jovanovich, 1930.

Packard, Vance. *The Hidden Persuaders*. New York: McKay, 1957.

Postman, Neil, Charles Weingartner, and Terence P. Moran, eds. *Language in America*. New York: Pegasus, 1969.

Reusch, Jurgen, and Weldon Kees. *Nonverbal Communication*. Berkeley: University of California Press, 1961.

Salomon, Louis. *Semantics and Common Sense*. New York: Holt, Rinehart and Winston, 1966.

Sanderson, James L., and Walter K. Gordon, eds. *Exposition and*

The English Language: Introductory Studies. 2nd ed. New York: Appleton-Century-Crofts, 1969.

Scott, Robert L., and Wayne Brockried. *The Rhetoric of Black Power.* New York: Harper and Row, 1969.

Sledd, James. "Bi-Dialectism: The Linguistics of White Supremacy," *English Journal, 58* (December 1969).

————. "Doublespeak: Dialectology in the Service of Big Brother," *College English, 33,* No. 4 (January 1972)

Sledd, James, and Wilma Ebbitt, eds. *Dictionaries and That Dictionary.* Glenview: Scott, Foresman, 1962.

Smith, Arthur L. *Rhetoric of Black Revolution.* Boston: Allyn and Bacon, 1969.

Sondel, Bess. *The Humanity of Words: A Primer of Semantics.* Cleveland: World Publishing, 1958.

Thurman, Kelly, ed. *Semantics.* Boston: Houghton Mifflin, 1960.

Weiner, Norbert. *The Human Use of Human Beings.* Boston: Houghton Mifflin, 1950.